$2.00 ıg

Place

Edited by
Casey Boyle
and **Jenny Rice**

INVENTING PLACE

*Writing Lone
Star Rhetorics*

Southern Illinois University Press
Carbondale

Southern Illinois University Press
www.siupress.com

21 20 19 18   4 3 2 1

Cover illustration: "Texas Store," image cropped. Photo by Brian McNely.

Library of Congress Cataloging-in-Publication Data
Names: Boyle, Casey Andrew, editor. | Rice, Jenny, editor.
Title: Inventing place : writing Lone Star rhetorics / edited by Casey Boyle
   and Jenny Rice.
Description: Carbondale : Southern Illinois University Press, [2018]
   | Includes bibliographical references and index.
Identifiers: LCCN 2017038651 | ISBN 9780809336500 (paperback)
   | ISBN 9780809336517 (ebook)
Subjects: LCSH: Rhetoric—Social aspects—Texas. | Place (Philosophy)
   | Language and culture—Texas. | English language—Texas—Rhetoric.
   | Discourse analysis—Social aspects—Texas. | BISAC: LANGUAGE ARTS
   & DISCIPLINES / Rhetoric.
Classification: LCC P301.3.T49 I58 2018 | DDC 808/.04209764—dc23 LC
   record available at https://lccn.loc.gov/2017038651

Printed on recycled paper. ♻

CONTENTS

Inventing
Place

Casey Boyle
and Jenny Rice

INTRODUCTION: BODIES, PLACE, AND *POIESIS*

At one extreme a favorite armchair is a place, at the other extreme the
whole earth.   —Yi-Fu Tuan

That's right, you're not from Texas. But Texas wants you anyway.
                                                           —Lyle Lovett

Being There

We, the editors of this collection, grew up in Texas. We did not know each
other as we were growing up, even though we did not live far from each
other in the suburban sprawl of Dallas–Fort Worth. Growing up in Texas
gave us some common experiences: the face-melting heat of summertime
that extended so late into October that Halloween never looked like autumn;
learning the grammatical difference between *y'all* and *all y'all*; the passions
ignited by our "guv" Ann Richards; multiple Texas history classes. Over the
years, we have traded stories about our Texas experiences.

However, growing up in such physical proximity has not meant that the
landscape shaped us similarly. Jenny, eleven years removed from Texas, still
does not own a proper winter coat. Even when freezing cold, she wears sleeve-
less summer clothes far too long into the winter in the colder climate in which
she now lives. Casey, on the other hand, hates wearing short sleeves, even
on the hottest days of Texas summers. Our drawls are different, and so are
our tastes for all the regional foods of Texas. Even our associations with the
state merge together and apart: East Texas holds uncommonly bad memories
for Jenny, West Texas reminds Casey of gathering storm clouds, but Austin
holds meaningful histories for both. Texas forges each one differently. But
one thing is solidly true for both of us: we were *there*.

Being there is a strange concept, for many reasons. The very phrase evokes
the phenomenology of Heidegger's *Da-sein*, a notion that stretches the commonplace definitions of both *being* and *there*. The *being there* of *Da-sein* is not
about bodies who find themselves in a defined place. For Heidegger, it would
be entirely feasible to *be there* (in Texas, let's just say) without ever experiencing

1

the kind of care and involvement that is central to *Da-sein*. In colloquial terms, we might slightly alter a bumper sticker that is commonly seen around parts of South Austin: "We're all here because we're not all there." For Heidegger, you might be there, but that doesn't mean you're all here. This phenomenological perspective has led critics to question the epistemic privileging of the body as knower. Proximity to any particular object does not offer a closer, purer, or less biased view into the truth of that object. The dispassionate discourse of the scientist does not offer her a more unfiltered view of the world any more than being from Texas means we have a clearer grasp of its "truth" than someone from Oklahoma. In fact, Kenneth Burke's discussions of occupational psychosis and trained incapacities suggest that *being there*, pressed up close to your particular scene, can inhibit a broader view of that scene's full complexity. In that case, proximity can actually become an epistemic hindrance.

Although bodily presence does not grant a body any epistemic privilege, we still might want to think about what, if anything, is special about bodies that live and move in particular places. If two bodies who grew up in Texas are not accorded any *purer* knowledge about the state, then what sort of knowledge or rhetorical effects are generated from *being there*? One possible response is to point out how *being there* helps create a kind of embodied knowledge of space. Here we might think of humanist geographer Yi-Fu Tuan's arguments that abstract space becomes place through human experience and affective attachments within those spaces. "Place is a special kind of object," he writes. "It is a concretion of value, though not a valued thing that can be handled or carried about easily; it is an object in which one can dwell" (12). As our own bodies and senses move through space, our encounters with those spaces form a kind of embodied knowledge and valuation of those spaces. The blast of scorching heat and humidity that hits the face of a long-gone Texan who has just exited DFW airport's air-conditioned building signals more than summer misery; it signals home, family, friendship, childhood memories. But to her traveling companion, who has never visited Texas, the sudden heat signals none of those things. Therefore, embodied knowledge arises from a bodily experience of *being there*, turning space into a place, whether that place is an armchair or the whole earth.

But there is another way of describing the kind of the rhetorical effects that happen as a result of a body's *being there*. This different perspective does not focus on knowledge of place as an epistemic artifact, nor does it focus on the body in terms of its embodied knowledge. Rather, this perspective focuses on what we might call the *poiesis* of a body-place assemblage, which is another way of describing the joint (but frictional) relationship of a body in a place. Therefore, in this perspective, we do not ask what a single body *knows* better because of the way it moves through space, nor do we ask how that space helps shape, police, or discipline bodies. Instead, we turn our focus to what kinds of rhetorical effects are created in and through that relationship. In this rhetorically inventive capacity, what new things can be said and written that happen as a result of *being there*?

We use the term *poiesis* to describe this inventional capacity partly because knowledge is overly identified with bodies and place in both an epistemic sense and the phenomenological sense. That is, knowledges that are created by *being there* tend to overly stress the knower herself or the place itself as an artifact. Although there are certainly good reasons to launch these types of inquiries, this is not what interests us about a body-place assemblage. Instead, we are interested in what is generated by a body-place collaboration of emplacement. The *what*, as we see it, is not knowledge but a kind of making or production. In Greek, ποιέω certainly has ties to poetry and literary arts. Beyond that, however, its etymological roots emphasize creation. As anthropologist James Clifford argues in the introduction to *Writing Culture: The Poetics and Politics of Ethnography*, *poiesis* can serve as a writing method for those who are engaged in many questions about culture. "Cultural *poiesis*—and politics—is the constant reconstitution of selves and others through specific exclusions, conventions, and discursive practices," writes Clifford (Clifford and Marcus 24). Such reconstitutions happen through writing, or what Clifford calls "textual experiment and emergence" in different ethnographic forms (24). As an anthropologist and ethnographer, Clifford seeks methods of writing about culture that allow for "rigorous partiality," or attention to the ways that cultures—in their historical, material, and political contexts—are always interfacing with bodies and language. The self-conscious and sometimes playful use of poetic language can emphasize the ways those interfaces shape our accounts of culture.

For those of us interested in writing studies, especially in writing about place, this method also opens up a new perspective on what some have called life writing or personal narrative. Indeed, because the authors' work in this collection is grounded in personal experience, we might hear echoes of what Candace Spigelman has called "personal writing." Spigelman cautions us to move past the binary that too often separates personal writing from academic writing. "Personal writing can do serious academic work," she explains; "it can make rational arguments; it can merge appropriately with academic discourse" (2). We take Spigelman's words to heart by honoring the ways personal writing can serve as ways of knowing place. Therefore, the *poiesis* we pursue does not only produce writing *about* place, as if we are separate from those locales. *Inventing Place* is a collection of essays that marks new approaches to writing rhetorics of place. It captures writing that emerges from the event of *being there*: the assembly of body in place.

3

A Note about Method: Writing Weak Theories

Since we are talking about this kind of writing as a form of method, it would make sense to spell out the methodology, providing a kind of how-to guide for those who wish to also practice this inventional approach. For those readers who are waiting for us to provide such a methodology, however, we risk some disappointment. This writing method might be best described as a "weak theory." A phrase like this might sound pejorative—and it might even be hurled in a pejorative way—but our take on "weak theory" comes from the ways Eve Sedgwick and Kathleen Stewart use this phrase. Describing Sedgwick's take on "weak theory," Stewart writes that this theory "comes unstuck from its own line of thought to follow the objects it encounters, or becomes undone by its attention to things that just don't *add up* but take on a life of their own as problems for thought" (72). The only guidance such writing has is to capture the textures of a singular encounter between body and place. Weak theories of place are never correct in their versions of place; they merely invent new views of a world opened up through a singular encounter. If there is a single unifying methodology to this kind of writing, then, it is this: become undone by the encounter of *being there*, not to bolster previous lines of thought but to witness the sounds, sensations, densities, rhythms, and *poiesis* of that encounter. In short, a weak writing theory of place does not aim to build conclusions about place so much as it aims to listen for the new problems created by the encounter.

This method of writing about place thus begins and ends with the encounter. But even that last phrase—writing *about* place—does not entirely capture the process we propose. *Method*, when examined etymologically, is *meta + hodos*, "about" the "way." *Method* is typically understood as an explicit statement through which someone explains the set of procedures through which she came up with her conclusions. But *meta* is not constrained to mean only "about" but can also mean "among" or "with." That is, *method* can mean—and perhaps this is the *poiesis* we are proposing—"with ways." A "being there" method avoids leveraging a removed position that *about* offers and instead embraces becoming *with* a place's ways. We compose *poiesis* of body *with* place: "being there" writing *poiesis*. It is a method for writing something *new*, new forms of knowledges, bodies *with* place. In other words, this method requires one thing: that a body live, move, and be *with* place. This method is not the only way to write about place—not by a long shot. Yet moving from *about* allows us to move method away from hierarchical claims of truth or validity and toward acknowledging the multiplicity of ways a place is written through *poiesis*.

As we have stated, this method begins from the premise that something happens in the physical adjacency between real bodies and real places. It is not necessarily a greater epistemic knowledge that happens in that clash. Rather, the experience between the two opens up new forms of knowledge and sensation. What is generated in the clash between bodies and places is something akin to what Deleuze and Guattari have called percepts, or blocs of sensation:

> Percepts are no longer perceptions; they are independent of a state of those who experience them . . . they go beyond the strength of those who undergo them. Sensations, percepts, and affects are beings whose validity lies in themselves and exceeds any lived. They could be said to exist in the absence of man because man, as he is caught in stone, on the canvas, or by words, is himself a compound of percepts and affects. (164)

A percept is different from a perception insofar as these affective qualities do not concern representation. As Deleuze and Guattari explain, "We paint, sculpt, compose, and write sensations. As percepts, sensations are not perceptions referring to an object (reference): if they resemble something it is with a resemblance produced with their own methods; and the smile on the canvas is made solely with colors, lines, shadow, and light" (166). The impact of bodies and place together generate percepts and sensations that are independent from representational meanings held by either the body or the place. The question for us, however, is how to invent a writing where the focus is neither on body nor on place specifically, but rather on the new insights that spill out of that clash between the two. How do we write with place using a "weak theory"?

One of the reasons we chose to pursue a "weak theory" of writing about place is that weak theory can offer a different kind of perspective on how *belonging* happens between bodies and place. As geographer Sarah Wright describes, "Weak theory promotes attention to affective assemblages, to the ways things, people, affects and places, with different trajectories, may come together, albeit in often tentative, inconclusive or evolving ways" (392). For Wright, attention to these assemblages can tell us something about the ways in which belonging is born (and reborn) through encounters of those emergent sensations of percepts that Deleuze and Guattari identify. Wright continues, "Things (or people or places) do not pre-exist, in static ways—their belongings are made through their coming together. . . . Here, belonging is not only created by people in places, or more-than humans in places, but actively co-constitutes people and things and processes and places" (393). Weak theories of writing do not tell the truth of place, therefore. If anything, the narrative truth of a place—what we might contrast as strong theory—is undone or unstuck by the encounter among people, things, processes, and place.

Dust: Weak Writing in Place

As a kind of illustration of what writing (with) percepts and sensations looks like, we point to the work of another Texan who has definitely *been there*. Jim W. Corder, a rhetorician and composition scholar, writes extensively about his own emplacement in West Texas. In his work, Corder does not so much write about West Texas as a cultural, historical, or personal place but instead more often diffuses the sensations that transverse body and place. One example is the way he writes *dust*. Corder's dust drifts across pages of his memoirs and books. In *Chronicle of a Small Town*, Corder recalls many dust storms that sprang up suddenly in his corner of West Texas. One afternoon, as a dust storm blew in, his brother lost his way when getting off the school bus. "Later," remembers Corder, "he swore to me that the sun was shining above the dust and the dust was thick and he saw his shadow in the air beside him." (28). Dust is a ubiquitous part of Corder's childhood fragments. "For a while there," he recalls elsewhere, "we had enough dust blow in to make a new county every year." Dust blows into the empty spaces of Corder's West Texas, creating new and shifting topographies with each dust storm.

In *Yonder: Life on the Far Side of Change*, Corder writes of dust as memory's manifestation. There he revisits his old notebooks that he kept as an adult when he attempted, long ago, to maintain a garden. While reading the old entries, he says:

> All I see of my own efforts is, at the first, traces of good intentions, and then, as the sun grew hotter, some evidence that I was mostly intent on getting through and getting back into the air-conditioned house. . . . I believe I thought that sooner or later the dust storms would come anyway. (194–95)

Corder goes on to write that the dust and its always-impending destructive arrival created other kinds of mountains. "Some 'they' told us to work hard, to . . . stay clean, to work slowly upward toward security; but the evidence suggests that the dust storms will always blow." (195). And yet they don't. Corder wrestles with unlearning the lessons he believed were right. Or, if not unlearning, at least learning how to reconcile the dust that always blows yet never arrives.

In Corder's writing, *dust* becomes sensation, one that reflects his own emplacement in West Texas. "The skies I remember, the skies I think about, are dark skies, full of the dust beating down off the Caprock," he laments. "Life will go on, but I'll be lost in the dust . . . and never find my place, or have one" (220). The very real dust of Corder's West Texas is a very real condition, but its textual image here is not object but what Kathleen Stewart, in her afterword to Melissa Gregg and Greg Seigworth's *Affect Theory Reader*, calls a refrain or a worlding: "a scratching on the surface of rhythms, sensory habits, gathering materialities, intervals, and durations" (339). What is captured by Corder's dust is not anything *about* dust or even West Texas. What is captured is the "surface of rhythms" moving through both place and body—moving through "bodyplace." "A worlding is an attunement to a singular world's texture and shine," writes Stewart. "The body has to learn to play itself like a musical instrument in this world's compositions" (341). Whether we describe it in terms of writing percepts or as a worlding, this method of writing place (or writing *about* place, *with* place, or *in* place?) calls for the writer to attune to the singular world's texture. That is, she is not looking to discover *the* world as a historical object. Neither is she attempting to tell of her own perceptions of feelings about this world. She is instead attuning to a kind of singularly empirical encounter between body and world. And by writing that attunement, the writer diffuses this attunement across a sensational composition.

Corder's dust is what Stewart might call a "weak theory" of place. The dust covering his pages causes him to *unstick* from his own line of thought. He encounters it, follows it, and treats the commingling as a problem for thought. To borrow Wright's phrasing, Corder turns his attention to the ways dust, personal history, memory, and place come together in tentative ways. The result is a kind of writing about West Texas that is not simply unique or original but that captures *poiesis* of a body-place assemblage. It is the attunement to a singular world's texture and shine, as Stewart says.

Why Texas?

One of the challenges with *Inventing Place* is that not everyone reading this collection has a connection with, or even concern about, Texas. Yet as Lyle Lovett sings, "Texas wants you anyway." We borrow Lovett's line to suggest something not just about Texas but about place in general. In this way, Texas is simply a fragment of any place our bodies might find themselves. There is no denying that Texas has become a social imaginary for people around the world, even for those who have never crossed its borders. As Manny Fernandez writes in a *New York Times* essay called "A Look at What Makes Texas Texas":

> As the world grows smaller, as technology obliterates the significance of where we live and work, as Americans become more transient, Texas resists. It declares, to itself and the nation: Place matters. . . . We tattoo Texas on our arms, buy Texas-built trucks and climb fire escapes with Texas dirt in our pockets. Place, we are unsubtly suggesting, matters. (A14)

Texas is a metonymy in this way. It stands in for places that have stubbornly brushed up against the bodies who live there, leaving sensational traces of those encounters. But the same could be said of any space whatsoever. It might be the city where you live. It might be the building where you work. It might be the country where you lived as a child. It might be the corner of a room where your favorite armchair sits. As Fernandez concludes, Texas matters because place itself matters. And as we propose though the following essays, the singularly empirical encounter between body and world matters—no matter where that world happens to be.

Rather than start from the position that places are fixed locations with histories and ideological structures that must be uncovered, this method of writing takes the encounter of place as inventional sites. This is why all the authors in this collection have some connections with the places they are writing about. It is not that their experiences with these places give them some greater authority or authentic ethos. But *being there* is essential to writing this particular kind of attunement. We chose Texas as a unifying theme because, well, we have *been there*. But also, as a familiar *topos* that has spanned so many social imaginaries, Texas has already been written *about* so often. Countless popular fiction works—whether Larry McMurtry's novels or James Michener's sweeping sagas—have helped create a literary landscape for a wide range of readers. H. G. Bissinger's journalistic *Friday Night Lights*, about high school football culture in small-town Texas, eventually became a wildly popular TV series. Although the televised version of *Friday Night Lights* was a national sensation, the show even managed to make the quote "Texas forever" a common refrain among its fans.

In a more critical vein, McMurtry's *Walter Benjamin at the Dairy Queen* reads Benjamin's critical theory (literally) inside a Dairy Queen in Archer City, Texas. McMurtry notes that Dairy Queens began dotting the small-town Texas landscape around the same time that Benjamin's essays began to appear in English translation. And as anyone who grew up in small-town Texas can attest, McMurtry is quite right in his observation that Dairy Queens served as the kind of "storytelling" space that Benjamin imagined. More recently, there have been a landslide of books about the "spread" of Texas. The titles alone suggest a kind of national Texasification: *Lone Star Nation: How Texas Will Transform America*; *As Texas Goes . . . : How the Lone Star State Hijacked the American Agenda*; *Big, Hot, Cheap, and Right: What America Can Learn from the Strange Genius of Texas*. In short, Texas has become a *topos* that stands in for much more than the physical space it inhabits. For this reason, we also found Texas fitting for our discussions of writing, bodies, place, and invention.

Nineteen Ways of Writing Texas

Although a significant body of work and scholarship exists on Texas and its sociological imaginary, that's not what we got our faces fixed for, as Jenny's Texan grandma used to say. Instead of focusing primarily on place-based or autobiographical details, the writing in *Inventing Place* attunes to the singularly empirical experience of *poiesis*, capturing the rhythms that emerge from those encounters. The essays in this collection relay a "weak theory" of place through their deployment of multiple methods. What results is not some kind of truth about Texas, as if the authors' experiences have given them a better vantage on the histories, cultures, or discourses found there. Rather, the nineteen essays share the results of nineteen singular writing experiments, nineteen different attempts to bear witness to what happened when the authors adopted a "weak theory" in this place.

We have divided the essays according to a particular set of spatial locations—Central, East, North, South, and West Texas—each of which tends to signify different mythologies for many Texans. This map of contents could look quite different if we imagine another set of poetics that do not rely on directional spaces. For example, many of the essays engage a sense of mobility, moving the reader along streets, highways, and corners. Other essays engage spaces that are decidedly less mobile: cement walls, bar stools, hallways. We could easily map these essays according to the motions and movements that each author describes. Or, drawing on an entirely different set of poetics, we might imagine a way of mapping the essays according to their temporalities, moving from past to future. Yet we decided on the current arrangement because these are referential points that resonate with us as bodies in place.

Central Texas

The chapters emerging from Central Texas—authored by James J. Brown Jr., Megan Gianfagna, Anna M. "Amy" Young, Nate Kreuter, and Casey Boyle—all begin in what Texans sometimes refer to as Hill Country. The authors of the small histories in this collection write about place not with the bookends of a beginning or a conclusion, but instead starting in the blocs of sensation that pass through the bodies of writer, reader, text, and place. For example, James J. Brown, Jr.'s essay, "When You're Pretty," generates sensations between space and body as he writes about getting his arm inked with a copy of Daniel Johnston's infamous "Jeremiah" graffiti, which adorns the side of an otherwise nondescript Austin building. Brown writes of movement, appropriation, networks. His tattooed arm now becomes part of this network of spaces, including his arm itself, which becomes for him something more than a tool to write with.

9

We should probably mention that Brown got his tattoo as a condition of his essay's acceptance into this collection. His essay, then, does not document what exists but becomes a kairotic point of invention. The writing generates creation.

Likewise, Megan Gianfagna's "Figments of a Future Austin" looks to engage creation. In this chapter, Gianfagna explores the Imagine Austin initiative, which seeks "to create space for weighing possible futures." While Austin might fairly be described as having an extremely nostalgic ethos, Gianfagna shows that this initiative pushes the boundaries on how a place can leverage the community to reinvent itself. Amy Young presents the spatial concept of terroir through the practice of Texas barbecue in "Rhetorics of Smoke and Cedar: The Terroir of Texas BBQ." Texas differentiates itself from other locales of barbecue, first and foremost, by understanding barbecue not as a noun, but as a verb. Young then uses the term *terroir*, meaning "make" and "does," to unpack place as a deeply rhetorical phenomenon.

Nate Kreuter takes us to the bar in "Drowning at the Poodle Dog." Showing how some places hide in plain sight, Kreuter explores the Poodle Dog Lounge as a place within a place, an oasis in a city hustling with technological change. He complicates proximity, discussing the out-of-time features of a style of leisure that the lounge offers when one knows it is destined to end all through the specter of the Iraq War. In "The Complete History of Parlin Hall (Abridged Version)," Casey Boyle explores place through bureaucracy, or place as kind of a bureaucratic machine. Examining a single building on the University of Texas campus, Boyle traces how remnants, abridged features, of the building's long history offer concepts for thinking about place in general. In studying a place as a kind of media archaeological site, he shows how any place is subject to and an object of dynamic temporal layers.

East Texas

East Texas is difficult to locate. Even growing up in Texas, it is hard to differentiate between what lies east beyond Dallas and what becomes Louisiana or Arkansas. Indeed, as in many places whose geographic character ignores official borders, people and places in that region meld into one another freely. In this shortest section in our collection, James Chase Sanchez and Jenny Rice offer essays that explore how boundaries of race and religion, community and individual overlap and often overstep their bounds. In "Recirculating Our Racism: Public Memory, Folklore, and Place in East Texas," James Chase Sanchez interrogates the racist past of Grand Saline. The nexus of race offers a powerful way to show how a place is preserved through memory and atrocity. Sanchez's essay then remembers racism to recover possibility beyond it. Jenny Rice's chapter, "Archiving Devils," explores memory as well, but not for the sake of preservation. In her chapter, Rice relays her story of being committed to a Christian youth camp for wayward teenage girls. Rice writes about expelling demons and disclosing archives—through shared memories, emails, letters—that are both of the self and beyond it.

North Texas

North Texas cities are legion. The region is home to Dallas, Fort Worth, and Denton and extends far up into the famous Texas panhandle. Perhaps best known, though, is the metroplex area of Dallas, which includes several major cities and their suburban sprawl of secondary and tertiary suburbs. North Texas alone would offer enough places to fill a volume or two of essays. The authors for this section—Cynthia Haynes, Doug Eskew, Jordan Frith, Michael Odom, and Ryan Skinnell—explore the region's places of music, growing up in its suburbs, its changing political climate, and the reluctance to accept Texas as home. In "Fort Worth by Day, Cow Town by Night: It's All to the West of Adios," Cynthia Haynes describes Fort Worth as "home," which means not so much the place where she lived but the place she kept "leaving." Haynes recalls the music and the bars, the restaurants and the schools that accumulated into her sense of place. Doug Eskew, in "(White Trash) Pantego," also writes about Fort Worth, along with its suburb Arlington and the suburb-within-suburb Pantego. Eskew's essay limns the not-quite-middle-class existence of "white trash." While the term often describes the economically downtrodden, Eskew shows it is instead a general term for those "unbelonging" sorts regardless of economics. Place here proceeds against the grain, where growing up on Country Club Lane marks not privilege but disadvantage.

Jordan Frith's "Denton and the Rhetorical Appeal of Authenticity" lands us in a city that sits in the shadow of two much larger cities to its south. Frith engages the space of Denton as host to a multiplicity of partial places but whose staying power, whose authenticity, is subject only to a small subsegment of the place's residents. The authenticity of any place, Frith proposes, should be rhetorical; it should *depend*. In "*Walnut Hill Story*: Memory, History, and the Built Environment in the Experience of a Place," Michael Odom explores the psychogeography of several intersections along the artery of U.S. Highway 75, Dallas's North Central Expressway, calculating the characteristics of a place—its landscape, buildings, development, terrain, flora, fauna, history, memories, and economic conditions—and their effects on a person's behavior and emotions. Odom's chapter explores the accumulations of city roads circulated within our memories and sense of place. Ryan Skinnell's "Reconciling Texas; or, Inventing (a) Place Out of Place" brings us a reluctant experience of place. Skinnell's essay represents the many people whose distaste of Texas is their only taste of Texas. Interestingly, though, Skinnell finds that Texas offers itself up to invent non-Texas and that any place is reconfigurable and subject to reinvention despite a long history.

South Texas

From the Gulf of Mexico to the Mexican border, South Texas folds together a multiplicity of cultures that form a place distinct from the rest of the state. The essays in this section—authored by William T. Burdette, Victor Vitanza, Jennifer D. Carlson, and Donna Dunbar-Odom—examine place through food, septic tanks, monuments, and the oil industry. Together they present a region of Texas known for its memory as much as its industry. In "From Bespoke to Baroque: Folding and Unfolding the Burrito in San Antonio," William T. Burdette sits at the table with a distinctively Texan dish, the burrito. In San Antonio, Burdette folds together the baroque façade of the San Jose Mission with the burrito to show how social historical and economic networks of place and being hospitable find their way into the food we make and eat, remaking what we consider to be "authentic" in the process. Victor Vitanza, in "Texas without Texas: The Septic Tank *Where Houston* Became Modern . . . in *Paris, Texas*," also folds together two unlikely Texas places, Houston and Paris, with two unlikely genres, essay and film script. Through a knot of notes, Vitanza dramatizes growing up, culturally and intellectually, in places with indistinct boundaries, a place he calls "Texas without Texas." Working across genres and places, Vitanza traces flows of electricity, family, friendship, and shit to show place emerges from a kind of release of/relief from buildup, a relief that comes from becoming unstuck.

It would be difficult to discuss Texas without also discussing oil. In recent years, the flow of oil has been redirected toward new techniques for extracting the precious resource. Jennifer D. Carlson's "Eagleville" ethnographically examines how one such new technique, the practice of fracking, invents multiplicity between surface and mineral place and makes the amorphous physical place cohere, incorporating all its surrounding places into the activity of oil. In "We All Remember the Alamo: Materializing the Personal," Donna Dunbar-Odom takes us back to San Antonio and to the oft-repeated phrase that every Texan is charged with never forgetting: "Remember the Alamo." Dunbar-Odom's essay embraces the personal investments we have in any place. It offers an informed narrative for how we "perceive our lives materially in terms of place" and how often those places are the landmarks that build shared memory even in the face of rapidly shifting demographics.

West Texas

In West Texas, the immense stretch of land one sees is dwarfed only by the infinite sky that extends forever above and beyond the land. In some ways, West Texas exemplifies Texas with its connections to western culture and its endless spatial expanse. In this section, the chapters offered by Barry Brummett, Brian

McNely, and Jillian Sayre discuss the change, movement, and immensity that Texas seems to offers with intensity. Barry Brummett's "Notes from a Texas Gun Show" takes the reader to an infamously Texan place, the gun show. Brummett explores the working-class character exhibited by the western ideals of the gun show and in the process shows gun culture to be, like the gun itself, "a contradictory bundle of restrained potential." The essay then goes on to discuss how the frustrated potentials of being working class today find their way into the performances of being gun owners. Brian McNely's "El Paso, Plastic Bags, Aesthetics" tackles a ubiquitous condition that permeates not only West Texas but perhaps all developed areas of the Lone Star State. Localizing his analysis and imagery on the presence of wayward plastic shopping bags that litter the landscape, McNely examines the aesthetic encounters shaped by street development and circulation that "provoke and let things be."

Finally, Jillian Sayre's "Weary Land: The Space and Place of West Texas" transverses what is perhaps the quintessential Texas experience: long drives on longer roads. The places offered up by Texas space are best told as a travel story, Sayre proposes, as a spatial practice. Sayre shows how those travels induce a weariness that can become generative moments, breaking down boundaries and limits, which include the very grammar through which her chapter unfolds and the long stretches of text we must travel. Its exhaustion is not just figurative; it's literal. While we might understand Texas as offering a limitless place, Sayre shows how its size instead offers a multiplicity of limits whose tiring experiences wear away but also create space for novelty.

Texas Forever

Although our collection is segmented spatially, we end with a final comment about the timelessness of interventions into place. The pop culture refrain "Texas Forever," born from the television series *Friday Night Lights*, offers a productive final note with which to conclude our introduction. Spoken through a tinge of premature nostalgia, the characters in the series repeat the phrase to capture a sense of place as they are living in it. Often the words are uttered with the clink of beer bottles by two people sitting in lawn chairs overlooking a Texas horizon at dusk. By repeating the phrase "Texas Forever," the characters also implicitly acknowledge the moment and its place as already fading like that setting sun. We find resonance here between "Texas Forever" and any study of place. What we hope to offer here, then, are ways for place not to be captured and contained but to be invented anew.

Works Cited

Burke, Kenneth. *Permanence and Change: An Anatomy of Purpose.* U of California P, 1984.

Clifford, James, and George E. Marcus. *Writing Culture: The Poetics and Politics of Ethnography.* U of California P, 1986.

Corder, Jim W. *Chronicle of a Small Town.* Texas A & M Press, 1989.

———. *Yonder: Life on the Far Side of Change.* U Georgia P, 2011.

Deleuze, Gilles, and Felix Guattari. *What Is Philosophy?* Translated by H. Tomlinson and G. Burchell. Columbia UP, 2014.

Fernandez, Manny. "A Look at What Makes Texas Texas." *New York Times,* 8 May 2016, p. A14.

Heidegger, Martin. *Being and Time.* Translated by John Macquarrie and Edward Robinson. Harper, 1962.

McMurtry, Larry. *Walter Benjamin at the Dairy Queen: Reflections on Sixty and Beyond.* Simon and Schuster, 2010.

Spigelman, Candace. *Personally Speaking: Experience as Evidence in Academic Discourse.* Southern Illinois UP, 2004.

Stewart, Kathleen. Afterword: Worlding Refrains. *The Affect Theory Reader,* edited by Melissa Gregg and Gregory J. Seigworth, Duke UP, 2010, pp. 339–54.

———. "Weak Theory in an Unfinished World." *Journal of Folklore Research* vol. 45, no. 1, 2008, pp. 71–82.

Tuan, Yi-Fu. *Space and Place: The Perspective of Experience.* U of Minnesota P, 1977.

Wright, Sarah. "More-Than-Human, Emergent Belongings: A Weak Theory Approach." *Progress in Human Geography* vol. 39, no. 4, 2015, pp. 391–411.

CENTRAL TEXAS

James J. Brown Jr.,
Rutgers University—Camden

1. WHEN YOU'RE PRETTY

It must be a pain to be so pretty
It must be a strain to be so well liked
—Daniel Johnston, "When You're Pretty"

February 1999

During a 1999 art exhibition called "The Art of Ron English and Daniel Johnston" at CBGB's Gallery in New York City, curator Jonathan LeVine was stunned by the fan response to Daniel Johnston's drawings. LeVine had photocopied the drawings, keeping the originals protected in plastic for buyers. All the artwork sold almost instantly, but the photocopies also disappeared. LeVine was incredulous:

> "I can't believe they stole the copies! Now there's no other documentation that the work existed. Some of that stuff was 15 years old. It'll never be chronicled, it was never photographed. It breaks my heart. By the next day, every single photocopy was gone and the show still had another month to run. I was pissed because I had no other documentation of the work and also because I'd worked so hard on the layout and now I had a blank wall." (Yazdani and Goede 76)

LeVine posted signs that said, "Due to theft we were unable to show you the Daniel drawings." These signs were soon scooped up:

> "And they stole the signs too! They stole the label tags off the paintings! I'm glad I bolted [Ron English's] paintings to the wall or I'm sure those would have been gone too. I wasn't prepared for that kind of reaction. Those people were weird. Strange and freaky." (76–77)

December 24, 2013

On Christmas Eve 2013, Rebecca Guest was caught spray-painting the word *Fuck* over and over on Johnston's "Jeremiah the Innocent" mural on the side of a building at the corner of Twenty-first and Guadalupe Streets. The 11 thirty-two-year-old Guest told police that this mural and others around the city were offensive and that they "were directed specifically at her" (Alexander). She hoped that defacing the mural would cause the building's owners to remove it.

April 24, 2015

When I first moved to Austin, I lived in a small apartment in Hyde Park, a neighborhood just north of the University of Texas campus. My path to campus ran along tree-shaded streets, either by bus (the #5 down Speedway or the #7 down Duval Street) or by bike. When I moved to Austin's East Side, my commute was not as pretty or leisurely. Public transportation in Austin, as in many cities, tends not to serve those who need it most. East Austin was less affluent at the time (gentrification is quickly changing this), meaning that I would have needed to take two buses to campus. So I began to drive, parking my car in the streets south of campus and walking north along either San Antonio or Nueces Street and then east on Twenty-first. This walk took me directly past "Jeremiah the Innocent." Six years after I stopped making that walk on a regular basis, I had Jeremiah tattooed on my left forearm. At thirty-seven years old, this was my first tattoo.

There have been many appropriations of Daniel Johnston's work, even though as a musician and artist he is an acquired taste. Johnston's voice is high-pitched and lispy. His 1983 *Hi, How Are You* album was recorded on a boom box and features a Speak & Spell toy as well as Johnston playing a broken chord organ. That album was adorned with Johnston's drawing of "Jeremiah the Innocent" ten years before the mural's appearance. The painting was commissioned by the owner of Sound Exchange, a record store that used to occupy the building. The artist's compensation was $100 and as many records as he could carry out of the store. Johnston was already an Austin celebrity at that point. He was known for distributing his cassette tapes to customers who visited him at a McDonald's restaurant where he worked.

At first it's difficult to know what to make of a song like "Don't Let the Sun Go Down on Your Grievances" (he pronounces that last word "GREE-vee-ance"). But the song comes into focus when you hear it covered by the band Clem Snide. There is an entire album of such covers called *The Late Great Daniel Johnston: Discovered Covered* (Johnston isn't dead). This is the main indication of Johnston's mark on the music world. His songs call out for appropriation, and the covers of his songs demonstrate that his lo-fi recordings are built on innovative melodies. His mark on Austin is also clear, especially when we consider the "Jeremiah the Innocent" mural. The mural has had a similar effect on people. After some years in operation, the Thai restaurant that now sits at the corner of Twenty-first and Guadalupe changed its name to Thai, How Are You. What was once street art is now a billboard. It's difficult not to scoff. However, the restaurant's choice of name is only one in a series of appropriations. This is not to say that we can't or shouldn't judge or critique appropriations. Some appropriations are more appropriate than others, and this is the question that most bothers me as I attempt to understand what the ink on my arm has to do with the paint on that wall: Jeremiah calls; we respond. What do we make of that call, and how do we make sense of the multiple responses to it?

These appropriations stand as what Henri Lefebvre would call the "representational space" of Jeremiah, and they are not separate from the physical space of the street corner that features Jeremiah's greeting. The tattoo on my arm does not represent just my choosing to appropriate—there is something about Jeremiah (and about any space) that calls out for this type of engagement. We want to grab on to space, to freeze it in time, in order to make sense of it. The call of any space manifests in different ways at different times. How does one respond? How does one know what one is responding to? And as space changes over time, how do the responses change? Everything shifts and changes, meaning that today's appropriation is not tomorrow's.

January 5, 2004

The story of "Jeremiah the Innocent" almost always circles back to John Oudt, owner of a Baja Fresh franchise that was moving into the building after Sound Exchange closed. In early 2004, *Texas Observer* writer and Austinite Dan Solomon heard that construction workers were preparing to tear down Jeremiah: "They were scheduled to tear down the frog mural so it could be replaced with windows. I hustled over and found some workers taking pictures in front of the frog. They were sad, they said. Everybody in Austin liked the frog." Even the workers tasked with his demolition were drawn to Jeremiah. Solomon and friends began to organize, and they were successful in gaining national and local media attention. Oudt was surprised—he thought the image was little more than "an accumulation of graffiti," but he also knew that this kind of protest was something he needed to take seriously: "I've been involved in areas around universities before, and I knew that the attitudes that people have about you are extremely important if you're trying to open a business in an area like The Drag" (Solomon). Still, the plans were in place, and Oudt said his hands were tied. The protestors left, already composing eulogies for Jeremiah. But Solomon's phone rang the next day:

> "I couldn't sleep last night," [Oudt] said before explaining that he'd decided to save the mural. We held a press conference that afternoon, at

which he said he expected it to cost him $50,000 in architect fees and lost revenue to preserve it, but that it was important to him. (Solomon)

Oudt saw the writing on the wall—a bad relationship with the locals is bad for business.[1] Jeremiah was saved, and a glowing Baja Fresh sign eventually sat hovering over his head. Soon Jeremiah was on the sleeves of Baja Fresh workers, and Johnston had been commissioned to create artwork that would be displayed inside the restaurant (Gray). The heroic story of street protesters saving Jeremiah is one more in a long narrative of Austin's "weirdness." But it's worth noting that the cultivation of this particular site on the map was already under way before *Rolling Stone* or the *Austin Chronicle* wrote up the story of Baja Fresh and Jeremiah.

Jeremiah (as well as other street art in Austin) is often carefully preserved. When Jeremiah was defaced with graffiti in 2012, the radio station KUT ran a story about how Austin's street art is maintained. Murals on a Chevron station in South Austin and a "Welcome to Austin" mural on South First Street are well known to many, and the story asked who is tasked with cleaning up graffiti. Typically, the city handles it, but Austin has an agreement with Johnston, who repairs Jeremiah when necessary. Dick Clark, who owns property in Austin, suggests that the problem with street art is ephemerality: "The dilemma with graffiti is that it's temporary. . . . It's a different art form" (Connelly and Dunbar).

However, the stories of Jeremiah show us that all graffiti is not created equal—Jeremiah is anything but temporary. Protests to save Jeremiah have ensured that he now sits inside a frame, like a painting in a gallery (figs. 1.1, 1.2). But what sits outside the frame? Or more accurately, what once sat outside that frame? What was sacrificed for the preservation of Jeremiah?

Before Sound Exchange closed, Jeremiah was part of mural-covered wall, bookended by other works of art. Here's how the wall was described by the *Austin Chronicle* in 2003:

> The visual splendors of ex-pat Austin artists, musical fringe legend Daniel Johnston and punk rock poster man Frank Kozik, include a flying eyeball, two spiky, four-eyed, lovable geckos (think: Keith Haring on acid), a faded image of Jack Nicholson from *The Shining* ("Heeeeeeere's Johnny!"), and our personal favorite: a froggy extraterrestrial welcoming you with a "Hi, how are you." Guess our space friends are still working out punctuation. ("Best of Austin")

Today Jeremiah is all that remains. His "Fly Eye" companion (which also dons the cover of Johnston's *Continued Story with Texas Instruments*) is gone.

Figures 1.1 and 1.2. *Top*, Jeremiah as seen from the opposite street corner, making clear how the mural has been put in a kind of frame. Prior artwork surrounding the mural has been destroyed. March 2008. Photograph by Dawn Danby, creative commons license (www.flickr.com/photos/dawn/2320492956/; https://creativecommons.org/licenses/by-nc-nd/2.0/legalcode). *Bottom*, the mural as it appeared in March 2005. Photograph by Philip Kromer, creative commons license (www.flickr.com/photos/mrflip/8917476/; https://creativecommons.org/licenses/by-sa/2.0/).

A mural by poster artist Frank Kozik that was once around the corner from Jeremiah (near the entrance of the record store on Guadalupe) was removed during the early stages of Baja Fresh's remodeling. One commenter on the Connelly and Dunbar story about preserving Austin street art puts it this way:

> I love how this article fails to mention the 2/3rds of the mural that is already missing. (eyeball, bat, etc.) Most of the original wall and mural was torn down by one of the location's post Sound Exchange owners. Q: What happens when iconic Austin street art is completely destroyed by greed and gentrification? A: No one lifts a finger.

This response is not surprising, and others similarly mourn an Austin that has been replaced. Here's a blog called *Chronological Snobbery* reflecting on Jeremiah: "These days, though, the mural [is] a relic of an Austin which no longer exists, but for in the minds of its current (and former) citizens who are at least a decade older than the undergraduates who walk past it every single day" ("Daniel Johnston Frog Mural"). Jeremiah carries the weight of all these identifications. Solomon recognizes this:

It means something different to them than it does to me, I'm sure. Just like it means something different to Daniel Johnston himself, or to the photography students at the University who shoot pictures of it every semester, or the guy on YouTube who put up a video of himself standing in front of it and explained that, "Standing before Daniel Johnston's mural in Austin, Texas, was a highlight of my trip across the United States."

"It must be a strain to be so well liked." After all these years, pulled in all these directions, Jeremiah remains. The rest of the artwork at the corner of Twenty-first and Guadalupe has been cut away. Until workers started poking holes in Jeremiah and preparing for demolition of "the People's Frog," no one stopped this from happening. But people did take away pieces of the Kozik mural after it was destroyed (Onorato).

March 16, 2005

Daniel Johnston is scheduled to play a free show during the South by Southwest music festival. I don't know who he is, and I've never heard his music. As we enter the store, an overweight, gray-haired man is leaning against the outside of the store, smoking a cigarette. Hushed voices. Pointing. We wait about an hour before realizing he's never going to play. We leave, and I press the friends who brought me there: "Who does this guy think he is?"

Space appropriates, and it only makes sense to address this appropriation head on. The term *appropriation* connotes extremes: one who appropriates another culture is a culture vulture; one who appropriates an image or a sound or a text without permission is a thief. But what if appropriation were refigured as a way to highlight exactly what it supposedly erases? What if it were an attempt to directly engage the problem that space is in constant movement and flux? Space is cultivated, groomed, managed, held together (just barely, it often seems) by relations, forces, and powers. But even this definition doesn't fully capture how space operates, since it still suggests that space is bounded and boxed in. How do we continually remind ourselves that this is not the case, even when we live a life that feels as if space is a container? One way is to grab on to space and remake it, remold it, put it into other contexts and ecologies.

Texas seems an ideal site to understand appropriation as a research method, given that Texas is appropriated and appropriates. It fascinates. It draws people in. Sometimes it repels, but even this response signals an attempt by the Lone Star State to grab us. For most of my life, I never understood Texas's fascination with itself. My first encounter with "Texas" (as an idea) was at Lone Star Steakhouse and Saloon in Monroeville, Pennsylvania. You could order a T-bone and throw your peanut shells on the floor. This was a marketing team's idea of Texas. I remember a massive Texas flag on the wall, and my first thought was how rare it was to see the Pennsylvania state flag anywhere. Being proud of a state was a foreign thing to me. Growing up, I was surrounded by Pittsburgh pride, but no one was waving Pennsylvania's hideous flag.

I carried this same response to the music and artwork of Daniel Johnston, who seemed to me to be little more than a curiosity for hipsters. Have you heard of Daniel Johnston? No? You just failed the indie rock litmus test. My experience at the Escapist Bookstore only reinforced the idea that the fascination with Johnston involved everything that made me uncomfortable with the indie rock music scene (a scene I sit right in the middle of): "This guy's voice is weird. I think I'm supposed to love it . . . yeah, I think I *do* love it." The documentary *The Devil and Daniel Johnston* solidified this for me, as it details how Johnston's mental illness was used to build the myth of a mad genius who recorded lo-fi songs and distributed them on cassette tapes.

But Texas appropriated me, and so did Johnston's work. I watch establishing shots on the television show *Friday Night Lights* and miss the Texas prairie. I listen to Johnston's songs and other artists' covers of them, and I miss going to shows at Emo's and the Red Eyed Fly. My initial response to this appropriative pull was to hold both Texas and Johnston at arm's length, to attempt to stand apart from them. But I now see this as a response that is not only impossible but also counterproductive. Space appropriates, and our responses might as well acknowledge it. What would it mean to understand scholarly engagements with space as appropriations, as attempts to make space into something else? And how might we take up this method carefully, thoughtfully, and ethically? My own response to Texas, to Daniel Johnston, to Jeremiah sits alongside all these other appropriations—scholarly or otherwise. A number of scholarly treatments of space have addressed how space is appropriated—how "users" of space are able to reimagine it, to hack it to their own ends. These appropriations happen in response to the designs and logics of architects, and they reveal that every space is a possibility space, one that welcomes tinkerings. Skaters appropriate parks. Graffiti artists appropriate walls. Pedestrians make their own walkways, wearing down grass even when cement paths exist. But what of the scholar of space?

Lefebvre's *The Production of Space* introduces three key concepts for scholars of space: spatial practice, representations of space, and representational spaces. Spatial practices demonstrate how everyday social interactions infuse and are infused by physical spaces. The analyst of a society's practices learns to decode them by "deciphering its space" (38). Representations of space, on the other hand, reveal the "conceptualized space . . . of scientists, planners, urbanists, technocratic subdividers and social engineers" (38). Finally, representational spaces describe the lived experience of "inhabitants and users," and it is the "dominated—hence passively experienced—space which the imagination seeks to change and appropriate. It overlays physical space, making symbolic use of its objects" (39). Space emerges from a dynamic interplay among these three sets of forces.

Lefebvre argues that the tension between representations of space and representational space is of particular interest. In fact, he sees this tension as "the *entire* problem" when it comes to understanding space (365). If representations of space reflect the discourses of designers and technocrats, then any thoroughgoing attempt to understand representational spaces must somehow reflect lived experience without falling back on the representations of those designers. The map is not the territory, but the map's power in shaping experience and articulations of experience is such that it is difficult to envision the territory:

> One of the deepest conflicts immanent to space is that space as actually "experienced" prohibits the expression of conflicts. For conflicts to be voiced, they must first be perceived, and this without subscribing to representations of space as generally conceived. A *theory* is therefore called for, one which would transcend representational space on the one hand and representations of space on the other, and which would be able properly to articulate contradictions (and in the first place the contradiction between these two aspects of representation). (365)

Appropriation presents a starting point for the theory that Lefebvre calls for here. However, it doesn't quite operate in the way he might have envisioned it. First, appropriation does not transcend anything—it would sit in space and be of space. Second, it would not necessarily articulate contradictions—it would perform them. Much the way a remix or a mashup appropriates a song, showing us its different possibilities, or a port of a video game demonstrates the affordances and constraints of software platforms, an appropriation of space does not argue representationally.

The complaints that Jeremiah is a relic of an Austin that no longer exists require a response, since those complaints assume that such a space exists. And it does, of course, in what Lefebvre would call representational space. It matters how people experience, conceive of, and appropriate space toward their own ends. This is part of the complex matrix of space, which is always in motion. But without tying that representational space to the other two legs of Lefebvre's triangle, to the design of space and to spatial practices, we are left with the idea that a space (Austin, "the Drag," Jeremiah, or any other space) could somehow be free of appropriation or cultivation.

The arguments for a pure "Austin" (perhaps the one that is reflected in the film *Slacker*) rely on a notion of space that must constantly be disrupted, if only because it is built directly into our perception of space. If, as Doreen Massey argues, the complexities of a space are "by no means all included within that place itself," then it makes no sense to draw clean distinctions when addressing the various appropriations of a space. My own tattoo sits alongside Rebecca Guest's spray paint:

> The identities of place are always unfixed, contested and multiple. And the particularity of any place is, in these terms, constructed not by placing boundaries around it and defining its identity through counterposition to the other which lies beyond, but precisely (in part) through the specificity of the mix of links and interconnections to that "beyond." Places viewed this way are open and porous. (5)

Appropriation lets go of the possibility that the frame around Jeremiah cuts him off from a gallery wall in Grenoble, France, where Jeremiah was reproduced as part of an "Art in Pop" exhibition, or from the iOS app that features him. More than this, it lets go of the possibility that my tattoo is external to my attempt to understand the forces at play on this particular street corner in Austin. Lefebvre says that "it is only *in* space that such conflicts come effectively into play, and in so doing they become contradictions *of* space" (365). This suggests that we must put ourselves into space to best understand its contradictions and that we are better served by appropriating space than by falling back on the "fetishization of communication," which always leads back to and is co-opted by the technocrat's representations of space. And yet here I am, writing about space. Maybe the tattoo can at least save me from the *complete* fetishization of communication.

Massey argues that the flux of space-time is constant, that our experience of space is stable and still is just that—an experience. A fiction. Still, we have few other options than writing more fiction:

> All attempts to institute horizons, to establish boundaries, to secure the identity of places, can in this sense therefore be seen to be attempts to stabilize the meaning of particular envelopes of space-time. They are attempts to get to grips with the unutterable mobility and contingency of space-time. (5)

The Jeremiah on my arm stands as a testament to the extension of this space beyond the frame, beyond the wall, beyond the trees that shade the sidewalk on Twenty-first Street. Perhaps a simple image search isn't enough evidence that this space is contested, fluid, multiple, in motion. Perhaps it's not enough to notice that every image of Jeremiah is slightly different. New graffiti emerges and disappears. Jeremiah's bottom lip was once a bit bigger than his top lip. Maybe the very fact that constructing a timeline of what was

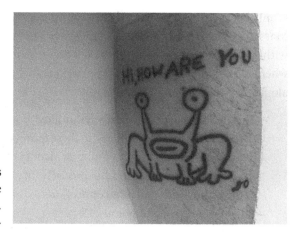

Figure 1.3. The author's tattoo, based on the March 2005 image. Photograph by author.

on that white brick wall at specific moments in time (When was that window built? Why didn't anyone care about the fly eye?) isn't enough to demonstrate that this space is in constant flux. Fine, then I will show you my tattoo, which reflects a very particular version of Jeremiah, one that appears to have been signed by an artist with the initials "D. O.," since at some point the lower loop of Johnston's "J" was painted over (see fig. 1.3 for images of both the tattoo and Johnston's initials).

When did Jeremiah look like this? I honestly couldn't tell you. I chose this image because it has been on my computer's desktop for more years than I can count. It is an entirely arbitrary choice, which seems odd given the permanence of a tattoo. But it's the one I grabbed when placing it on my desktop. The permanence of tattoo ink meets the impermanence of space, but even this isn't quite right. Skin stretches, and ink fades and bleeds. Years from now, the top loop of Johnston's "J" that now looks like an "O" will probably just look like a dot on my arm.

Appropriation signals two contradictory forces at once. First, it points directly to the iterability of any space. (You think I'm the only one with this frog tattoo?) But this same appropriation points to the unavoidable situatedness of space. Situatedness here should not be understood as some notion of authentic, physical space—as pointing to some single place that is easily circumscribed. Quite the opposite. Here, the tattoo is situated in a constantly moving network of space-time. Appropriation creates something new and sheds new light on that which is appropriated, and in any appropriation worth its salt, the source material asserts itself. In his discussion of two vandals dumping paint on the Joe Louis monument in Detroit—a large black fist—Marback reminds us that rhetoricians should be concerned with much more than just our responses to an object or a space. The Joe Louis fist might trigger a range of responses, and it might mean different things to different audiences (the vandals saw it as a symbol of black power), but these different meanings don't mean that the fist is "an empty gesture in need of interpretation to stabilize its signification (52). Our responses are important, but they aren't the end of the story:

> If response does matter more than the object itself, then we are at a real loss to make sense of the vandalism as a response to some thing the vandals perceived as outside themselves, some thing that has such weight they cannot but take extreme action against it. (51)

Marback argues that we must "give the object its due" and that we should recognize the "mutual vulnerability" among objects, spaces, and people. This means "[forgoing] the claim to agency we make when we project our sovereignty over objects" (59). Neither the physical thing we call "Jeremiah" nor my attempt to make sense of it stands alone, and neither sits still either. But all we really have are brief moments of arrest, appropriations that freeze time and space in order to make sense of things. This is more than a recognition that I speak from some perspective or that the object means different things to different people—it's a recognition that I am not here and Jeremiah is not there. The appropriative method I have in mind suggests not only that I transform a space to understand it but also that it transforms me into a different person in the interaction. I am situated in space, which extends outward and beyond 21st and Guadalupe.

Consider this essay my cover of Johnston's song "When You're Pretty." (To my knowledge, no cover of this song has ever been officially released.) It's easy to miss, but in this song, Daniel Johnston is singing about time and space. Otherwise, the song would have been called "Because You're Pretty."

Note

1. The press release announcing this change of plans is telling in this regard, since it makes no secret of what the company and Oudt hoped to gain from this publicity:

> "Our partner, John Oudt, shares the Baja Fresh philosophy—that it's our mission to provide fresh flavorful food and support the lifestyles of our customers," said Greg Dollarhyde, CEO of Baja Fresh. "John's a Texan and understands that this community wants to Save the Frog. He's incurring this expense because it's so important to the people of Austin."
>
> Baja Fresh prides itself on its no compromises approach when it comes to freshness and flavor. The restaurant uses No freezers; No microwaves, No can openers; No MSG or lard; and only uses boneless, marinated chicken breast, and lean USDA choice steak for their unique burritos, tacos, enchiladas, fajitas,

and ensaladas. For its signature "Baja-style" fish tacos, only fresh fish will do. The self-service salsa bar at each location offers salsas freshly prepared several times daily using top-quality produce. ("Baja Fresh Saves the Frog")

Works Cited

Alexander, Heather. "Police: Iconic Austin Frog Defaced by Woman Who Thought It Spoke to Her." *Houston Chronicle*, 26 Dec. 2013, www.chron .com/news/houston-texas/texas/article/Police-Iconic-Austin-Frog-defaced -by-woman-who-5094160.php. Accessed 13 May 2015.

"Baja Fresh Saves the Frog: Texas Entrepreneur Spends Personal Dollars to Save Culturally Important Austin Artwork." *The Free Library*, 7 Jan. 2004, *PR Newswire Association LLC*, 15 Aug. 2017 www.thefreelibrary.com/Baja +Fresh+Saves+the+Frog%3b+Texas+Entrepreneur+Spends+Personal+Dollars ...-a0111945984. Accessed 24 Mar. 2017.

"Best of Austin: Best Mural: Soundexchange." *Austin Chronicle*, 2002, www. austinchronicle.com/best-of-austin/year:2002/poll:readers/category: architecture-and-lodging/sound-exchange-best-mural/. Accessed 19 May 2015.

Connelly, Kelly, and Wells Dunbar. "What Happens When Iconic Austin Street Art Is Defaced?" *KUT*, 12 July 2012, kut.org/post/what-happens-when-iconic -austin-street-art-defaced. Accessed 18 May 2015.

"The Daniel Johnston Frog Mural in Austin, Texas." *Chronological Snobbery*, 27 May 2010, www.chronologicalsnobbery.com/2010/05/daniel-johnston -frog-mural-in-austin.html. Accessed 18 May 2015.

Gray, Christopher. "TCB: *Austin City Limits*, Cannonized!" *Austin Chronicle*, 23 Apr. 2004, www.austinchronicle.com/music/2004-04-23/207600/. Accessed 19 May 2015.

Lefebvre, Henri. *The Production of Space*. Wiley-Blackwell, 1992.

Marback, Richard. "Unclenching the Fist: Embodying Rhetoric and Giving Objects Their Due." *Rhetoric Society Quarterly*, vol. 38, no. 1, 2008, pp. 46–65.

Massey, Doreen. *Space, Place, and Gender*. University of Minnesota Press, 1994.

Onorato, John. "About the Frog." *Austincommunity*, 7 Jan. 2004, austincommunity .livejournal.com/976809.html. Accessed 19 May 2015.

Solomon, Dan. "The People's Frog." *Texas Observer*, 5 Nov. 2010, www. texasobserver.org/the-peoples-frog/. Accessed 19 May 2015.

Yazdani, Tarssa, and Don Goede. *Hi, How Are You? The Life, Art, & Music of Daniel Johnston*. 2nd ed., Last Gasp, 2006.

Megan Gianfagna,
University of Texas—Austin

2. FIGMENTS OF A FUTURE AUSTIN: IMAGINATION ON THE RISE

It is often said that if something is conceptual, it is only an idea, but that is missing the point. It is because it is an idea that it is important.
—Anthony Dunne and Fiona Raby, *Speculative Everything*

After the dream, they set out in search of that city; they never found it, but they found one another; they decided to build a city like the one in the dream. —Italo Calvino, *Invisible Cities*

*W*e begin in Comuna 13 in Medellín, Colombia, two thousand miles and thirty years from the imagined place where we will end. Comuna 13 has a story that reads like fiction, an entry in Calvino's famous and absorbing novella.[1] It's a vivid place that feels at once sharply present and intangible, known until recently for its inaccessibility to outsiders and its inhospitable iron grip on inhabitants. It looks like a dreamscape. Built into a steep hillside, the neighborhood consists of technicolor shanties that are crammed and layered upward as far as the eye can see. From a distance, the ascent is stunning. But for two decades, a darkness sat among the colors, claustrophobia marked by abject poverty and violence that lurked around "invisible borders," as Michael Kimmelman calls them in his *New York Times* profile of the city, erected by those in power. Pablo Escobar and his cartel had oozed into the barrio, slow and sticky. The mess remained long after Escobar's death in 1993.

Underlying the manmade drama of the scene were the hardships imposed by the hill itself. As people pieced together their lives each day, most trudged ahead on foot, climbing hundreds of stories up and down the hill as they moved to and from the city. The long, slow journey kept the people weary and made them incidental to the rhythm of life below. Even so, how many times at the end of a long day must those living in Comuna 13 have daydreamed of ways to float back to their homes high above but had no means to give those dreams form?

Then, finally, a change came. It happened in 2011 through "a mixture of ideas and bricks," according to Alejandro Echeverri, director of urban projects   29 under Medellín's former mayor Sergio Fajardo and the person on the ground carrying out Fajardo's mission to make life better in Comuna 13 (Vulliamy). With conviction, the city carved six wide, bold ribbons into the hillside. The world's first massive outdoor escalators now zigzag up the hill, gleaming silver in the Colombia sun as they carry inhabitants quickly to and from the center of town. The escalators act as surrealist artwork and as giant magnets, pulling tourists looking to ride the wave of progress into the bleeding heart of history. They come looking for signs of an insurmountable past from the safety of the stairway, but what they see is its slow, winding trail as it begins to evaporate into the blue sky above. The people are changing, in increments, with the hill, trading war for peace of mind, jobs, and mobility in and around the barrio.

Placemaking as Risk-taking

A collective dream by city officials to spur economic growth and improve quality of life in Medellín gave rise to the escalators and other works of public architecture such as libraries and parks. The work of Medellín's architects, policymakers, and urban planners is what designer Anthony Dunne and designer-architect Fiona Raby call "critical design," which aims to be "intentionally at odds" with the present (17) to facilitate change "by generating alternatives" (44). Comuna 13's story shouts of the transformative powers of a speculative act—one that dreams of new ways forward and seeks to change the existing framework rather than simply hoping to survive within it (9). But even the most ordinary cities are built by and evolve through everyday acts of risk, curiosity, and imagination.[2]

Change constitutes places as much as their material elements or maps do. As Calvino writes, "There is the city where you arrive for the first time; and there is another city which you leave never to return" (125). Intentional interventions in place are just one catalyst of change among many, including natural processes and alterations in the patterns of our daily lives that we make for ourselves but that alter, with varying degrees of subtlety, the energy and interactions around us. I focus here on the potential of change to be precipitated by intentional choices made through critical design and discourse, primarily because those types of changes shape and are shaped by the felt identity of the place itself, making them a key factor in both social and economic health.[3]

Two defining features of critical design are its intent to anticipate the needs of a future state of being and its way of inviting conversation that "can help people construct compasses rather than maps for navigating new sets of values" (Dunne and Raby 44). The goal, then, is not to stabilize a future or prescribe a path, but rather to create space for weighing possible futures. In the case of Comuna 13, the most fully present needs in 2011 were increased safety and income. To those ends, people kept their heads down, valuing anonymity and silence in the face of ever-present danger. Two other needs were not as manifest then—the need for public gathering space and the need for extra leisure time as a vast improvement to quality of life—but according to residents of Comuna 13, those have been the most powerful effects of the escalators (Reimerink). The escalators moved people to reimagine themselves in relation to a future they didn't know they needed.

Austins for Everyone

Like Medellín, Texas's capital city of Austin sees itself as defiantly different. Basques colonized Medellín, while Spaniards settled most of Colombia. Echeverri notes that the people are "fiercely proud" of this distinction as well as all that has arisen from it, be it Escobar or dignitaries, because they couldn't have come from anywhere but Medellín, a city so bold and full of energy that it "replace[s] its own cell structure" (Vulliamy). Austin's quirky, laid-back, trendsetting, liberal identity largely gets constructed from the ways it's thoroughly Texan without resembling the rest of Texas.[4] Now the city is spending a lot of time and resources facilitating a conversation around what it should become. The most crystallized idea at this point, as expressed in the "Imagine Austin Comprehensive Plan," is that it wants to be vibrant, livable, and connected. Those are the words that city officials hope will be associated with Austin's brand and that have colored the conversation in social media campaigns and community forums. What a vibrant, livable, connected city really looks like is what the city is still working out for itself, and where city officials, private consulting groups, and Austin's inhabitants are making critical interventions.

The process of inventing a future Austin began in 2009, when the city launched its initiative with a name that reads like both a public invitation and an imperative. Imagine Austin is an ongoing, large-scale effort to shape Austin's brand, character, and infrastructure. This is happening through wide-ranging efforts from residents sharing accounts of the kind of city they'd like to live in to a wholesale redesign of the city land use code. At many points along the way, inhabitants have provided input into the plans by participating in public workshops around specific issues such as transportation, the creative economy, and environmental health; by sharing their priorities for Austin on Twitter and on whiteboards posted at city events; and by using toolkits provided by the city to conduct surveys of their individual neighborhoods' defining features.

Imagine Austin is a thoroughly speculative enterprise. The word *speculative* comes from *specula*, for "watchtower" ("Speculative"), and Imagine Austin has the desire for a sweeping view of the city and for guardianship over what it becomes. Imagine Austin, like Medellín's larger-than-life escalators, 31 makes visible vital, ongoing placemaking processes that seem remarkable when they surface but are in fact part of the very structure of place. Places are always imagined, in a sense. Kevin Lynch writes that "our images of past and future are present images, continuously re-created" (65). Take Comuna 13 for example. There the Escobar years will always seep into memory and be a reference point for progress, the thing that made the barrio what it was, the thing it overcame to become a new version of itself.

Places, then, are never fully present, never cohesive or reliable or still. But they are rich material from which people construct for themselves a reality, coextensive with a mythology, that puts them in actionable and meaningful relation to its elements. Even what we think of as place's linchpin, its geography, is a moving target. Edward Said writes that geography is "a socially constructed and maintained sense of place" (180) that "stimulates not only memory but dreams and fantasies, poetry and painting, philosophy . . . fiction . . . and music" (181). These kinds of creative works reflect that places exist in multiplicity, and voicing the time-places one wishes to see or wants to avoid make that multiplicity visible. That visibility allows for more effective critical interventions, helping inhabitants imagine Austins and in doing so helping destabilize the branded version of that city to make space for other accounts that help hold other possible futures open.

Designing a Future Place

Dunne and Raby argue that imagination is a necessary catalyst for change, one that to be effective must be given the space for expression and applied to even the most mundane aspects of everyday life (44). For them, critical design, whether it's expressed visually or verbally, begins with two words of speculation—What if . . . ?—that launch us out of the present and send us sailing over uncharted territory without a net. The purpose of that experience (or perhaps many iterations of that experience over time) for both designer/writer and audience is to open up space for debate and discussion. By mapping and reacting to future scenarios, people weigh alternatives and iteratively construct a personal and social compass to help guide future attitudes and behavior. Because speculative work anticipates and attends to future needs and not the present, the map that emerges as a product of the what-if work is less important than the process of orienting oneself to desired outcomes. It is an exercise in imagining how we will need to change ourselves to fit the vision as we choose to set it. Who would we have to become to inhabit this future "now"?

To achieve these ends, the what-if scenarios of critical design are "by necessity provocative, intentionally simplified, and fictional. Their fictional nature requires viewers to suspend their disbelief and allow their imaginations to wander, to momentarily forget how things are now, and wonder about how things could be" (Dunne and Raby 3). Lynch also calls for speculation presented as fiction. He writes that "the creation of fantasy is a way of exploring future alternatives and suggesting new modes of action. Any open society will have some means for generating and communicating these dreams" (95). To participate in placemaking in a way that honors the centrality of change and the risks it demands is an uncomfortable scholarly pursuit and an exciting one. When we speak of methods for rhetorical research, "risky" and "not based on fact or investigation" aren't attributes that come to mind. Method implies a kind of rigor and certainty that provide a safety net: even if the outcome isn't what one expected, the approach and data can still be good.

For rhetoricians exploring places and their possible futures, critical design is quite a fitting, if unfamiliar, lens that can help put the safety net out of focus. In advance of cities instituting massive public works, city officials and residents engage in the rhetorical speculation of framing the future. In Medellín, safety and public gathering spaces were guiding ideals. The tagline for Imagine Austin—"Vibrant. Livable. Connected."—and the way present-day Austin is described in published reports around the project mean that from the onset, more value gets attached to some of the ideas than others produced by the collective reimagining of the city's identity. Before city officials and residents know what the city will become, they have characterized its evolution. The necessary fictions created around urban change influence material shifts in the environment; those material changes, in turn, reinscribe the articulated vision with new meaning.

The vignette, as a form, fits Dunne and Raby's criteria for a critical design project. Vignettes are brief and evocative, yet they seem to exceed their boundaries, inviting the reader to wonder what else is at play in the world he or she just caught a quick glimpse of. They are a useful form for thinking many diverse things together in quick succession. Vignettes lend themselves to reflecting the experience—past, present, or future—of life in a place. They value subtle but striking details over the careful definition of one idea. The beauty of vignettes is that they do not carry the burden of painting a cohesive picture or providing actionable information. Instead, they help relay the way place is often encountered: in flashes, traces, and affects.

What-if-based design work also offers the benefit of allowing the writer to be flagrantly contradictory in order to create a friction with the familiar. Friction is necessary to start new ideas in motion. The vignette offers a particularly neat way of achieving this, as its brevity makes it perfectly acceptable, if not expected, to leave some holes in the story. These holes can be invitations for further speculation, whereas in a longer form piece, the expectation is that the author will trace out details and tie up loose ends. When employed in succession, as Calvino demonstrates, vignettes invite

33

comparison with reality and among possible futures. This allows the collaborative vetting of something that has made an impression on the designer/writer prior to its existence.

So, taking seriously Dunne and Raby's claim that "rich and thought-provoking fictional worlds can be developed from idiosyncratic starting points" (86), and believing that these minutiae are the real impressions from which we construct a sense of place anyway, I offer up three future Austins. Each was seeded by an idea that constellated around the Imagine Austin effort, and they do not necessarily exclude one another. They are speculative interventions into the collective public work of imagining possible futures for a city whose future is important to me, a former resident and big fan. Because I see the preapplied characterizations of the future city as in need of particular scrutiny and playful recasting, I have organized my contributions under these banners.

Vibrant Austin

They found themselves drawn to the sounds floating out of doorways and up into the warm, blue sky. They had come to hear a city alive with sound and stayed because of how they could taste the grit, the twist, and the joy of it in their three square meals, how they could smell its smoky breath through every open window. They built their houses right in the middle of it all, high above the rooflines, where they imagined they could see the most and catch even the stray notes as they floated away. They felt invigorated there, as if they could be people who were part of that energy. So there they stayed.

It's hard to say exactly when the charm wore off, when they started to see the surfaces without the glow of neon and moonlight, or when they began to analyze decibels rather than absorb the ambience. They shouted loudly enough out their windows that the people on the streets grew tired of the interference. So now, as they stand in front of a coffee shop platform or a stage flooded in dancing lights, they all hear the music and feel the beat in their heads. You'd think that such a thing would seem strange, so many people bobbing together to a silent but palpable melody. But when tourists came to the city billed as offbeat, they chose to see a cool new kind of audience and clamored to be part of the performance. When the tower dwellers have visitors from their old lives ask what brought them to this place, they say they saw the opportunity to stake their claim in a city that's growing up. The visitors nod their heads in understanding but know that really the answer floated away long ago with the last loud, bluesy note.

Livable Austin

The day the traffic stopped for good, it took people a while to realize what was happening. At first they sat patiently as if it were just another Tuesday rush hour, an accident at worst. But the longer they sat, the more their imagination ran wild and the more restless they became at not knowing what was ahead. Because of the nervousness and the long wait, some had to pee, and they did so as discreetly as possible, crouching by the back tires of a semitruck. When the news eventually came on the radio, the reporters announced it matter-of-factly, speaking just as much to commuters in Arkansas or Abilene as to the people sitting right there on those newsworthy highways. No instruction was given on how the commuters should proceed. No one was supposed to be surprised.

So, no longer drivers, they improvised their way along the highway that night. Some picked up their briefcases and ran full speed down the median, hoping they could still make the tail end of happy hour. Others climbed down to the surface roads and flagged down a passing biker, hitching a ride on the handlebars. Still others, disoriented, wandered along the endless line of cars, staring straight ahead, their legs moving when their minds would not. A few simply slept there, unwilling to leave their property behind and hoping the morning sun would dissipate this terrible dream.

The next day, the sun gleamed off the windshields of that endless line like a secondary sunrise. People got up. They rode and ran and walked to work, many jumping from trunk to hood, playing out an action movie fantasy along that strange trail. Then, sweaty and late, they sat smiling at their desks until the first ding of a new email snapped them back into the rhythm of the day. Later, families satisfying a need for fresh air and a firsthand look strolled down the open boulevard, passing people selling tacos and doughnuts and coffee who dotted the route. The whole thing had the air of a parade. It only grew in familiarity and fanfare week by week, quickly becoming a favorite place to see and be seen. Meanwhile, on the lower roads, the crowds at the bus stops spilled out into the street, anxious and irritated at the delays. The train, deemed a luxury meant for a fussier city, never came.

Connected Austin

When the ground begins to sag in spots, under a dog's paw or the weight of a bike tire, and people walking to brunch begin to stumble inelegantly on the turf, a practiced crew sweeps across the promenade, injecting foam beneath the green expanses to return the structure to its proper lift. There is no sign but this of the unconventional origin of downtown's newest neighborhood, the West of East District. It straddles what was once the edge of downtown and the . . . ahem . . . "up-and-coming" neighborhoods to its east. The idea was to increase mobility for people wanting easy access to more of the city, but so far, years later, the traffic has only been one-way.

Few remember how WofE was made possible by the creation of a tomb. To create the booming, walkable boulevard above, the city buried what was

Megan Gianfagna

once the most congested highway in the state and the fourth worst in the country, a noisy, ugly thing. Even fewer would know the full weight of the concrete corridor below as a divider, keeping East Enders east of the city whose name, they thought then as now, still applies to their neighborhoods too. When the city buried the offensive concrete mass and the congestion it bore, its citizens celebrated loudly the unification of the business districts as rising rents matter-of-factly pushed the divided people farther east and out of sight of all but those who had a curiosity for new frontiers and a craving to see different-colored faces at the grocery store. People in WofE walk the shops along the promenade or do sun salutations in the park's morning dew, enjoying unobstructed views of a city moving into the future. When the ground sinks just a bit beneath them, they smile quietly to themselves at how well loved this place must be to already be so well worn.

Notes

1. *Invisible Cities* is a short work that explores the nature of place in a series of vignettes. In each of the surreal accounts that Marco Polo, the novel's main voice, gives to Kublai Khan, he uses one aspect of Venice's history, culture, or landscape to craft a city that feels entirely like another world.

2. A mundane example might be that someone opens a shop, with no true precedent and no guarantees. Maybe one by one people realize that they are or want to be the kind of people who need what it sells. The city is changed, and so are they in some small way. If the venture fails, then still something has been said about the future direction of the city, and others to come will reference that failure. In recent years in Austin, where we are about to arrive, this has been a frozen "fruit poop" stand, any number of massive mixed-use developments, and a dog park–bar combination.

3. See Ash Amin and Nigel Thrift on London and Jim W. Corder on West Texas.

4. See Jenny Edbauer's account of how Austin's identity has been constructed around the "Keep Austin Weird" campaign.

Works Cited

Amin, Ash, and Nigel Thrift. *Cities: Reimagining the Urban*. Polity Press, 2002.
Calvino, Italo. *Invisible Cities*. Translated by William Weaver. Harcourt, 1974.
Corder, Jim W. *Yonder: Life on the Far Side of Change*. 1992. U of Georgia P, 2011.
Dunne, Anthony, and Fiona Raby. *Speculative Everything: Design, Fiction, and Social Dreaming*. MIT Press, 2013.
Edbauer, Jenny. "Unframing Models of Public Distribution: From Rhetorical Situation to Rhetorical Ecologies." *Rhetoric Society Quarterly*, vol. 35, no. 4, 2005, pp. 5–24.

36

"Imagine Austin Comprehensive Plan." AustinTexas.gov. 2012, amended 2016, ftp://ftp.ci.austin.tx.us/npzd/IACP_amended2016_web_sm.pdf. Accessed 3 Mar. 2015.

Kimmelman, Michael. "A City Rises, Along with Its Hopes." *New York Times*, 18 May 2012.

Lynch, Kevin. *What Time Is This Place?* MIT Press, 1972.

Reimerink, Letty. "Medellín Made Urban Escalators Famous, but Have They Had Any Impact?" *Cityscope*, 24 July 2014.

Said, Edward. "Invention, Memory, and Place." *Critical Inquiry*, vol. 26, no. 2, 2000, pp. 175–92.

"Speculative." *New Oxford American Dictionary.* 3rd ed., 2010.

Vulliamy, Ed. "Medellín, Colombia: Reinventing the World's Most Dangerous City." *Guardian*, 9 June 2013.

Anna M. "Amy" Young,
Pacific Lutheran University

3. RHETORICS OF SMOKE AND CEDAR: THE TERROIR OF TEXAS BBQ

*T*exas governor Greg Abbott ordered the Texas State Guard to monitor the U.S. military as it conducted Operation Jade Helm because he felt it ushered in an Obama-imposed martial law. Abbott delayed a request for federal aid through FEMA after the worst flooding in Texas history. But his most egregious offense? The one that drove thousands of people to comment on sites like Eater Austin? Greg Abbott believes that "Austin is ground zero for barbecue" and that "the most important thing about barbecue is the sauce" (Chaudhury). Although Austinites' slavish devotion to Franklin's and Mueller's, barbecue institutions with lines beginning at 8 A.M. and that are featured on every travel food show imaginable, including Anthony Bourdain's *No Reservations*, helps in some way to support Abbott's first claim, his second is blasphemous. Texas barbecue is a sauce-on-the-side variety for two main reasons. First, if a pit master spends fourteen hours smoking a brisket to achieve the Maillard reaction, the crisp browning on the outside of the meat, and the sought-after smoke ring that ought to be about a quarter inch thick all the way around when you slice into it, that pit master wants you to taste the brisket in its unadulterated, smoky, wonderful glory. Second, many Texas pit masters are somewhat antisauce because they feel it is too often used to cover up bad barbecue or to dress up something that is grilled to make it seem as if it were barbecued.

To the outside observer, all this fuss over barbecue sauce likely seems superficial, if not downright insane. After all, there are certainly much more important things to worry about than barbecue. And yet barbecue is not merely a food—it is a symbolic and material instantiation of a place. Chef, author, and travel guru Anthony Bourdain has argued that the only food truly native to America and invented by Americans is barbecue. Of course, this claim is factually inaccurate—like other food traditions that we call "American," barbecue is a colonized food—but that is hardly the point. Barbecue occupies significant cultural space in America, and experts stake claims in four physical barbecue territories: Memphis, North Carolina, Kansas City, and Texas. Although dozens of books have been written on which barbecue is best (Texas), and although I am not interested in answering that question (actually, I am; it is Texas), I am invested in exploring the rhetorical dimensions of the barbecue terroir of Lockhart, Texas.

In 2003, the Texas Senate followed the Texas House in conferring the title "Barbecue Capital of Texas" on Lockhart (*City of Lockhart, TX*). In other words, Lockhart has staked its public identity on barbecue. In this essay, I argue that Lockhart's terroir is particularly Texan, a response to territory in smoke and flesh. Lockhart's terroir is also deeply rhetorical—it is about a history, a culture, a discourse, production and consumption, a mode of invention, and a style. While this terroir makes barbecue, barbecue in many ways makes Texas—a food destination, the Wild West, a cowboy aesthetic, a vernacular, an outsize pride. A territory, in other words, becomes a state.

The "Barbecue Capital of Texas"

Because this volume is a collection of essays about Texas as a place and the ways rhetorical scholars and scholarship can approach the study of place, it makes sense to provide a little background on Lockhart, the self-proclaimed and legislatively approved "Barbecue Capital of Texas." Lockhart is a small town of about thirteen thousand residents situated on Plum Creek and the Chisholm Trail, approximately twenty-five miles south of Austin. Just before the Civil War, Central Texas generally and Lockhart specifically suffered a massive drought. Crops would not grow, so enterprising farmers started raising cattle instead. On Lockhart's charming and folksy website, we find an invitation:

> The story of historic Lockhart is an ongoing tale of human endeavor, proudly nurtured by her citizens. Lockhart warmly invites you to sample its unique brand of small town hospitality. Step back into the past as you tour beautifully preserved buildings and homes and browse the antique shops. Stay for lunch or dinner. Sample the best barbecue in the world. Come to Lockhart! (*City of Lockhart, TX*)

The visitors' guide separates barbecue restaurants from all other types of eating establishments, and although Chisholm Trail Barbecue is on the list, the highlights are the big three: Black's, Kreuz's, and Smitty's Market. Black's is the oldest of the three and almost the oldest in Texas continuously operated by the same family. Lyndon Johnson served Black's barbecue on the grounds of the U.S. Capitol. A story of passion and drama, Kreuz's and Smitty's are owned by a brother and sister, respectively, who could not agree on how to carry on their family's barbecue restaurant together. Visitors to Lockhart are fiercely loyal to their favorite.

Central Texas is topographically distinct from the rest of the state. Dubbed Hill Country, Central Texas is rolling and green, dotted with German- and

Czech-influenced food- and beverage- and tourist-centered towns where visitors can eat barbecue, drink wine, and still be within easy reach of major cities such as Austin and San Antonio. People tube the lazy rivers, floating coolers of Shiner along for the ride. The vibe of Central Texas is hipper, younger, and decidedly more progressive than the rest of the state. There is a real warmth about the region. I am not from Texas, but I lived in Austin for six years during graduate school, and the pull is still very real. So though this essay is about Texas and terroir and barbecue, it is also something of a love letter to a place that shaped me as a person and as a rhetorical scholar.

Terroir

Terroir is a viticulture term for the influence of environment on wine, "the total impact of any given site—soil, slope, orientation to the sun, and elevation, plus every nuance of climate including rainfall, wind velocity, frequency of fog, cumulative hours of sunshine, average high temperature, average low temperature, and so forth" (MacNeil 21). Terroir explains why Syrah and Shiraz, made with genetically identical grapes, taste so very different: Syrah is a "guy who wears cowboy boots with a tuxedo. Rustic, manly, and yet elegant," whereas Shiraz is defined by a "rich, sappy, berry taste, seductive aromas, and thick, soft texture" (788). The exact translation of *terroir*, though, is "territory"—the notion that land, shaped by culture, by natural environment, by history, by politics, and by those who tend to it, gives rise to a specific, identifiable, and distinct flavor and style.

When viticulturists, enologists, and sommeliers talk terroir, they are talking about earth in two interrelated ways. In one regard, they mean the physical earth from which grapevines grow. That incorporates everything from plot size in hectares to dirt to slope and many other variables. Pinot noir, for instance, is a notoriously finicky grape to grow. It grows well in tremendously challenging earth—rocky, treacherously sloped. Most grapevines would never make it in that kind of earth. But terroir is not only about earth but also about region. Wine culture refers to both region and appellation (*appeller* is French for "to call" but connotes "to name"). So the sparkling white wine from California you served at your anniversary dinner is not and technically cannot be a champagne, because it is not from the Champagne region and it is not appellation d'origine contrôlée. That does not mean it is not a good bottle; it just means we cannot call it champagne because that is a legal classification given by l'Institut national de l'origine et de la qualité in France.

Barbecue may not be overseen by a government organization designed to legally protect Memphis or Kansas City or North Carolina or Texas, but it most certainly has terroir. If we think about the two ways in which viticulturists speak of earth—physical and regional—we can identify barbecue analogues. The physical analogues would include what type of animal and what part of that animal, the kind of wood used for smoking the meat, the amount and type of moisture added to the wood, dry or wet rub, temperature, time on indirect versus direct heat, and the savoir faire of the pit master. In Lockhart, as in most of Texas, the preferred meat is beef and the preferred parts are brisket and ribs. Texas pit masters tend to use native oak and pecan woods to smoke their meats, but other regions such as North Carolina use hickory or fruit woods. Every pit master has her or his rub, which can be wet or dry (dry in Texas), and every pit master has a particular way of controlling temperature, moisture, wind, heat, and cooking time to produce a barbecue that is identifiably from Lockhart, Texas, or High Point, North Carolina, or Memphis or Kansas City. In a material and embodied sense, barbecue is tethered to place.

And in another analogy with wine, while you may prefer red, within the broad category of red there are significant variations in fruit, mouth feel, body, and weight such that you may favor an Old World Bordeaux while I'm more partial to a New World Zinfandel. With barbecue, you might like the general category of smoked meat, but within that, people have distinct preferences for pork versus beef, for sandwiches versus meat with sides, and for sauced versus unsauced. The physical and topographic aspects, climate, and earth of a place all contribute to the barbecue it produces. In this way, Lockhart produces a barbecue that other "earths" will not and cannot.

But perhaps the more intriguing and certainly more rhetorical element of terroir is this notion of region. Region is very political. How do we draw the boundaries, for instance, of what I am referring to as Central Texas? Who lived there? Who lives there now? Do they care for the land or are they razing it for industrial development or polluting it with toxins? How do they care for their animals? How do they vote? What sorts of traditions do they uphold? If physical earth dictates cow rather than pig and pecan instead of hickory in Lockhart, region asks us to consider the cultural traditions that surround barbecue, the economics of raising animals and running a restaurant in rural Texas, the politics of land use, the dynamics of serving the local versus the tourist community, and so on. As Jeff Rice explains, "terroir, as a rhetorical process . . . aggregates a number of meanings" (162).

Let's unpack this notion of *region* in terroir a bit in terms of Lockhart, because understanding what it means, how it is negotiated, how it is articulated, and how it circulates are inherently rhetorical concerns. Texas is somewhat slippery to distinguish as a region. Some would argue that Texas is the South—after all, it was a member of the Confederacy, and it retains in its culture both the beauty and the ugliness of the post-Reconstruction South. Others would argue that it is the Southwest—like New Mexico and Arizona, it has been shaped profoundly by native and Mexican peoples, traditions, and cultures. Still others would label Texas as something entirely its own—a nation within a nation, a state so expansive geographically that it makes classification nearly impossible. Central Texas, where Lockhart sits, is no different. How do we draw borders? Officially, Central Texas is the region surrounding Austin, bordered by Brady, Kerrville, La Grange, and Waco. Yet there are maps that include even cities such as Lubbock in Central Texas. So it is a geographic area that is somewhat contentious even to other Texans. Just because the state or the local chamber of commerce draws boundaries in definite ways, rhetorical terroir asks us to consider Central Texas as a region in dotted outline as part of the aggregate meaning of the region.

Lockhart negotiated its terroir as the "Barbecue Capital of Texas" beginning nearly two decades ago. Using Jeff Rice's notion of terroir as an aggregation, we might interrogate the decision to pursue this very formal distinction. On May 26, 1999, the Texas State House passed Resolution 1024, identifying Lockhart as the official "Barbecue Capital of Texas." In 2003, the Texas State Senate affirmed the resolution, and Lockhart claimed its mantle. We can really only speculate why Lockhart would pursue a legal designation. In all my research, I have never found an explicit rationale. Yet if we think about the origin of the term *terroir*, and we think about countries such as France, Germany, and Italy, where region and appellation are highly sought-after designations, we might trace in dotted outline an explanation. Names matter. If Texas is already a place that is recognized by any worthwhile barbecue aficionado as a seat of barbecue excellence, Lockhart's move to be legislatively official as the "capital" ensures its inclusion on almost any foodie's map. A useful analogue is the Michelin system of stars. In 1900, the Michelin tire company began the system of rating restaurants to encourage road tripping around France. Today earning and keeping Michelin stars is a priority among chefs and restaurateurs because these stars mean recognition, acclaim, and perhaps most significantly, traffic. The same is likely true for Lockhart—being *named* means they always make it onto the map.

However, this negotiation of terroir did not end with Lockhart's pursuit of and designation as the "Barbecue Capital of Texas." Indeed, identifying the "best" barbecue is a cottage industry. There are barbecue competitions, such as the prestigious Memphis in May. There are guides to barbecue. There are pilgrimages to the top spots as if seeking Mecca. And there are competing interpretations in this negotiation of terroir-as-meaning. Gary Jacobson wrote an article on the *Texas BBQ Posse* blog in 2013 asking the question, "Is Lockhart Losing Its Title as the BBQ Capital of Texas?" Jacobson writes, "Yes, we know that's borderline smoked-meat heresy. But on our recent Best of Texas Tour, we ate at three Lockhart joints and only one—Kreuz Market—made our top tier of six. The others—Smitty's Market and Chisholm Trail Bar-B-Que—were well off the pace." *Texas Monthly* magazine has a regular section dedicated to barbecue and is decidedly more pro-Lockhart, naming Black's and Kreuz's among the fifty best barbecue joints in the world ("BBQ"). Michael Park of *Epicurious* devoted a day to eating at each of the four barbecue restaurants in Lockhart and found delights at each. Yet with the popularity of some barbecue places such as Franklin's in Austin bordering on hysteria (the lines begin at 8 A.M. for an 11 A.M. opening), the negotiation of social and cultural capital is ongoing even if Lockhart is still the "capital."

The ways Lockhart's terroir gets articulated are multiple and layered. Barbecue culture has a lexicon just as wine culture does, though it is not nearly as overwrought sounding. True Texas barbecue devotees, for instance, think of the "bark" and the "burnt ends" as perhaps the tastiest eating. "Bark" is the crispy sort of crust that surrounds a brisket, and "burnt ends" are pieces of meat cut from the point of a smoked brisket. I introduced the terms *smoke ring* and *Maillard reaction* early in this chapter. Wood can be "split," in "chips," or in "chunks." In many parts of the United States, the terms *barbecuing* and *grilling* are synonymous and interchangeable. Should you use the term *barbecuing* in Texas for anything other than cooking a piece of rubbed meat "low and slow" over indirect heat from a wood fire, however, you will be in grave danger of being the recipient of a series of soapbox speeches from natives and knowledgeable transplants. You will never make that mistake again. Part of articulating terroir, then, is deploying an insider's vocabulary on the subject.

Lockhart does quite a bit of its own horn-tooting. The town's website discusses barbecue on its home page and devotes an entire page to Central Texas barbecue and to its four barbecue restaurants. Similarly, the Lockhart Chamber of Commerce, like the town's website, calls Lockhart by its full name, "Lockhart: Barbecue Capital of Texas." In its section on "BBQ Capital of Texas," all four barbecue restaurants in Lockhart get write-ups. And of course, there are countless publications, food-related television shows, foodie blogs, and social media sites and posts that help articulate Lockhart's terroir as distinctive and special, even in a state that is already considered a station of the cross for barbecue.

Intrinsically related to the articulation of terroir is its circulation. In other words, how does the aggregate meaning of Lockhart's terroir get distributed among expert and lay publics? Jeff Rice argues that networks are central to the circulated meaning of terroir (160). In his book *Craft Obsession*, Rice speaks to the significance of social media and digital sites as networks for craft beer terroir. Being able to rate a beer, finding out what is on tap at your favorite watering hole, learning of a new release, and talking about beer with other enthusiasts contribute to a networked circulation of terroir. Barbecue is no different. There are several *Facebook* pages devoted to Lockhart; food blogs about Central Texas barbecue such as *Texas Monthly BBQ*, *Texas BBQ Posse*, and *Full Custom Gospel BBQ*; and *YouTube* videos featuring the culinary delights of Lockhart. Rice also argues that "persona" is an "important actor in the network that generates terroir" (162). Travel and food expert Anthony Bourdain has raved about Lockhart, but the persona of Texans is really what sells. Texans are interpellated as fiercely proud of their state, as cowboys, as ranchers, as western, and importantly to this project, as people who know barbecue. So if Texans speak of Lockhart with reverence or in hushed tones, their persona helps circulate terroir's meaning through networks.

Visual imagery is also meaningful in the circulation of Lockhart's terroir. Amateur and professional photographs of sliced brisket and glistening sausage are almost invariably associated with Lockhart. Piles of pecan wood, waiting to be split, chipped, or chunked, rest outside the rustic façade of Kreuz's. An enormous open fire pit is tended by a weathered, tan man in Wrangler jeans, a cowboy hat, a belt with a huge silver buckle, and shit kickers. It is Central Texas tradition to eat barbecue on a piece of butcher paper. Meat is surrounded by slices of old-fashioned white bread, beans, slaw, potato salad, and pickles. A bowl of Wet-Naps sits atop a table dressed in a checkered tablecloth. Dozens of people wait in line in a historic Texas town just to get a taste of the good stuff. All these images create and circulate meaning. In "Rhetoric of the Image," Roland Barthes relays a story about an advertisement for Italian products as having "Italianicity"—that is, the gestalt of colors (red, green, yellow) and pictures of foods like garlic, tomatoes, and pasta "make up a sentiment of being Italian even if one does not know how to use the ingredients to make Italian food" (165). We might call the visual meaning of Lockhart's circulated terroir "Lockharticity" or "Central Texanicity"—that is, we may not have eaten barbecue in Lockhart, or we may not be from Texas, or we may be new to barbecue as a food and as a culture, but we understand this "message without a code" (Barthes 36).

That's Right, You're Not from Texas (Texas Wants You Anyway)

In the traditional sense of terroir, the sense in which it is used in France, Germany, and Italy to designate region and appellation, it is deeply and intricately tethered to place. Terroir in this sense, then, excludes. In fact, the very purpose of region and appellation designations, like the purpose of the Michelin star system, is to tie beverage and food to an exclusive plot of earth, as in the case of the above-mentioned champagne. And though there may be legitimate reasons for the system of appellation, it works to locate a wine absolutely. In locating it so specifically, it gives rise to an understood set of predictable tasting notes. A champagne bottle has a uniform look. The association between a few hectares on a map and the bottle of wine it produces is strong.

To some degree, barbecue has this same kind of association with the literal earth of a place. Texas is cattle country, so Texas barbecue is beef-centric. Lockhart has a lot of live oak and pecan trees, so those are the woods that are burned in the pits. Lockhart's pit masters are all natives. Indeed, Black's, Smitty's, and Kreuz's are all family-owned and family-run establishments. We might speculate, too, that Lockhart's decision to pursue through legislative action the title "Barbecue Capital of Texas" is to tie rhetorically the standard of barbecue to Lockhart. In turn, when people think about Lockhart's literal earth, their association is with barbecue.

And yet, in a rhetorical sense, terroir *means* and *does*. In *Craft Obsession*, Jeff Rice talks about how lambic beers used to be located only in a small area around Brussels, Belgium. The definition of lambic, in other words, was (for some) or is (for purists) about the literal earth around Brussels. Yet we can now get lambics in the United States, not just in Belgium. As Rice explains, "Lambic as a sense of terroir has evolved and changed, moving physically and conceptually out of Payottenland and into homes and bars across the U.S." (163).

Lockhart's terroir is similarly networked and mobile from a rhetorical perspective. I mean that in several ways. The first is that most barbecue restaurants in Central Texas, including those in Lockhart, will ship their barbecue all over the country in a cooler on dry ice. Services such as Air Rib pick up Texas barbecue and do this kind of shipping. When your barbecue order arrives, it comes with explicit instructions on reconstituting, heating, and serving your barbecue. So Lockhart's barbecue no longer stays in Lockhart. But beyond the "real thing," Texans make Central Texas barbecue outside the state, barbecue classes specialize in different regions taught all over the country, and cookbooks and online recipe collections are available for those who wish to re-create Lockhart-esque barbecue at home. I bought my husband a smoker for his birthday last year and promptly spent an hour on the phone talking to my cousin Gabe in Central Texas about his recipe for ribs and brisket. Eating Central Texas–style barbecue at my home in Tacoma, Washington, is not the same as eating it in Lockhart because it is not the same earth, but rhetorically, terroir has mobility through meaning making, articulation, and circulation in networks.

Terroir is a deeply rhetorical phenomenon both as a marker or characterization of place and as an articulation and circulation of meaning. Scholars of region and place, such as those writing in and reading this collection, may not have used the term *terroir* because it has such a specific denotation, but they most certainly argue for and about what makes a neighborhood, a city, a state, or a region special, distinctive, particular. Using the viticultural meaning of terroir, we can think about place as earth. The number of days of sunshine, rainfall, wind, temperature, land use, and local savoir faire are terroir.

What I hope to contribute in this essay is a more expansive notion of terroir, one that recognizes the importance of place in its physical manifestation, earth, but also one that sees terroir as rhetorical, cultural, political, and even personal. That is, terroir is what makes a place special, but those coordinates and that place and that creative process also affect people (Young 271). And it is about how place gets communicated and how it gets passed around. If Jeff Rice is right, and I think he is, that terroir aggregates meaning, terroir has more ingredients than just the earth at a certain longitude and latitude. In the end, terroir is about the interplay among place, people, and meaning. It is the way place creates meaning and the way meaning creates place. When I think of Lockhart, I think of graduate school in Austin, I think of friends, I think of discovering Texas barbecue after having lived in Tennessee for eight years, I think of hot sun, and I think of the smell of smoke. That place created those meanings for me, but those meanings, in turn, create my sense of that place—a sense of place not defined by longitude and latitude, but by its function as a form of rhetoric, of cultural production, and of political identity.

Works Cited

"BBQ." *Texas Monthly*, www.texasmonthly.com/bbq-home/. Accessed 30 May 2015.

Barthes, Roland. *Image-Music-Text*. New York: Hill and Wang, 1978.

Chaudhury, Nadia. "Texas Governor Boldly Proclaims Love for Barbecue Sauce." *Eater Austin*, 14 May 2015, austin.eater.com/2015/5/14/8606343/texas-governor-boldly-proclaims-love-for-barbecue-sauce. Accessed 28 May 2015.

City of Lockhart, TX, 2014, www.lockhart-tx.org/. Accessed 29 May 2015.

Jacobson, Gary. "Is Lockhart Losing Its Title as the BBQ Capital of Texas?" *Texas BBQ Posse*, 14 February 2013, texasbbqposse.com/2013/02/is-lockhart-losing-its-title-as-bbq.html. Accessed 29 May 2015.

MacNeil, Karen. *The Wine Bible*. Workman Publishing, 2000.

Park, Michael Y. "Eating Lockhart: BBQ Capital of Texas." *Epicurious*, 28 March 2013, www.epicurious.com/archive/blogs/editor/2013/03/eating-lockhart-bbq-capital-of-texas.html. Accessed 29 May 2015.

Rice, Jeff. *Craft Obsession*. Southern Illinois UP, 2016.

Young, Anna M. "Quaffable, but Uh . . . Far from Transcendent: Wine, Rhetorical Style and Politics." *The Politics of Style and the Style of Politics*, edited by Barry Brummett, Lexington Books, 2011, pp. 263–78.

Nate Kreuter,
Western Carolina University

4. DROWNING AT THE POODLE DOG

I met a guy who told me about a bar called Trash Hill near the
Oklahoma-Texas line. He says he went in there one night and sat at
the bar next to a redneck who had a towel wrapped around his hand,
which was bleeding. After closer inspection, the guy realized the
redneck's thumb had been bitten off in a bar fight.

"You probably ought to have that looked at," the guy said.

"Aw, it'll be awright," the redneck said.

> —John Kelso, "Continental Club, Sir, Is No Dive"

The Poodle Dog had to die. The Poodle Dog was a bar, a lounge technically
under Texas law, on Burnet Road, just north of the intersection with
FM 2222. It was a cinder-block building, painted a long-ago-faded pink, with a
large mural of a white poodle dog on the front, no windows or air-conditioning,
and a decidedly nonhip clientele in a decidedly nonhip part of Austin. I
will explain why it had to die.

Every current and former Austinite can refer to a specific moment when
the city stopped being the hip oasis that he or she once knew and was finally
overrun by trust fund hippies, by refugee yuppies from coasts east and west,
and the precise moment at which, at least for that individual, the city was
finally loved to death. Even the act of pointing out the ubiquitous Austin
"back when I arrived" or "before you got here" narratives, which are inevitably followed by the individual's tales of just exactly what has gone wrong, is
itself a cliché. You can just about date a person's arrival to or departure from
Austin based on the "things were better when" tale that he or she offers you.

For me, a late arrival to the city's economic and cultural boom, the death
of the Poodle Dog Lounge is my mark of Austin's spiritual death. It was a
certain coup de grâce, that death.

John Kelso's column titled "Continental Club, Sir, Is No Dive," cited above,
appeared in the *Austin American-Statesman* about six months after I had
moved to town. A friend clipped it from the newspaper, so quaint, and gave
it to me, which is the only reason I encountered it (he's dead now). Kelso

wrote his column, in which he defines a "dive bar," after taking exception to a *Stuff* magazine (headquarters: NYC) article that had listed the Continental Club, a definitely hip music venue in Austin's equally hip South Congress district, as one of the top twenty dive bars in America. In the article, Kelso wrote, "I love the Continental Club, and it used to be a dive. That was in the late '70s, when you could find people drunk in the place well before noon." Kelso offers readers a proximity of time, the late 1970s, and place, the club itself, as a means of legitimizing his curmudgeonly opinion, with which he will set the dive bar record straight by explaining why the Continental Club of the 2000s, where a New York writer even felt safe to enter, is not a dive bar.

Kelso's column is a response to Austin's boom itself. Many of the non-Texans who move to or vacation in Austin seem to be seeking a sort of approximation of Texas, a version of their stereotypes of the state, and Austin has been happy to oblige, roughing the edges of its ultramodern technology centers and rising glass and steel condos with cowboy kitsch. Those who don't know any better get to experience the thrill of slumming it cowpoke style, without any of the risk of getting bucked, leaving cantankerous townies like Kelso to gripe about the affectation that allows a New York journalist to classify the Continental Club as one of America's top twenty dive bars without even realizing the gratuitous irony of attempting to compose such a list. You can't send tourists to bars like Trash Hill if even the locals are getting their thumbs bitten off.

It may have been a dive, but the Poodle Dog wasn't really a dangerous place. The only time it, by which I mean its clientele, became a little more perilous was during the day, and on rainy days in particular. When a hard rain settled over Austin, not really a common thing, it was not uncommon during those rare weather events to find day laborers drinking away their frustrations over a day without wages inside the Poodle Dog. They were predisposed, by the lost wages I presume, to be a little testy. Trash Hill it was not, though. The Poodle Dog catered to a clientele of regulars, working-class and hard-bitten Texans who came by several times a week, some of them daily, precisely some of the populations that Austin has most effectively marginalized and shunted off to the edges of the city as property values continue to explode and the cancers of hip and kitsch continue to metastasize across the city.

I discovered the Poodle Dog in 2004, shortly after I arrived in Austin to begin a PhD program in English at the University of Texas. I did not begin my career as a graduate student specializing in rhetoric and composition, my current area of specialization. I arrived at UT–Austin expecting to focus on literature and cultural studies, the only parts of English studies that I was familiar with from my undergraduate career. I would say that I entered my graduate program with hostility. That may even be an understatement. I despised graduate school, most of my cohort, the classes, and a sizable population of our faculty from the get-go, for reasons not really having to do with any of them at all. Perhaps needless to say, it made for a bumpy transition.

Before showing up in Austin, I had spent the previous two years, 2002–4, working as an imagery analyst at the National Ground Intelligence Center (NGIC), the army's national strategic intelligence facility. I was originally hired straight out of college as a civilian employee of the Department of the Army, which commands the NGIC through the Information and Security Command. With the defense appropriations bill for the fiscal year 2004, my employer changed, and though I continued to work at the main NGIC facility in Charlottesville, Virginia, I became an employee of the National Imagery and Mapping Agency (NIMA). The director of NIMA at the time, Lieutenant General James Clapper (ret.), demanded that the agency's name be changed based on the logic that we were a sister agency of the Central Intelligence Agency (CIA) and thirteen other agencies that all had three-letter acronyms (NSA, NRO, FBI, DIA, and so forth). Clapper felt that NIMA's four-letter acronym amounted to a slight, a subtle indicator that we were somehow below the thirteen other agencies that, with our own agency, the U.S. intelligence community comprised at that time.

But no one could come up with a name that had a three-letter acronym and that accurately described the nature of the organization, which deals primarily in intelligence and mapping derived from "overhead platforms" (spy planes and satellites). So the never-before-hyphenated phrase "geospatial intelligence" became "geospatial-intelligence," and we were suddenly a glamorous three-letter agency, the National Geospatial-Intelligence Agency (NGA). The Department of Defense appropriation for the name change was millions of dollars, money that was spent replacing logos (not *logos*), stationery, and plaques, the trappings of petty bureaucracy, at a time when soldiers serving in Iraq were jerry-rigging armor for their vehicles from scrap metal and publicly begging for body armor (Mazzetti; Lenz).

While Clapper, who went on to become the director of National Intelligence, was jockeying for political position, my coworkers and I were, from the comfort of our stateside desks, prosecuting the early stages of the war in Iraq through our satellite feeds. The short of it is that before I enrolled full-time as a navel-gazing graduate student in English, I had worked as a mostly deskbound spy. Concurrent with my time as an imagery analyst with Top Secret clearance, the NGA's stateside bureaucracy was ascending among policymakers and military leaders as the go-to intelligence agency, with its whiz-bang satellite capabilities, while the workaday desk-jockey spies helped vaporize Iraqi tank divisions and inconvenient civilian obstacles, along with probably committing an occasional fratricide.

The work had not sat well with me even as I undertook it, but neither had my departure after relatively little time—but what an exactly opportune and inopportune time—on the job. When I arrived in Austin, something, as a result of that work that I had done and all that I had witnessed from afar, was quite broken inside of me, but I didn't know it yet. I was already angry, but at what or why I didn't exactly know. There was a very clear calculus that had dominated our work at the NGIC. Nobody drilled it into us. It was more of a presupposition, so deeply embedded within our conversations, our work, our whole approach, that I was entirely blind to it until well after I had left. The math was simple: American lives are worth more than Iraqi lives. There wasn't a ratio, no precision to that math, but the philosophy of a disproportionate equation dominated our decisions. I was mad at myself when I arrived in Austin, paradoxically angry over many of the things I had done, and angry to have quit the job, to have left more and similar work undone. I just didn't know it yet.

Only at the very beginning stages of processing what I had been involved in and what we had done, when I arrived in Austin I was mentally prepared neither for "Keeping Austin Weird" (keep away from me, you weird fucking yuppies, hippies, you yippie motherfuckers) nor for the self-indulgent analysis of contemporary literary studies (critically theorize that urinal, jackhole). Emotionally, I had not even a landmark to orient myself to, so to speak.

Some landmarks, like the unremarkable Poodle Dog, hide in plain sight, while others declare themselves. Iraq's Monument to the Unknown Soldier, a spot I knew well, in a virtual sense, and where several other public monuments and their open spaces are quickly visible along a bend in the Tigris, declares itself. It is an easy spot to find, from the bird's-eye view of a satellite. I used the monument as my starting landmark to walk through Baghdad via satellite. There were essentially two ways to navigate satellite imagery. If you knew where you wanted to go, you simply typed in the coordinates, and our viewing software would snap us to that spot on the imagery. But more often than not, we didn't know where we were going. We were on a hunt, either actual or scavenger. In these cases, we needed to orient ourselves. I would find the tomb and then begin my "walk" through the streets of Baghdad, usually first thing in the morning, bleary-eyed in the dimly lit section of cubicles used by the imagery analysts, slurping coffee. Just as casually as I would later slurp the first slosh of foam off painfully cold Lone Star cans at the Poodle Dog when it all finally hit me.

Even though I lived near it, the Poodle Dog wasn't the first of Austin's lounges that I came to know. The first was Carousel Lounge, another cinder-block building north of downtown, at pissing distance from I-35. What's remarkable about Carousel is its commitment to a theme—the theme of the circus. Every surface of the building inside and out is painted in elaborate, Crayola-colored circus motifs, and inside, the circus murals are complemented by papier-mâché circus animals. For all the years that I lived in Austin, there was a waitress, in at least her sixties when I first encountered her, who would make you tuck your dollar bill into her garter when you tipped her. Even when I arrived in the summer of 2004, the joint was thoroughly infested with irony-seeking hipsters, Austin's self-appointed connoisseurs of cool. It was a place where I could have a drink, as I did many times with fellow graduate students, but not the sort of joint I could fall in love with.

Neither was the Poodle Dog the last lounge I patronized regularly. Once I moved south to the much trendier environs of the 78704 zip code, the Horseshoe became my new neighborhood lounge. It certainly was convenient, a shorter drive from my new home than the Poodle Dog had been from my old one. But like much of 78704, which rode and still rides on the coattails of the neon-illuminated South Congress district, much of the Horseshoe felt slightly like a large-scale affectation, inauthentic, but in a very subtle way, because all the bar paraphernalia and tchotchkes were carefully authentic and carefully placed so as to appear that they weren't carefully placed, curated. But, I'll grant, the place still had its grit. One every-night regular was an old, cranky vet who sat at one end of the bar and nursed Pearl Light that he drank on ice from a plastic cup. Nobody fucked with him. I've since learned that even the approachable Horseshoe Lounge has been forced by rising rents to relocate, no longer able to afford the South Austin rent.

The plight of Austin's lounges is an analogue for the larger changes that have beset the city. Its technology scene, cultural cache, and almost ceiling-less wealth make Austin a city that is frequently visited, often scrutinized, and widely written about. A booming local economy combined with a vibrant, distinct local culture have made Austin an eminently desirable city for broad swaths of demographic groups. Lounges are unique within this Texas and Austin social landscape and also unique within the actual landscape. They occupy a niche within Texas's liquor laws, and this also explains to a degree why they are so different from what are, at least in Austin, far more ubiquitous bars, which are not the same, legally or socially, as lounges.

Texas is one of several states that regulate the on-premises consumption of alcohol in a tiered system. A mixed beverage permit allows the establishment to sell distilled spirits in addition to beer and wine, whereas a beer and wine permit allows the establishment to sell only these lower-ABV drinks. But an establishment with only a beer and wine permit can still—and here is where Texas is a little weird—allow its customers to drink distilled spirits, so long as those spirits are provided by the customers themselves. These are the lounges. A series of awkward protocols unfolds from this apparent weirdness in the Texas law. In a lounge, it is not at all unusual to see a patron walk in carrying his own bottle of liquor. But the patron may not simply enter and begin swilling. At most establishments, he must purchase a cup of ice, locally referred to as a setup, from the lounge. Consumption of neat liquor is strictly forbidden, and this is one of the few rules I've seen regularly enforced by lounge barkeeps. My point is simply this: the Texas lounge is a unique institution that lends itself toward "dive" status as Kelso sets it forth, a low-overhead, no-frills establishment offering relatively cheap beer and the occasional dust-covered single-pour bottle of wine to a coterie of locals who largely remember when Austin was such-and-such, and who are largely being left behind as chic Austin expands north and east into formerly working-class and ethnic neighborhoods, gentrifying away not only the former residents but also the grubby watering holes where they might have been inclined to drink away such sorrows. Lounges are, by the definitions set forth in their licensing, modest institutions.

Each lounge is a subculture, catering to an ultraspecific aesthetic and clientele, maybe catering exclusively to a neighborhood or another demographic. All are subtly different. That was their charm. Plenty of other lounges call to other people than myself, such as Beverly's and the G & S Lounge, to name but a couple of those bars meeting the technical definition of Texas lounge (no spirits served). A host of other dives, both legit and aspirational, have full liquor licenses. The Poodle Dog was my environment. I felt possessive of it, didn't want it to be discovered by the same irony seekers who had muffed the vibe at the Carousel.

Living up north in a soulless apartment complex with more residents than the town I had grown up in, I soon found the nearby Poodle Dog. It was thoroughly decorated in a combination honky-tonk and Marilyn Monroe motif. I don't know why Marilyn Monroe. Magazine spreads were cheaply framed and covered large portions of the walls, along with the promo crap that beer companies like Budweiser give out. Without AC, big industrial fans in each corner pushed air around during the nine warm months of the Texas year. It was dusty, not in a desert but in a cobwebby sort of way. It was the only place in town I knew of that simply ignored the city smoking ban, and its thick clouds of incinerated nicotine made my eyes weep. There were two rooms: the bar area and a larger area with about half a dozen poorly maintained pool tables. Sometimes the concrete floor was wet from a recent hosing down. Beer was kept on ice hauled in each day. Cheaper in some respects, I guess, than refrigeration. Every now and then, I took a woman there, but it was never a date so much as a test. I wanted to see how she would react—to the eye-burning smoke, the hot air, the dirty floors and foul restrooms, the narrow selection of American beer iced down to a painful level of cold. And most of all, how she would react to patrons, to the leer of a man twice her age with half her education, to the good-humored ramblings of an overweight and over-friendly laborer, to the pregnant barmaid working the whole bar alone, and to me.

The Poodle Dog was an unaffected oasis in a city built on affectation. When "Keep Austin Weird" is the slogan of the local business bureaus and tourism boards, you ain't weird anymore. Hell, Austin even has a bar called Dive Bar, which is about all one needs to know about Austin's attempt to market its own former grit.

Enter rhetoric. I started spending a couple of evenings each week alone at the Poodle Dog, and I persisted in graduate school, abandoning literary study for rhetorical inquiry. As I was educated and professionalized, I began to see a set of theories, a perspective on the world, that explained the human behaviors I had witnessed as an imagery analyst. The lure of rhetoric for me was that it offered an explanation, a set of theories for understanding the world that I had seen and was only beginning to process in my own mind. Rhetoric explained to me the conspiracy of the war and my own unintentional complicity, and that of hundreds of other analysts without actual skin in the fighting game. It allowed me to unpack a set of experiences that I had no terminology to describe.

It explained how people with the best of intentions could unwittingly collaborate to write our nation, through deeply flawed intelligence reports, into a foreign policy disaster that will haunt us for generations. It explained how political leaders could dupe us while maintaining plausible deniability. Finding rhetoric and applying it to the national decision to go to war, which became the subject of my dissertation, wasn't therapeutic, though, unless perhaps you consider self-immolation a form of therapy.

In 2006, I went through an extended period of not sleeping. Because I couldn't sleep, I spent most of each night, for a period of months, watching a propaganda war unfold on YouTube. It was the period of mounting U.S. casualties that led to the surge. My best friend had just returned from a tour as the director of mortuary affairs for all U.S. forces in the Mideast. I had begun to combine my study of rhetoric with my processing of guilt, working on two presentations on how coalition and insurgent forces were waging a proxy war against one another on YouTube. Antioccupation militants in Iraq were reaching the heights of their own success, perfecting the clever and increasingly sophisticated IEDs that took an increasing toll on U.S. forces. The insurgents, students of rhetoric themselves, frequently taped their exploits and edited footage of attacks on Americans in videos of middling production value, which they then uploaded to YouTube to recruit fighters and donors to their cause. American troops, carrying increasingly cheap and portable cameras throughout their tours, posted their own propaganda films, outside of any formal military PR channels. Over a period of months, I became expert at finding and authenticating videos, honing my navigation of both coalition and insurgent videos to the point that I could with some frequency find competing video narratives of the same incident or urban battle.

And it was driving me fucking crazy. I was having nightmares for the first time, recalling things I had been a party to, those recollections in turn combining with the bloodbath I had continued to watch in the compilation of video narratives of the war. During this same period, a five-and-half-year-long relationship of mine imploded. I drifted into the Poodle Dog more and more frequently, unable to sleep, my home unwelcoming, and sometimes feeling unsafe alone around myself. Throughout, the Poodle Dog served as my sanctuary. On the night of my big breakup, it was the first place I went and where I stayed the night, sleeping in my car in the parking lot, not because I was drunk (though maybe I should have been), but because I had no other place to go. It became that sort of a place for me, just by being the place that it was, where it was, and not because of who was inside but because of who wasn't—the hippies and yuppies and fellow grad students.

I tore myself apart over a war I had participated in, taking place in a country that I had never set foot in. Proximity legitimates experience. "I was there" is the ultimate bona fide, whether one is saying, I was there when tanks crossed the berm into Iraq or I was there was Austin was still cool. Although the two have nothing to do with one another, the rhetorical function of proximity is the same in both cases. In declaring oneself proximate, we undertake a special witnessing, as well as playing a rhetorical trump card among our interlocutors. In declaring our own proximity, we dare others to match the legitimizing forces of our own proximity. Either they can respond, "Yeah, well, I was there when . . ." and declare an even closer proximity to essential events (and that proximity may be in time, space, or both), or they can cede, to a degree, the point. They cannot match our proximity. My experience of the war was both proximate to it and not.

On the one hand, it is entirely obvious and self-evident how proximity, how nearness, in space or time, legitimates the experiences we claim and the opinions we hold. By implication, it is perhaps also initially unremarkable that a lack of proximity reduces the legitimacy of experience. Imagine a resident of the north Burnet area saying to a developer, "I don't care what you want. You don't live here. I do." The soldier's claim of "I was there" gives his opinions on war—for better or worse—a gravitas that cannot be matched by those who didn't walk the sands themselves. But on the other hand, the gradations through which proximity functions are somewhat strange. Despite having occurred in one of the most densely populated areas of the country, only a minuscule percentage of Americans can claim geographic proximity to the attacks of 9/11. In terms of time, a vastly greater percentage of Americans can claim proximity, for the wonders of satellites and video feeds made most of us who are old enough to remember virtual witnesses as we watched events unfold in real time, proximate in terms of both *chronos* and *kairos*, even if not in terms of location. Technology has altered what proximity means. Were all those people watching TV present at the 9/11 attacks? Of course not. But they all were.

Within the literature of rhetoric, proximity has been theoretically linked to empathy, an irony that is not at all lost on me, given my own crises of proximity. Dennis Lynch, after demonstrating the bond between empathy and proximity, which empathy both produces and is produced by, argues

> that empathy can be the discrete event of an appeal, that is, a momentary effort absorbed into the body of a speech in order to achieve a step along the way; that it can be a tool of invention for preparing a speaker to face an audience and endure if not succeed; and that as part of the framework of argument it establishes conditions that make argument possible, or give it sense. (19)

Proximity, like empathy, is a facilitator of identification, in the Burkean sense.

Proximity is a function of memory and emotion as well. I couldn't possibly expect a reader to feel the linkage that I articulate here between a quintessentially modern experience of war and a defunct Austin dive bar. But that linkage is forged permanently in my own brain, for my experience of retreating into the dirty, unwelcoming cinder-block confines of the Poodle Dog corresponds temporally and experientially with the time in my life when I began to reconcile and process my own contribution to events in Iraq.

I was never proximate to the war in Iraq, at least in space. I certainly was in terms of time. But the strangeness of my experience, and one of the new strangenesses of modern warfare, is that I fought the war from home, without ever having been exposed to the dangers of warfare. I had been there, and had been complicit, a cog in the machine. Even while I had not been there. My proximity indicated my guilt, as did my lack of proximity. In the time since my own departure from federal service, the airmen who fly combat missions via drones, while they remain safely on U.S. bases, have advocated for status as combat veterans, and it has been well documented that they suffer from a new sort of battle fatigue. Whereas their compatriots physically located in war zones suffer from the relatively understandable trauma of witnessing war's tragedies firsthand, PTSD, the drone pilots prosecuting war remotely suffer from another kind of exhaustion and anxiety, borne largely out of the jarring transition from remotely conducted combat to ostensibly "normal" life just hours later. They also feel the guilt of seeing comrades engaged in combat, exposed to and suffering risk, while they remain safe, both shielded and deprived of the cauldron of combat. During the surge, I was wracked by a terrible guilt. My days, spent reading and sitting often silently through graduate seminars, felt entirely frivolous. I had abandoned a righteous undertaking to focus on my own needs, my own wishes and dreams for the future. By quitting to attend graduate school, I had abdicated a responsibility. I felt guilty not only for what I had done in the past but for having done it remotely, from a point of safety, and for not doing more of it in the future.

Our taskings had sometimes seemed fickle. When it was reported that insurgents were using white pickup trucks, we were sent on scavenger hunts for white pickup trucks. We found a bunch, a whole bunch, pretty easily, for they stood out well on the imagery. When taskings weren't specific, or early in the day before new taskings had come in, we were at liberty to poke around on our own. The next morning, on my "walk" through Baghdad, I decided to swing by the pickups. Not white anymore, but black charred.

> For decades the model for understanding PTSD has been "fear conditioning": quite literally the lasting psychological ramifications of mortal terror. But a term now gaining wider acceptance is "moral injury." It represents a tectonic realignment, a shift from a focusing on the violence that has been done to a person in wartime toward his feelings about what he has done to others—or what he's failed to do for them. The concept is attributed to the clinical psychiatrist Jonathan Shay, who in his book *Achilles in Vietnam* traces the idea back as far as the Trojan War. The mechanisms of death may change—as intimate as a bayonet or as removed as a Hellfire—but the bloody facts, and their weight on the human conscience, remain the same. (Power)

I am haunted by the paradox of my proximity to the Iraq War, of having inflicted profound destruction from a computer terminal in a cubicle, without ever having exposed myself to the risks of the American troops that we supported or even, frankly, of the insurgent forces that they battled on the ground as we watched on feeds from low-earth orbit.

Proximity also invades memory. Readers will have already deduced that the only proximity between the Poodle Dog and the war in Iraq is the simultaneousness of my memory and experience. Dealing with the war, beginning to deal with it, while I was hiding in the Poodle Dog several nights a week is a synthetic proximity, uniquely my own. Many others endure. I will forever associate bowling with an Iraqi tank regiment hidden in the date palms. Sesame bagels with Daniel Pearl having his head sawn off in Pakistan. Springtime and the videos their captors made of Jessica Lynch and her compatriots. Helmud province and a lone set of footprints in the snow. I'm not being flippant. Proximity sutures disparate experiences, and this is part of where emotional trauma arises from: the irreconcilable juxtapositions. The Poodle Dog and guilt.

One of the beauties of the Poodle Dog—and any institution of a similar ilk—is that there is a certain psychological entry fee. All sorts of institutions make themselves intentionally and explicitly uninviting to particular demographics—the members-only country clubs, the gated communities, which have physical and legal barriers to the entrance of undesirable demographics backed by the sanction and force of law. The Poodle Dog, and any number of places like it, was similarly exclusive, but its exclusivity, its exclusion, enforced only by informal measures, was subject to change. Its location was a start, awkwardly set back from the road between a Church's Chicken and a used-car lot, and then there was its appearance, uninvitingly painted that pink that had long ago faded, no windows, little signage of any type. You cannot claim any proximity to it unless you were willing to walk inside.

Kelso, in his rancor, approved of the Poodle Dog, writing, "The Poodle Dog Lounge on Burnet Road has some dive traits. Beverly's on far South Congress is a dive. If the place isn't listed in the phone book, and the Poodle Dog and Beverly's are not, it could be a dive." While it may seem a subtle distinction to note that the cinder-block Poodle Dog Lounge closed and re-opened as the Aristocrat, the Poodle Dog is dead. My Austin is dead. The hell of the matter is that my "Austin used to be great" narrative—focused around what was, to most folks, a shitty and forgettable bar in a perilously unhip neighborhood—would just as quickly be dismissed by an Austinite of ten or twenty or thirty years earlier, when the Broken Spoke was literally on the southern edge of town, surrounded by little more than Hill Country scrub oak. It now sits between condo high-rises, and one would need to drive south through overpass-stacked highways for another fifteen miles to find the alleged "edge of town."

All of this makes me quite hesitant to claim any proximity to a "true" or somehow purer experience of Austin. To be sure, my landmark is gone. Not bulldozed, the way that many landmarks in Austin have been, but renovated and rebranded as a slightly less shitty, more approachable lounge. The edge is gone, the experience purified, in order to comfort more customers. The Poodle Dog didn't solve anything for me. There's no grand narrative here about how a run-down bar that most people would find too seedy to enter offered me my sanctuary and cured me of my internal ills. I didn't find my Texas Cheers. No grizzled, old vet that I met at the bar set me straight and put my mind at ease.

But the Poodle Dog is my Texas, one of the parts that I loved most. It will in my own memory and experience always be proximate with my guilt, a decade-long unraveling and reweaving through which I have tried to reconcile my contributions to one of the most foolhardy and destructive foreign policy decisions in U.S. history.

Perhaps Austin's lounge scene isn't worth saving or even worrying about. For the most part, I'd agree with that criticism. Trees and green spaces, affordable housing, displacement of the poor and ethnic minorities—all of these are far more meaningful problems than whether the Poodle Dog does or even did exist, I'll grant. In the end, I liked the Poodle Dog for precisely the reasons that so many others didn't. It was rude and unwelcoming. It offered a home, a sanctuary, where those I least wanted to face rarely wished to enter. It will live in my memory for the juxtapositions created by my own experiences. Ultimately, for me, the Poodle Dog had to die. I loved it, and I'm glad it's gone.

Works Cited

Kelso, John. "Continental Club, Sir, Is No Dive." *Austin American-Statesman*, 20 Feb. 2005, p. B1.

Lenz, Ryan. "Soldiers in Iraq Still Buying Their Own Body Armor." *Turkish Daily News*, 28 Mar. 2004. *Factiva*, global.factiva.com/aa/?ref= TURPR00020040401e03s00000&pp=1&fcpil=en&napc=p&sa_from=. Accessed 13 Oct. 2009.

Lynch, Dennis. "Rhetorics of Proximity: Empathy in Temple Grandin and Cornel West." *Rhetoric Society Quarterly*, vol. 28, no. 1, 1998, pp. 5–19.

Mazzetti, Mark. "Bush Acts to Defuse Furor on Armor." *Los Angeles Times*, 10 Dec. 2004, articles.latimes.com/2004/dec/10/world/fg-armor10. Accessed 12 Oct. 2009.

Power, Matthew. "Confessions of a Drone Warrior." *GQ*, 22 Oct. 2013, www .gq.com/news-politics/big-issues/201311/drone-uav-pilot-assassination. Accessed 19 May 2015.

Casey Boyle,
University of Texas—Austin

5. THE COMPLETE HISTORY OF PARLIN HALL (ABRIDGED VERSION)

*m*ore than the classes I took, course projects I composed, friends and mentors I met, or parties I might have some scant recollection of having attended during my undergraduate education at the University of Texas, I remember Parlin Hall. It was, and somewhat still is, the location for the English Department (and now the Department of Rhetoric and Writing), its faculty, and many of its courses. Constructed in the early to mid-1950s, Parlin Hall is one of the "Six Pack" of buildings that housed many of the university's liberal arts departments and programs. Anyone who has spent any time in Parlin Hall immediately remembers its aesthetic. Its exterior limestone facade contained an expansive geological history that directly clashed with the momentary fashion statement made by its everlasting interior green-tiled walls and floors. With faculty offices and classrooms and department offices, Parlin Hall hosted me for four years as an undergraduate English major. I'd arrive early to classes, and while sitting on hallway benches to catch up on that day's reading, I'd overhear professors' meetings with students about the novels they'd read and papers written in response. During long breaks between classes, I'd get lost in its halls reading the many items posted to bulletin boards and the various posters affixed to the faculty's office doors.

More than anything, I recall how much bureaucracy shaped my sense of the place. For years, I held on to a single piece of yellow paper that listed each of my degree requirements, and every semester, following an advisor's advisement, I would cross off each completed degree requirement. That paper coordinated all the other papers and gave them certain roles: posted course descriptions, semester projects, novels and other readings, teacher-student correspondence.

I returned to that bureaucracy when the institution I had attended for my undergraduate degree hired me as faculty. Being assigned a faculty office in the same building where I had spent so much time as a student was not a return home so much as an opportunity to continue wandering. *This return was not seamless.* Instead of that yellow paper listing my degree requirements, I now crossed off items from an online list of human resource requirements that included employee-training videos for tasks that I would never need to do. I learned rules for animal research, how to reserve and request a vehicle from the motor pool, the proper procedure for accepting gifts, and many other tasks for which my job was not qualified or positioned to entertain. Unlike the seemingly efficient and planned bureaucratic hoops I'd jumped through as a student, those of the newly hired faculty member seemed to be the result of a layering of successive procedures and practices since that building had opened.

Only one thing bridges my experiences from student to professor: Parlin Hall. What gives me pause about my connection to Parlin Hall, and place in general, is that I do not just feel like a mere *part* of the place. While the place's educational mission suggests I have a complete story—I was a student and now am faculty—my life and Parlin Hall's time do not coincide. Nedra Reynolds, outlining how we typically engage place, writes that places "cannot be treated as singular or stable; neither can the identities that are shaped within them. Places (or territories) are contested, with competing and shifting interpretations of their meanings" (58). Implicit in this statement is that all accounts of place are partial and that we must contend for our partiality over or with others. Do these two mutually exclusive positions provide enough space for how we might inventively engage place? Are we really barred from having a complete account of a place? It is fact that the building's expanse started well before I came along and will most likely extend far after I walk through its doors for a final time. That said, does place exceed any one of us? How do our complete experiences contribute to place? How might the bridges and halls that connect my *partial* experiences of a place work their way into composing a complete *place* that is also a part? In what ways might my own place that is Parlin Hall not be merely partial yet not claim completeness?

Places as Bureaucratic Machines

As much grief as I might express about bureaucracy, it gives purpose to Parlin Hall. Bureaucracy not only informs a sense of place but also can serve as an image of the machines that make and sustain place. Jim Corder writes around this idea. Fighting the same bureaucratic entanglements I worked through as faculty, Corder proposed a course at his institution that would explore place. In "I Proposed a New Geography Course, but the Curriculum Committee Turned It Down," Corder explains, "I recommended it as sort of a geography course, though I thought it should bring together literature, history, art, and geography into a place to think about place, what it has meant to us, why a sense of place is strong in some of us but not in others" (128). The course, Corder continues, would respond to a number of questions:

How and why do we acquire so much misinformation about places and their relationships? How do we rhetorically construct a geography for ourselves (the prepositions we use for directions often locate the center of the universe near our various belly buttons)? Why do some people become attached to places while others don't? When and why do we humans begin to think about place? What are our personal geographies? (129)

So many of his questions address why and how we are drawn to places, and they chip away at my own questions of place. Place has something to do with our own embodiment, our own sense of belonging, our own understandings about a space. We construct personal geographies that are both *a part of* and *apart from* a place and its expansive histories.

To pursue these questions, students taking Corder's course would have proceeded "to learn about places, using the resources available to a citizen— atlases, travel guides, county, state, and federal maps, painting, photographs, poems, novels, histories" (129). All those various media products Corder turns to remind me of the variety of media that turn to me every day and help construct my own personal geography, which is, again, *a part of* and *apart from* Parlin Hall. Maps, photos, classrooms, office doors, course descriptions, committee reports, student papers, my writings, annual reports—and on the list goes, stretching farther than any one person could or should read. Corder's intuition about the variety and multiplicity of media that give sense to place is apt. A place becomes place by virtue of how its relations and their rhythms are mediated through the function of a kind of bureaucratic machine. Roads, newspapers, music, buildings—all work together to generate place by structuring its rhythms. Scooping up all the various media products as a way to explore a place is a practice for extending a place's events beyond its times or exact physical location. It is also dangerous. We err by looking to the meditations themselves as the place where place is to be found. Sadly, Corder's course was turned down because it failed to find its place among the heavily divided and parceled space of his then university's bureaucracy. As always, bureaucracy seems to have the final word.

Frank Zappa once said, "It isn't necessary to imagine the world ending in fire or ice. There are two other possibilities: one is paperwork, and the other is nostalgia." We can feel how nostalgia ruins our sense of a place. It would be easy for me to recall my time as a student in Parlin Hall in ways that would dampen or undermine my present experience. We often adhere to a nostalgic vision of a place, and our adherence to that vision ruins a place. "Keep Austin Weird" continues to work against the urban development that all places undergo, despite also working *for* that exact urban development (see Edbauer). As we revere restaurants closed long ago or listen only to music created decades before, new places emerge and layer onto those older places like the paperwork that piles up on my desk in Parlin Hall or the fossilized outlines that adorn its exterior limestone walls. Somehow, addition becomes subtraction.

It's also not hard to imagine paperwork as a suitable end to a place. I mention Zappa because he hits on something interesting I sense about bureaucracy in general and place in particular. There is a considerable temporal dynamic at work in places and more so in our most mundane of bureaucracies. In addition to having to endure the heft of paperwork and mind-numbing hurdles to accomplish even the smallest of tasks in a bureaucracy, one also must wrestle with and against time. While Zappa positions paperwork as bridging the great expanse between nostalgia and the end of times, bureaucracy and nostalgia function by using the same mechanisms for trying to ensure a place remains.

To put the matter in another way: bureaucracies, like all places, try to suspend and elongate time as a kind of future nostalgia. *We will have preserved.* Places function as bureaucracies: historic districts regulate against replacing certain buildings; monuments are erected to preserve one time in perpetuity; zoning determines what gets built. Despite these attempts, or perhaps because of them, material remainders of place's bureaucracies vary temporality in ways that actually work to sustain a place through change rather than against it. In *What Time Is This Place?*, Kevin Lynch discusses how temporality shapes a place's character and understands the place as a kind of material memory at work: "Every thing, every event is 'historic.' To attempt to preserve all the past would be life-denying." While we might select and preserve certain elements of the past to serve the present, "some random accumulations" are necessary "to enable us to discover unexpected relationships" (36). This same kind of randomness often confronts us in our deepest bureaucratic moments. These random moments not only represent opportunities to discover unexpected relationships but also are when we invent those relations that then elaborate a place.

Bureaucracy as Baroque Place

Many have written extensive histories of bureaucracy as a managerial form, but Ben Kafka offers the most productive engagement with bureaucracy that resists simply chalking it up to an obstacle. Oddly echoing Zappa from a moment ago, Kafka states that "modern political thought was both founded and confounded by its encounters with paperwork" (10). Instead of treating paperwork in the negative, Kafka quickly points out that "paperwork is full of surprises." Indeed, in Kafka's project, as well as almost any other take on bureaucracy, paperwork is usually the leading actor in bureaucracy. My own experience as a student and teacher in a place is managed by the papers I am responsible for producing and receiving. It's hard to imagine bureaucracy, or a typical university workday in Parlin Hall, without immediately recalling the mountains of folders and ledgers that house stacks and stacks of paper.

In contrast, however, what I'd like to consider is how paperwork itself might be an exaggerated middle of the bureaucratic enterprise. Etymology helps explain this notion. Bureaucracy's root word, *bureau*, usually means two things. As a desk, a bureau is a place where we write, and a bureau is also a series of cabinets and cubbies where we place writing. This double meaning positions writing to be the mediator, and not just the mediation, of places. In our common understanding of bureaucracies, however, we mistake the metonymy for the entire enterprise, not unlike our understandings of place. Paperwork *becomes* the bureaucratic place. What about its other mechanisms? What roles do the bureaus play in bureaucracy? What are the bureaucratic features that sustain any given place?

With "Bureau of Bureaucracy," artist Kim Schmahmann mimics the cabinets of curiosities that spread throughout Europe during the seventeenth century. Instead of traditional curiosities, Schmahmann collects documents: birth certificates, graduation diplomas, licenses, medical reports, financial statements, and marriage certificates. These documents mediate our bodies through place. "Such documents," Schmahmann notes, "result from our interactions with the many bureaucracies that, over our lifetimes, register our existence, certify our competence, authorize our practice, describe our health and wealth, permit our movement, and sanction our union." In addition to the fact that she acknowledges the productive value that these papers have for creating identity and place, I'm fascinated by her foregrounding of bureau, whose place usually is backgrounded.

Schmahmann notes that in the bureau, we find a bottomless drawer, a false drawer, a glass ceiling drawer, a half drawer, a reflective drawer, a drawer of measures, a drawer within a drawer, a secret drawer, a locked drawer, a drawer accessible only through a particular hidden procedure, and so on. It is tempting to search the bureau and exhaust all its contents, but that would be to elide just how the bureau is designed to be overwhelming. *More than complete.* Its secret compartments and drawers within drawers offer abundance in the same way that cities and spaces are temporally layered, as described by Lynch. The bureau, a city, Parlin Hall, and any other place all contain folds that envelop some of their features while allowing use of and engagement with others. These envelopments, though, should not be considered lost or missing. The fold tucks away and provides another coherent version.

Schmahmann's contraption materializes place in a way that Gilles Deleuze understood the baroque and its attendant practice of folds. Paraphrasing Leibniz, Deleuze writes in *The Fold* that a flexible or an elastic body still has cohering parts that form a fold, such that they are not separated into parts of parts but are rather divided to infinity in smaller and smaller folds that always retain a certain cohesion. Thus a continuous labyrinth . . . resembles a sheet of paper divided into infinite folds or separated into bending movements, each one determined by the consistent or conspiring surroundings. (6)

The "Bureau of Bureaucracy" actualizes the folding and subdivisions that Deleuze writes about in terms of tapestry and architecture through his example of paper. When we approach bureaucracy, the folds are not necessarily removed from the places entirely but provide a mechanism for random relations. Parlin Hall, or any place, has the same features found in these bureaucracies. Some have access to some of its parts while others access other parts, without anyone losing coherence. No one's place is *the complete* place, but neither does any one place suffer incompleteness.

Media Archaeology and Abridgment

In an article published by the University of Texas alumni association's journal, former English professor Don Graham writes about his experiences in Parlin Hall from the 1960s all the way into the twenty-first century. Graham tells the story of a former student returning as a professor. His story took place well before mine, but it resonates with my own. Graham narrates his story as a graduate student roaming Parlin's halls until he returned as a professor. Throughout his account of his time in Parlin, Graham references different media that populated the building. His present self notices the laptops and smartphones, but his memory speaks of manual typewriters being replaced by electric typewriters. In fact, he writes that in the 1970s, "the English Department had no outside telephone service in individual offices." The faculty did not get telephones until the 1980s, when donors learned of the need. "They promptly changed the way we were able to communicate," says Graham, "supplying bright new shiny phones for each office. We still have landlines in our offices now, but of course we all carry cell phones along with our students."

After noting all the changes in the technologies that managed the place, Graham ends his account with a new observation of a building he had spent decades inhabiting. "I still discover things about Parlin that I hadn't noticed before," he marvels. "I happened to look up above the entrance . . . and there I beheld a wonderful bit of architectural decor, a finial book with its pages spread open in stony splendor. Imagine that: a book."

Graham's account of Parlin Hall, steeped in the mechanisms of bureaucracy, elaborates the example of the bureau and places as bureaucratic machines. Neither Graham's account nor my own, though, can be productively engaged by tracing out a linear history of technological development. We need a new method for exploring place and its temporal layers that offers complete stories without the need to resort to partial accounts.

As we accumulate and fold away media through which our places operate, it becomes apparent that we need methods to understand the materiality of machines. An emerging method for media-based research is media archaeology, which might be useful for thinking about place as a multitemporal bureaucratic machine. Media archaeology is a method, first and foremost, designed to trace media history away from its overwhelming progressive narrative often attributed to technological progress. In some ways, media archaeology is also about place itself. Like media, place cannot merely be described by a linear narrative. Recent work in media archaeology associates the method with productive speculation on the material aspects by offering media different possibilities that are not part of a historical record. Bureaucracy as place, then, would not *just* be a series of innovations for organizing and managing people arrived at through a steady progression of technocratic solutions to organizational problems. Instead, any place would also be a complex meeting of differing and competing media trajectories whose future deployments would help determine its evolutions.

Jussi Parikka writes that "media archaeology is . . . a way to investigate the new media cultures through insights from past new media, often with an emphasis on the forgotten, the quirky, the non-obvious apparatuses, practices and inventions" (2). Erkki Huhtamo and Parikka write that media archaeology offers "a constant interchange, a cruise in time. The past is brought to the present, and the present to the past; both inform and explain each other, raising questions and pointing to futures that may or may not be" (15). Like the field of archaeology in general, exploring place has a lot to gain from exploring the variegated temporal histories of its mediations. Corder unknowingly attempted this with his proposed course. By gathering and examining all kinds of interdisciplinary mediations associated with a place—songs, maps, poems, stories—Corder was actually on his way to establishing an archaeological relation to the place. If he had pitched his course as sort of an archaeological course instead of "as sort of a geography course," perhaps it might have found its place.

It is often written that media archaeology attempts a nonlinear approach. It is averse to a strict historicism that the past is given and out there waiting for us to find it; instead, it attempts a radical assembling of history and histories. In short, media archaeology would understand my notion of place as a bureaucratic machine to be a site for the proliferation of future possibilities at least as much as a site for the retention of any past. Such an account of a place and its mediated folds would offer both a complete and also a partial characterization.

Abridged Invention

Thinking about complete and partial not as mutually exclusive would lead us to an *abridged* account. Not unlike the *Reader's Digest Condensed Books*, abridgments that offered a way to read and be in conversation with a great many works without having to account for *all* the popular work, so too does understanding place as an abridgment allow for us to be on the same page while experiencing difference. This is not a gesture to mere relativism. Each abridgment would work only if it were able to augment a place and affect its other abridgments. Augmentation (see Boyle and Rivers) contributes a different version of a place that is not a quantitative addition but a space for qualitative change. Abridgment is inventive. Abridgment offers a way to understand our own places as both complete and partial, turning mutually exclusive terms into occasional inclusivity. My abridged place does exists even if, as Corder writes, "the small geography that each of us is the center of does not always appear on maps drawn by others" (147).

For an understanding of the abridged, I looked to Parlin Hall's many media remnants of past bureaucracy and its former versions of place. As Lynch discussed regarding the varied development we can witness in any long-standing city, Parlin Hall has grown and changed in strange topologies while remaining the same. It should be of little surprise that one would need to look no further than an academic setting to explore bureaucracy as a site for media archaeology. Built in the mid-1950s, Parlin Hall bears marks of what might be considered the golden age of bureaucracy. The building sits as one of six intended to house the majority of the liberal arts programs for the university. As products of those times, the buildings adhere to some of the central tenets of bureaucracy. The buildings' intercoms and centralized clocks (fig. 5.1) are attributes for what Max Weber considers to be an important part of bureaucratic sites, the coordinated attempt to rationalize an organization. However, in addition to this traditional read on bureaucracy, Alexander Styhre frames "bureaucracy as a productive organizational method where centralized control is perhaps the least of its attributes" (xx). Styhre argues that bureaucracies are multifaceted and always in need of recruiting a multiplicity of unlikely allies to accomplish even small tasks. Just like the temporal layers in Lynch's cities, the drawers within drawers of Schmahmann's bureau, or the folds of the expanded surface in Deleuze's account of the baroque, so too is Parlin Hall a place for multiple abridgments.

I was confronted with this site's multiplicity when I first arrived on the job while the entire building was under construction. In addition to getting a peek behind the curtain of my own undergraduate institution, I was also privy to a peek behind its ceiling tiles and walls (fig. 5.2). Along with the kinds of bureaucratic experience one undergoes as a new faculty member in a large

institution, I was immediately made aware of the many different mechanisms for its communication, as it was all foregrounded. Electrical conduits, alarm bells, internet cables all hung above me as I carried my first boxes into my office. Although I was not present when it was built, nor was I even alive, I formed a relation to Parlin's construction through its reconstruction.

Figure 5.1. Parlin Hall hallway

Figure 5.2. Parlin hallway reconstruction

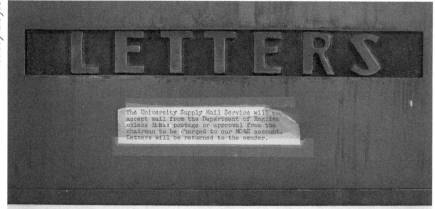

Figure 5.3. Mail drop

I quickly found multiple instances in which the bureaus of this particular bureaucracy had become unmoored from its present (or past) operations. That is, several medial components necessary for past practices have remained far beyond their original use. Elaborating on Jussi Parikka and media archaeology, and perhaps elaborating on Corder's method, we might use an approach that we could call *archaeology of the bureaucratic machine*, attempting to trace out and reassemble a place without regard to its direct historical line of development. One such archaeological feature in Parlin Hall is the mail system that once constituted the building's communication network (fig. 5.3). All throughout the building, elaborate brass mail drops remain. Janitorial staff occasionally polish the brass, though no one has used the system in decades. Even prior instructions remain, directing users to get the "chairman's approval before sending out any communications." It is unclear how long that directive has been there, but decades might be a starting place.

Not all archaeological remnants are mere adornment. Toward a media archaeological examination of place as abridged, we can look to those elements of outdated bureaucratic machinery that remain but have new purpose. For instance, long before I arrived, as mentioned in Graham's narrative, the only available phones in the building were in phone booths installed in each floor (fig. 5.4). These small closets, still marked with "For Staff Use Only," made the phone conversation a public event, as the closet was too small for an adult to close the door. Today the booths serve as conduits for internet service and other wiring. The prior uses folded away and present an abridged place to engage.

Figure 5.4. Telephone room

Another example of an abridged place is that every door in the building is equipped with a nicely designed mail slot (fig. 5.5). You can easily imagine that this mechanism once facilitated the passing of papers, term papers, exam books, and interoffice correspondence to professors. You can probably also imagine this pretty wide opening becoming a way for just about anyone to pass anything through. For this reason, all the mail slots were boarded up and sealed twenty years ago. However, we can see how an abridged account, one that folds together a prior tool with a new use, would allow for an example of how place temporally functions. Throughout the building, different appropriations of the mail emerge as reenacting the mailbox's function but in a slightly different way. Each of the attempts to reclaim and redeploy an older medium for even a related purpose shows an inventive aspect of bureaucracy and place that typically gets elided when we think of bureaucracy only in terms of the obstacles and barriers it places before us. Each of these mechanisms offers a range of possibilities not determined by former use or original intent.

In my last example of remnants of bureaucracies past, we find an abridgment that is difficult to ignore even as it is often literally papered over. It is kind of hard to see in the picture, but behind those course descriptions that are still posted to walls throughout the building, there's a button connected to an operating bell (fig. 5.6). When the building was constructed, it was planned that any faculty member or administrator might press the button to summon janitorial staff to assist in something. Every floor has two or three similar buttons, and *all the buttons still work*. Today this remnant is not simply an interesting feature, but a material occasion that rings several

Figure 5.5. Repurposed mail slot (*left*)

times a day when someone finds the button and presses it out of curiosity, as would happen with any unlabeled button. Fact: no one's curiosity is satisfied with only one press of the button. Two, three, four times the button is pressed, until the interested party realizes that no one will come to answer the bell.

This abridgment is perhaps the most interesting. There is no longer a purpose for the bell, as with the mail slots, but it does enact an effect. It gives every bell-ringer an experience to take away from Parlin Hall. Taking an idea from an old *Twilight Zone* episode, I put up a little sign below the one that's right outside my office that reads, "If you Press this button, someone in the world will die" (fig. 5.7), and then waited to see how many people would actually press it. Many more people did press the button. More than simply resuscitating a long-forgotten bell, however, the sign spurred a conversation that marks this as a place of writing. Weeks after I had put up the sign, someone added another, asking if they could pick who was killed. After that, someone else put up a sign to correct the grammar, and then, as it goes, someone followed up correcting the correction. These abridgments, mechanisms of old bureaucracies, are examples of how places fold and unfold. The slots in doors, defunct mail systems, repurposed telephone closets, and a reinvented bell are all examples of how places accumulate dimensions by folding and unfolding their relations.

Looking for Nothing Lost

Jim Corder writes that "it's hard to find places and to know them" (128). Corder's essay about proposing a class to explore place came about because

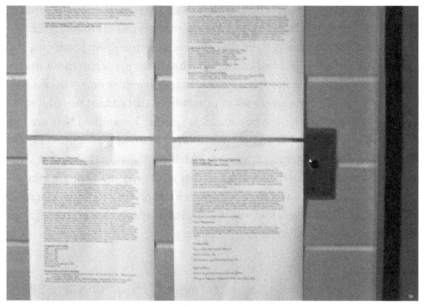

Figure 5.6. Partially papered-over bell button (*right*)

place was lost to him. Place was wrapped in loss, nostalgia, and wandering, and he sorted through maps, songs, novels, and physical locations as a way to find it again. What if, instead of thinking about place as a puzzle to piece together, one understood it as a set of bureaucracies for exploring and reinventing place through its temporal layers? Examining even one place, an academic building named Parlin Hall, offers multiple opportunities for navigating alternative routes around the idea that any place needs a neat totalizing narrative, which so often bears on how we understand the character of any place. The remnants of past mediations layer atop one another, folding past uses into present inventions. These layers of mediations abridge places and develop novel relations. I was not privy to a complete history of Parlin Hall, no one is, but my own history of the place continues to be invented and reconstructed through the multiple abridgments that emerge.

Figure 5.7. Signs about the button

My place in Parlin Hall is both complete and partial. Both terms capture place as it exists around me. This is not to say that any place is wholly reducible to my own time. Of course, there are others whose time spent producing the place of Parlin Hall aligns and converges with my own. Each of those stories is abridged inasmuch as it is space from which to inventive new relations. We actualize a place from a larger set of possibilities that cannot be reduced to a *mere* piece in a puzzle. The bureaucratic vestiges I examined here are but an example of the routine and extraordinary dynamics that unfold in any given place. Surely other examples would tell similar stories. A coffee shop might accumulate varied coffee cups, and its tables and chairs might take on differing characteristics over time as they are broken, repaired, and replaced in varying ways. These layers fold together and offer spaces to explore or ignore by composing abridged accounts of a place.

Works Cited

Boyle, Casey, and Nathaniel Rivers. "Augmented Publics." *Circulation, Writing, & Rhetoric*, edited by Laurie Gries and Collin Brooke, Utah State UP, forthcoming.

Corder, Jim. "I Proposed a New Geography Course, but the Curriculum Committee Turned It Down." *Yonder: Life on the Far Side of Change*, edited by Jim W. Corder, U of Georgia P, 1992, pp. 123–48.

Deleuze, Gilles. *The Fold: Leibniz and the Baroque*. U of Minnesota P, 1993.

Edbauer, Jenny. "Unframing Models of Public Distribution: From Rhetorical Situation to Rhetorical Ecologies." *Rhetoric Society Quarterly*, vol. 35, no. 4, 2005, pp. 5–24.

Graham, Don. "The View from Parlin." *Alcalde*, 18 Dec. 2014, alcalde.texasexes. org/2014/12/the-view-from-parlin/. Accessed 3 Feb. 2015.

Huhtamo, Erkki, and Jussi Parikka, editors. *Media Archaeology: Approaches, Applications, and Implications*. U California P, 2011.

Kafka, Ben. *The Demon of Writing: Powers and Failures of Paperwork*. Zone Books, 2012.

Lynch, Kevin. *What Time Is This Place?* MIT Press, 1972.

Parikka, Jussi. *What Is Media Archaeology?* John Wiley and Sons, 2013.

Reynolds, Nedra. *Geographies of Writing: Inhabiting Places and Encountering Difference*. Southern Illinois UP, 2007.

Schmahmann, Kim. "Bureau of Bureaucracy." *Kim Schmahmann*, 17 Dec. 2012, www.kimschmahmann.com/pages/g_bureau.html. Accessed 3 Feb. 2015.

Styhre, Alexander. *The Innovative Bureaucracy: Bureaucracy in an Age of Fluidity*. Routledge, 2007.

Weber, Max. *Economy and Society: An Outline of Interpretive Sociology*. Vol. 1. U of California P, 1978.

EAST TEXAS

James Chase Sanchez,
Middlebury College

6. RECIRCULATING OUR RACISM: PUBLIC MEMORY, FOLKLORE, AND PLACE IN EAST TEXAS

The ache for home lives in all of us. The safe place where we can go as
we are and not be questioned.   —Maya Angelou

*M*y home relocated to Grand Saline, a small salt-mining town between
Dallas and Shreveport, in 2000. I moved to the town a few weeks into
my seventh-grade year and stayed there until I left for college at eighteen.
Though I still have a few childhood friends from other places, most of my
lifelong friends are from Grand Saline, and I still refer to the town as my
home. Maya Angelou, in the quote above, finds home to be the "safe place"
for being asked no questions, and during my schooling years, I would have
easily appropriated her definition of home as my own for Grand Saline. However, the idea of home changes over time, and all safeness can disappear too.

I say this because before the summer of 2014, most people who knew me in
town also would have said that it was my home. But things changed. On June
23, 2014, a white preacher, Charles Moore, self-immolated in Grand Saline's
biggest parking lot to protest the town's racial history. The self-immolation
received little news coverage, but I felt Moore's death deserved more recognition. So I solicited a few newspapers to cover the event, and a few of them
did. Residents of my town knew I provided this information, and many of
them afterward labeled me as a traitor. One childhood friend, in particular,
called me "a self-righteous, uninformed, self-serving pseudo-academic" who
"used this town [and] defamed it" ("Racism in Grand Saline?"). Needless to
say, my relationship with my hometown changed.

Reading Moore's suicide note, "O Grand Saline, Repent of Your Racism,"
reveals that his death involved more than some vague remorse or discon-
tent—Moore specifically felt pain over the town's racist history. In his letter,
he describes a precise memory that affected the outcome of his life:

When I was about 10-years-old, some friends and I were walking down
the road toward the creek to catch some fish, when a man called "Uncle   75

Billy" stopped us and called us into his house for a drink of water—but his real purpose was to cheerily tell us about helping to kill "niggers" and put their heads on a pole. A section of Grand Saline was (maybe still is) called "pole town," where the heads were displayed. It was years later before I knew what the name meant.

Charles Moore was born on July 18, 1934, and was "about 10-years-old" over forty years before I was born. Nevertheless, when I moved to Grand Saline in the early 2000s, I heard similar stories of "Pole Town" from friends and peers, except they were not firsthand experiences; rather, they were third- and fourth-generation stories (at the earliest). Legends of Pole Town, the site of black decapitation and massacre, extend at least a century, and the same stories that led Moore to self-immolate made me believe during high school that being racist was cool and normal. Now I reflect on my past with disgust.

My time in Grand Saline appeared normal enough even as I left for college in 2006. But it was only when I left this closed-off culture that I slowly began to see how my town's past had traumatized me. Pep rallies before football games would end with the entire team shouting with pride, "We're all right cuz we're all white!" A coach once told me to not piss off the black boys on the other team because "black kids become better athletes when they are pissed." In hindsight, I desperately attempted to become white in high school, to disassociate all of my brownness, so I would not be the point of ridicule for many peers. Still, my nicknames were "Beaner," "Wetback," and "Sancho." These names did not hurt me at the time because it was a playful way for me to fit in with my friends, but I see now how this was a way for me to cope with the color of my skin, to be the whitest brown kid in school. Racism, in one way or another, had constructed my reality.

The story that Charles Moore refers to does not just present a racialized folklore of one specific location. It represents a larger legacy for the entire area when combined with stories of Clark's Ferry and the Sundown Town. More specifically, each legend corresponds with a particular place: Pole Town with a small section of the town on the southwest side, Clark's Ferry with a spot seven miles north of town on the banks of the Sabine River, and Sundown Town with the entrances to the town from both sides of Highway 80. All these stories situate three or four particular sites of memory, and they designate place in the town of Grand Saline too—a place for racism to continue breeding well into the twenty-first century. The racist stories of Grand Saline use a systemic structure to maintain power, producing a culture implicit in casual, "color-blind" racism.

Many scholars of race in the twenty-first century acknowledge that the use of "implicit racism," often referred to as neoliberal or color-blind racism, keeps white hegemony intact. Osagie K. Obasogie states, "Claims of post-racialism and colorblindness are exposed as premature expressions that only serve to conceal and further entrench racial subordination" (176). Eduardo Bonilla-Silva makes it clearer: "Most whites endorse the ideology of color blindness and . . . this ideology is central to the maintenance of white privilege" (14). My research aims to better understand how stories of Grand Saline's past exist as a color-blind racism that shapes place and race for residents and myself too.

To fully explore the implications of my hometown's public memory, I interviewed residents to better understand their memories of this folklore. I had the pleasure of interviewing nine different people about my hometown.[1] Half of these interviews were completed in person, and the other half were conducted via telephone and email. I solicited interviews through my website and *Facebook*, and particularly, I attempted to recruit people who I knew stood on various sides of the Grand Saline racial history (based on a recording of their public comments). Each interview focuses on questions about the public memory of Grand Saline. I asked respondents open-ended questions on these stories (such as "What is your memory of the story of Pole Town?) and racial relations in the town (such as "What do outsiders think about the town?"). The people I recruited represent a wide array of responses about the town's history and culture and were selected for this exact reason.

Public Memory, Place, and Race

My analysis of Grand Saline's folklore stems from recent scholarship in public memory rhetorics. In "Public Memory in Place and Time," Edward S. Casey asserts, "Public memory is both attached to a past (typically an originating event of some sort) *and* acts to ensure a future of further remembering of that same event" (17). Casey relates public memory to acts of tradition, consisting of a past and a commemoration of said past. Other scholars, such as Amy Heuman and Catherine Langford, use public memory to analyze traditions too. These authors study whiteness at Texas A&M University, claiming, "Memory constitutes identity and identity constitutes memory. Our analysis examines how ideologies get remembered and perpetuated through the traditions of an institution, a culture, or a community as a response" (121). To Casey and Heuman and Langford, public memory lives through acting out renditions of these memories, such as in reenacting a Civil War battle at a famous site. For my argument, I believe that people in Grand Saline "perform" their memories through retelling their folklore. Public memory develops because town residents keep these legends alive and tell them to new people who move into town.

My research does not just fit within a broad realm of public memory; it also signifies memory as placemaking. Greg Dickinson and colleagues declare emphatically on this subject, "Of course, real and imaginary places have long stood metonymically for grand ideas, satirical commentary, geopolitical histories, horrifying or scandalous events, idealized community, maligned political stances and so forth" (23). Their edited collection, *Places of Public Memory*, situates public memory with certain varying memorials. To these editors and their authors, actual sites of memorials embody public memory, such as in the National Jazz Museum and at Alcatraz Island. Gregory Clark believes that "rhetorical experiences, whether discursive or not, present powerful symbols of shared identity that teach people whom they ought to aspire, individually as well as collectively, to be" (5). His work expands "our awareness of the rhetorical resources that prompt the individuals who constitute a community to adopt a common identity" (8–9). Clark's book identifies certain sites, such as Yellowstone and the Lincoln Highway, that ask tourists to enact certain traditions to develop a communal experience. Whereas Dickinson and colleagues focus on how sites symbolize public memory, Clark finds that experiences and traditions at these sites often encompass a public experience, a new type of memory. The stories of Grand Saline correspond with particular sites of memory too, on the edges of town on Highway 80, at the bridge in Pole Town, and at the riverbank at Clark's Ferry. The stories, combined with the sites of these memories, work to maintain memorials of Grand Saline's racist legacy and mold place for storytellers and visitors.

Some recent works have connected public memory with race, which is vital for my own scholarship. In *Memory in Black and White*, Paul A. Shackel finds that "minority groups often struggle to assert their view through commemoration, although sometimes their views are overpowered by those of the dominant group," and often the control of a collective public revolves around intense debates between minorities and dominant groups (173–74). Race then becomes a lens through which to understand sites of public memory. Shackel's work opens the door for my study of how race can become a lens in rhetorical placemaking. Victoria J. Gallagher and Margaret R. LaWare use the public memory of race in their analysis of the Monument to Joe Louis, in downtown Detroit. The authors write, "Artifacts that memorialize individuals and events that are 'raced,' are essentially complicated, unfinished texts that . . . creat[e] a place and occup[y] a space that is ambiguous yet recognizable and, ultimately, rhetorical" (102–3). Race remains in an ongoing conversation of meaning because it has such a complicated relationship in America's history and future. Carl Gutierrez-Jones notes this, believing "the processes of defining race and racism must themselves be ongoing and incomplete because these terms have complex rhetorical lives," and thus the analysis of the monument makes sense: the authors comprehend the complexity of race's relationship with place as being the meaning behind the piece (27).

For my argument, I believe racialized folklore can embody this ambiguity at public sites of racism, especially as it relates to white people remembering racism publicly. I argue that for my hometown, the three specific stories of a racist past keeps the town's racist legacy intact. By simply retelling these stories and visiting these sites, the residents of Grand Saline continually memorialize themselves as being racist.

The Shadows of Our Sins

A windy backroad takes residents from the north side of Grand Saline to the Sabine River, a body of water that spreads from the border of Texas and Louisiana and meanders to near the Oklahoma border. Jack Kerouac referred to the Sabine as "an evil old . . . [r]iver" in *On the Road* (92). He could have written that line from Clark's Ferry, the spot where the old trail in Grand Saline meets the Sabine. From the center of town, the journey to Clark's Ferry is 6.5 miles of bumpy, rotting pavement, leading to a mile of dirt and then to the turnaround at the Sabine. As adolescents, we spent many nights drinking beer at this spot and trying to scare one another from these woods. But Clark's Ferry denotes more than childhood freedom; it embodies the legacy of racism as well.

Two legends of Clark's Ferry tie place and folklore together. One origin narrative states that a long time ago, a man named Clark helped schoolchildren cross the river on his ferry. Unfortunately, one day the ferry flipped, and the children all drowned. The story always seemed unreal to me because the riverbed is only a few feet deep, but nevertheless the spot received its name from this legend. Another story defines the space of Clark's Ferry. This one is still folklore but carries a more haunting tune. To many of us high schoolers, Clark's Ferry exemplified an evil pas. Growing up in this area, we heard the legends that it was a secret meeting spot for the Ku Klux Klan. Various residents in the area claimed to have seen people in the woody shadows at night, partaking in the rituals of the KKK.

People I interviewed about this folklore all narrated similar tales about the area. Sarah Dern, a woman who has lived in Grand Saline for twenty years, clearly remembers stories:

> I've always heard Klan activity takes place out there. I can remember my husband saying when he was in high school they were out on the back roads out there one night, and there was a tree across the road, and they got out to move it so that they could get through, and looked over in the pasture, and there was a Klan meeting with a cross being burnt. And when [my husband] saw [the Klan], they took off after [him], and [he] literally [was] doing like 80 down that blacktop road to get out of there. It scared [him] to death.

Dern also recalled that local kids in the late 1990s attempted to write a historical research paper on Clark's Ferry but were scolded by elders in the town. A previous resident of the town, Brittney Welch, whom I knew in high school, declared quickly when asked about Clark's Ferry, "Well, everyone says that is where the KKK is still active." However, not everyone I interviewed was as quick to remember this story. Another interviewee close to my age, Amanda Jones, stated that she had "never heard of a story about Clark's Ferry" but did remember "growing up hearing the usual stories we all did: the KKK used to have meetings, [and] someone's grandparents had white robes in their closet." The image of the KKK pervading Grand Saline's culture emerged in eight of the nine interviews from town residents, without their being directly prompted about the KKK in my questions. Though not everyone mentioned the story of Clark's Ferry, most could vaguely remember stories about the KKK being present.

Clark's Ferry exemplifies an interesting space for me. Every once in a while, my friends and I would drive there and find a dead hog or another animal that someone had displayed as a ritualistic sacrifice. I always assumed it had just been done by other high school students as a prank. The memory of the KKK is not explicit in the river's movement or in the trees blowing in the wind; the only hint of its racist past and presence exists in the stories of others. By retelling the origin tales of the KKK at Clark's Ferry, the people of Grand Saline perpetuate a racism. Though none of the storytellers would claim to be racists, the story embellishes the town's history and culture, indicting the culture as racist and also providing the place "with some lastingness," or a factor that makes Clark's Ferry memorable (Casey 39). The act of retelling folklore memorializes storytellers, appointing them participants in the tradition and denying them responsibility.

Another folklore transports us to the southwest side of town, across the railroad tracks, in one of the poorer parts of Grand Saline often referred to as Pole Town. To get to the area when I lived in the town, we crossed an old wooden bridge that shook the hell out of our vehicles. Each wooden plank wiggled with pressure from tires, and I held my breath each time I crossed it, knowing this would be the time I would fall onto the train tracks below. Sometime after I left the town, the bridge eventually fell but was not replaced. Brittney Welch and I talked about the significance of the bridge during our session. "They are not even rebuilding the Pole Town Bridge," Welch indicated to me. "It is down, but they are not going to rebuild it, which amazes me . . . they have no intentions of rebuilding it, even though it is the main access to the rodeo." The bridge and the tracks always felt strange to me as a kid, somehow reminding me of a past I could not explain, and as Welch noted, it remains the main access to a popular venue. Yet the town has yet to rebuild the bridge. I believe this directly relates to its racist symbolism.

The story of Pole Town conveys more explicit racial implications than Clark's Ferry. As the legend goes, residents of the town hung black people on the bridge and let trains demolish their dead bodies. Residents would then decapitate the bodies and place the heads on poles all around the area. As an adolescent, I heard this story and thought about it often as I trekked through Pole Town on the way to friends' houses. I associated the story of the lynchings with the roughness of the bridge—with every jolt in my car, I could imagine the deceased swinging below, bouncing off trains like my tires bouncing off the cracked wood.

Though not everyone recollected a specific story associated with Clark's Ferry, all the Grand Saline residents I interviewed recalled legends about Pole Town. Alan Greggory, a man who had gone to high school with me, hesitated to discuss more specific stories at first. He acknowledged, partially, the legend of Pole Town, though he seemed timid because of the volatile nature of the subject matter covered in the interview. He stated when asked specifically about the story, "Man, I feel like I have one story, and I can't remember it. Something pertaining to the actual pole." Alan remembered that there was a story connected to the area but did not move past this simple description. Maybe he didn't remember. Maybe he chose not to. Amanda Jones, another participant who pushes against Grand Saline's racial culture, clearly recalled the story, though: "I believe the name Pole Town originated from [stories that] black people would be hung by members of the KKK on poles" there. Other participants produced the stories with ease. Shirley Crawford, the only minority interviewee, articulated a clear pain: "I was told [members of the KKK] would sometimes torture [black people] by throwing rocks at them, cutting them, or making them watch their other family members die before they died." Welch went on to note, "When the Saline Café was open they still had pictures up of the bridge and I think it had a couple of lynchings in them." When I asked if she remembered specifically seeing those pictures, she nodded in agreement. This café closed down in the mid-1990s.

The story of Pole Town designates a place with a more lingering image of racism. Compared with Clark's Ferry, Pole Town remains a site of pain, focusing less on tales of the KKK and more on real images of decapitated black people. I can hear it in the interviewee's voices when they bring up the Saline Café and the brutal descriptions of the deceased. John Bodnar writes that pain often rhetorically situates war memorials because these memorials remind communities of their dead (156). I believe the bridge and site at Pole Town have a similar effect for those in Grand Saline, reminding them of a past pain of racism and lynching and a realization of the horrors of their ancestors. The bridge may have fallen, but that pain still peeks through the crevices of cracked road on both sides of the train tracks.

Though the previous two stories align strongly with actual places, one of the final stories about Grand Saline's racist history emerges in a more vague space. Highway 80 splits the town in half, running all the way to Dallas (about 60 miles west) and to Shreveport (about 125 miles east). The road parallels Interstate 20, which is 10 miles south of the highway, but for many travelers in the area, Highway 80 is the main access not only to the town but to larger cities as well. From the east, the town nestles behind three large hills. On entering the city limits, one passes an old abandoned steel plant on the left, followed by the skating rink, which was every kid's weekend outing in late grade school and middle school. From the west, one drives around a large curve with the train tracks on the right, tucked behind a small tree line. Rounding the curve, one encounters a large sign welcoming people to Grand Saline, followed by a large lumber store on the left side of the highway.

I explain these entrances to better imagine what Grand Saline looks like in the story of its being a "sundown town." Sundown towns are communities that forbade African Americans to live within their limits. James W. Loewen notes that they were so named "because many marked their city limits with signs typically reading, 'Nigger, Don't Let The Sun Go Down On You In ————'" ("Sundown Towns," 1). In his *Sundown Towns Database*, Loewen confirms that Grand Saline was one. An oral history in Loewen's collection claims that the town purged black residents after Reconstruction, "killing all who were unable to escape. . . . The mass killings were followed by mutilation of the corpses for public display." A former slave who traveled through town even said that "dey had a big sign dere wid 'Nigger, don't let de sun go down on you here' on it" ("Grand Saline in TX"). The history of Grand Saline's sundown town status seems well recorded through oral history, yet the actual place of the sign remains unknown in these oral stories.

Whereas nonresidents I spoke to were mostly unable to attest to stories of Clark's Ferry and Pole Town, many of them acknowledged stories of the sundown town signs. Latonya Winters, a black woman who grew up in Edgewood, a town ten miles west of Grand Saline, said, "I do believe I heard there was a sign in Grand Saline that stated, 'Niggers don't let the sun go down on you here!'" Leon Sylvester, a white reporter who worked for the county's newspaper for thirteen years and lived in Canton, a town twelve miles to the south, had spoken with many locals about the signs in the past. He asserted, "Most people in Grand Saline, however, seemed to deny the sign's existence and would not talk about it when asked. A number of people I spoke with, however, were certain of having seen it at some point in the past." For people outside Grand Saline, the stories of the sundown town sign seem real and historical.

Though the interviewees from Grand Saline remained uncertain about the sign's existence, they had all heard the stories (mostly from outsiders). One former resident, Lacey Michaels, spent her entire life in the town and remembered "being told, mostly by people from surrounding towns, that Grand Saline used to have a sign at the city limits." Though eight of the nine respondents recalled the sign, none had ever seen it, and many believed it was just another legend. This legend stays alive only through the tradition of retelling these stories and visiting the edges of the town where the signs might have existed. Heuman and Langford believe, "Traditions are customs and practices handed down from the predecessor. Tradition is not observed; tradition is enacted" (126). The people of Grand Saline breathe life into these stories, memorializing them, by keeping them in the public's storytelling imagination. Though there is little proof the signs existed, the stories make them real.

Together these three stories not only assign a physical place for racism, located in certain areas of the town, but also stay in existence through the public memory of the town. More specifically, the continual telling and re-telling of this folklore represents a twenty-first-century racist practice. I end this chapter by demonstrating how residents battle against these public sites of memory, how the sites fashioned my perception of my town, and how the stories situated place for me as well.

A Legend of Place

My interviews demonstrate that hardly anyone in the town would refer to himself or herself as racist or would label Grand Saline a racist town. Their logic pushes against an essentialist viewpoint. Critical race scholars Richard Delgado and Jean Stefancic state, "When we think of the term 'essentializing,' we think of paring something down until the heart of the matter stands alone" (62–63). Scholars typically use this term when discussing stereotypes of race; for example, believing that "all brown people speak Spanish" would be essentializing Latinx peoples, since many of us do not speak Spanish. In terms of the Grand Saline interviews, people of the town believe that calling the town racist essentializes them, and since they are not all racist, outsiders cannot label the town this way.

However, the stories many recollect from town imply something different. Whereas most of the residents' arguments against being called racist focus on the explicit use of racism, I contend that the town's culture postulates this racism by keeping these stories in the public sphere. Thus when I refer to the town in this chapter, I am pointing to its culture, not every single resident in the town. Many of the people I spoke to referred to these stories as being folklore or "things that kids just say." Others, such as Tracy Lunsford, a woman who left town and never looked back, see things differently. "Fear," she said. "By retelling these stories they are keeping the fear alive, thus keeping them cocooned in their 'white bubbles.'" These stories mold the town's understanding of race and keep black people as a distant "other." They also explain how the town's culture fears blackness, making them the victims of the town's racial power. The hegemony protects itself by continually demonstrating historically how they have oppressed black people. And without having any remorse within these stories, the culture of Grand Saline demonstrates their hegemonic prowess.

Each racial story revolves around not only a certain place but objects within these spaces as well. Clark's Ferry derives from the turnaround at the river's edge; Pole Town surfaces from the cracked bridge; and Grand Saline receives fame as a sundown town from the hateful signs. Yet the history of the sundown town signs remains ambiguous. The bridge at Pole Town fell a few years ago, and the city has not bothered replacing it. Even the turnaround at the Sabine has been closed off, gated by a private property owner tired of kids messing around in his woods. By taking away access to these sites of memory or by removing the symbols of each site, the town attempts to erase a racialized past. But it can't. The stories, the true power behind this folklore, keep them alive, even as the fences, fallen bridges, and destroyed signs call for erasure.

I am not the first one to talk about Grand Saline's racist culture. Mike Daniel, a Dallas attorney who filed suit against the town's discriminatory housing in 1985, acknowledged the problem: "The Ku Klux Klan hasn't bothered to go to Grand Saline because they know they don't have to. Nothing's going to change in Grand Saline" (qtd. in Stewart). What a powerful statement. And it seems to still hold true thirty years later. To me, and to some others who reside outside the town's perimeters, Grand Saline has a stain of racism unable to be cleaned in its culture; its residents continually try to cover this stain with preachings of inclusion and acceptance, but it still persists below the surface, breeding in the stories of their (public) memories. My own story attests to this.

During my years in Grand Saline, the town symbolized a home, a place for my friends and my single mother to remain safe. I never felt afraid in my hometown. Actually, I remember leaving doors unlocked at night, being able to walk the streets whenever I wanted, and having a space for freedom in my everyday living. Even now, ten years after I left, I still envision Grand Saline as a place of safety for its residents. For many people who live there, Grand Saline has been home to their families for a long time. I recall being one of the only outsiders during my high school years, and I knew many whose parents, grandparents, and further generations had grown up in the town or the area, which gives them a level of comfort.

But it is impossible for me to look back on my time there and have the same sense of belonging now. Things drastically changed. I see now that the stories told to me as an adolescent conjure a figurative and physical space for racism to exist. These physical places remain in the public memory of residents, expressed in the interviews above. Though not every resident would necessarily call these sites "places for racism," they still carry racially charged memories of lynchings, the KKK, and sundown signs, and by keeping these stories alive through folklore, the residents of the town memorialize these sites in the tradition of racism. As "Lost Cause" sympathizers celebrate the likes of Confederate Memorial Day and Robert E. Lee's birthday to "attest to the [their] heritage as a region," the people of Grand Saline travel to many of these sites and tell these stories to keep the racist legacy of their past alive, whether intentionally or not (Towns 145–46). However, whereas many sites of public memory persist through the acts of explicit tradition, the sites of racism in Grand Saline live implicitly, maintaining status through a storytelling that most dub untrue. I still uphold that this practice should be defined as racist as well.

Still, the people of my hometown are not "evil" racists. They follow the same principles as most of America, believing in color blindness (a different problem) and having fundamental American values. Main Street Baptist Church, the largest church in town, even recruited a black preacher to be its interim pastor, and he won "Man of the Year" honors from the Grand Saline Chamber of Commerce in 2015 (Fite). Overall, the residents could be the people of any rural city in the South. What prevents them from being more progressive is the persistence of racist folklore across the twentieth and twenty-first centuries. No one individual is responsible for the memorialization of these sites; we are all culpable merely by visiting them and retelling the stories. And as long as young kids go backroading at night and tell the legends of their ancestors' misdeeds, this sphere of agony will continue to thrive, even as the sites decay and lose symbolic value.

My mom no longer lives in Grand Saline. She moved ten miles east to the slightly larger town of Mineola. This leaves me no real reason to go to the town except occasionally to visit friends who still live there, or I may pass by on the way to visit my mother from the Dallas–Fort Worth metroplex. When I get close to the town's entrance, a tingle always shoots up my spine. I don't think it is nostalgia or a sense of home anymore, but a memory of the traditions I took part in—telling the legends, visiting the sites, keeping the folklore alive. The feeling soon dissipates.

Grand Saline may no longer be my home, but it will always represent a racialized place of my past, one I choose to remember so I can choose to do better.

Note

1. For the sake of anonymity, I have replaced interviewees' actual names with pseudonyms.

Works Cited and Consulted

Bodnar, John. "Bad Dreams about the Good War." Dickinson et al., pp. 139–59.

Bonilla-Silva, Eduardo. *Racism without Racist.* Rowman and Littlefield, 2003.

Callaway, Wendi. "Man Sets Himself on Fire in Public Parking Lot." *Grand Saline Sun*, 25 June 2014, p. 1.

Casey, Edward S. "Public Memory in Place and Time." *Framing Public Memory*, edited by Kendall R. Phillips, U of Alabama P, 2004, pp. 17–44.

Clark, Gregory. *Rhetorical Landscapes in America.* Columbia: U of South Carolina P, 2004.

Dean, Kenneth. "Madman or Martyr? Retired Minister Sets Self on Fire, Dies." *Tyler Morning Telegraph*, 1 Jul. 2014. www.tylerpaper.com/TP-News+Local /201968/madman-or-martyr-retired-minister-sets-self-on-fire-dies. Accessed 1 Jul. 2014.

Delgado, Richard, and Jean Stefancic. *Critical Race Theory: An Introduction.* 2nd ed., New York UP, 2012.

Dickinson, Greg, et al., editors. *Places of Public Memory: The Rhetoric of Museums and Memorials.* U of Alabama P, 2010.

Fite, B. R. "Chamber of Commerce Throws Annual Banquet Fundraiser." *Grand Saline Sun*, 2 Apr. 2015, gss.stparchive.com/Archive/GSS/GSS04022015p01. php?tags=fite|man%20of%20the%20year. Accessed 14 Apr. 2015.

Gallagher, Victoria J., and Margaret R. LaWare. "Sparring with Public Memory: The Rhetorical Embodiment of Race, Power, and Conflict in the *Monument to Joe Louis*." Dickinson et al., pp. 87–112.

Gutierrez-Jones, Carl. *Critical Race Narratives: A Study of Race, Rhetoric, and Injury.* New York UP, 2001.

Heuman, Amy, and Catherine Langford. "Tradition and Southern Confederate Culture." *Public Memory, Race, and Ethnicity*, edited by G. Mitchell Reyes, Cambridge Scholars, 2010, pp. 120–40.

Kerouac, Jack. *On The Road.* Viking P, 1957.

Loewen, James W. "Grand Saline in TX." *Sundown Towns: A Hidden Dimension of American Racism*, sundown.tougaloo.edu/sundowntownsshow.php?id =1213. Accessed 1 Apr. 2015.

———. "Sundown Towns." *Poverty and Race Newsletter*, vol. 14, no. 6, 2005, pp. 1–2.

Moore, Charles. "O Grand Saline, Repent of Your Racism." 23 June 2014.

Obasogie, Osagie K. *Blinded by Sight.* Stanford UP, 2014.

"Racism in Grand Saline? Comments." *Facebook*, 15 July 2014, www.facebook
.com/grandsaline.sun/posts/291551221025462. Accessed 15 July 2014.

Shackel, Paul A. *Memory in Black and White.* AltaMira P, 2003.

Stewart, Richard. "Desegregation: 'Nothing's . . . to Change in Grand Saline.'"
Houston Chronicle, 17 Oct. 1993, p. 1. *NewsBank*, www.infoweb.newsbank
.com.ezproxy.tcu.edu/resources/doc/nb/news/0ED7B2F41CDEBBC2?p
=WORLDNEWS. Accessed 16 Apr. 2015.

Towns, W. Stuart. *Enduring Legacy: Rhetoric and Ritual of the Lost Cause.*
U of Alabama P, 2012.

Jenny Rice,
University of Kentucky

7. ARCHIVING DEVILS

Pigs in the Parlor

In 1973, a friendly-faced Baptist minister and his wife from Plainview wrote a small book about their Christian ministry that would profoundly change the way millions of people came to think about not just their lives but life itself. Frank and Ida Mae Hammond's book *Pigs in the Parlor* was no ordinary book about Christian life, however. Theirs was a book about demons, demonic possession, satanic strongholds, and exorcism. *Pigs in the Parlor* is a catalog of the unseen demonic world that affects every corner of our everyday lives. Shortly after its publication, the Hammonds' manual for casting out demons became a kind of textbook for Christian charismatic ministries throughout the world that took on the work of demonic deliverance. In the forty years since its humble beginnings, *Pigs in the Parlor* is still one of the most widely circulating manuals for demonic deliverance and exorcism around the world.

New Boston, Texas, is 455 miles away from the Hammonds' house in Plainview. It was 157 miles from the suburban Dallas house where I lived in ninth grade. One hot summer day, my father carried my small suitcase into a car and drove me 157 miles from Dallas to New Boston. After a silent car ride, we turned onto a gravel road and drove down a long farm entrance. Small, white clapboard buildings dotted acres of land. At the center sat a tiny white chapel. The sign over the entrance read "Gateway Christian Farm for Girls." My father stopped the car in front of the chapel. "This is it," he said without looking at me. This was it. The end of the road. Any road. New Boston, Texas. 1990. I would live here at the farm for the next twelve months.

At fifteen, I was sent away to Gateway Christian Farm for Girls because I had become possessed by a spirit of rebellion. Or, at least, this is what the pastor at my parents' Pentecostal church had told them. After much prayer, God had finally led their pastor to the only answer: I needed deliverance from Satan's spiritual bondage. *For rebellion is as the sin of witchcraft, and stubbornness is as iniquity and idolatry.* Their pastor gave them the name of a ministry that specialized in delivering girls and young women from such bonds. It was a place for liberation. My only hope for salvation.

Nighttime chapel was the time when spirits of rebellion were cast out of the girls at the farm. When the demon was finally cast out, the Holy Spirit's redemption was clear. Deliverance was witnessed through speaking of tongues and dancing in the Spirit. During every session of deliverance, I was instructed to write down the demons that had been cast out:

> The demon of sexual impurity.
> The demon of fantasy.
> The demon of anger.
> The demon of despair.
> The demon of pride.

Over the course of a year, I witnessed many similar deliverances among the girls who lived at the farm with me. Spirits of infirmity were cast out. Spirits of idol worship and witchcraft, spirits of lying, spirits of immorality, spirits of alcohol and drug use. They left our bodies one by one, leaving us free to become pure servants of the Lord once more.

As strange as this account might seem, my experiences are not unique. In the middle of *Pigs in the Parlor*, Frank Hammond tells the story of a girl named Mary. Mary's father brought her to Hammond, complaining that "she was a most difficult child to handle, being very stubborn, self-willed and rebellious" (67). Hammond's description of Mary's deliverance unfolds over several pages with incredible detail. "I asked her to come sit on the bench beside me while I prayed. She did, but she was so restless that I had to take her on my lap to keep her near me. She sat on my lap with her back toward me" (67). As his prayer began, Mary voiced discomfort and rejection of Hammond's touch. Nevertheless, he continues, "The Holy Spirit very plainly told me . . . to consider every word hereafter that came out of Mary's mouth to be a demon speaking or to be demon inspired" (67). Mary was not silent, according to Hammond, continually repeating one phrase in particular: "I don't like what you are saying" (68).

After plowing forward with the prayers, Hammond then described Mary's attempts to free herself from Hammond's grasp. "The demons were making Mary struggle to get out of my lap although I was still able to hold her rather loosely in my arms. Eventually I had to resort to putting one of her legs between mine, thus holding her in a vise and bodily restraining her" (68). Meanwhile, the girl continued to fight with her words and body. "Mary began to scream one long scream after another and beg to be turned loose," Hammond writes. "She would say, 'Don't hold my leg! Don't hold my leg!'" (69). With Mary's small body restrained, Hammond continued to command the demons to leave her. The demons of fear, rejection, hate, defiance, self-will, stubbornness, madness, bitterness, and rebellion were all called forth in the name of Jesus.

Hammond describes how eventually Mary's ability to physically struggle was reduced with each demonic loosing: "She was softly crying and said, 'I don't like for you to hold me like that.' I said, 'Well, I'm sorry I had to hold you so tight, but the bad spirits were making you fight me.'" (70). After the final demons had been called out, however, a spirit of peace came over the girl. Hammond closes his account with great emotion. "The warfare was so tumultuous and the peace afterward so beautiful. I could not keep back the tears. To God be the glory!" (70). And with that closing, Mary's story comes to an end.

Yet, of course, her story does not end there. What happened to the demons who were cast out of Mary? Out of *me*? Where did they go? For that matter, what happened to the demons who were bound and rebuked from women's bodies in churches across the world? What archivable artifacts did those deliverances leave behind? These questions are nearly impossible to answer, since archives of deliverance are few and far between. Such archives would be spread across spaces and across time, stretching across every moment when a girl has been told she must give up her demons. Every moment when a physical, emotional, or mental need has been erased in the name of spiritual cleanliness. Every moment when a girl's desire for life becomes redescribed in terms of spiritual pathology. But there seem to be almost no such archives.

From Demon to *Daimon*

When an archive is missing, it is not because the materials do not exist. Perhaps what is absent is care. When I think about archives and care, I cannot shake the image of my daughter's archival fever every time she pores over family scrapbooks and baby books. Nine-year-old Vered is trying to learn her own story from these mad fragments. She turns the pages carefully to avoid damaging (and risk losing) the key that explains how Vered become Vered. Watching my daughter spend hours in a fitful state of archival fever, I also recall that care has less to do with love or compassion than with an entanglement and involvement. Martin Heidegger saw care (working from the mythos of Cura) as the mode of absorption in the world.

Several commentators have suggested that Heidegger's notion of care remains relatively underdeveloped. As an alternative, some turn to Japanese philosopher Tetsuro Watsuji to help expand on Heidegger's sense of care. Watsuji uses the Japanese term *sonzai* to describe the structure of being. *Sonzai* is derived from two parts: *son* for maintenance or subsistence against loss and *zai* as remaining within relationships (Shields 92). For Watsuji, the practical structure of human being is a dialectic that alternates between maintenance against loss (which signals time) and the desire to remain in relationships (which signals space). The *son* of *sonzai* relates to a threat that the *self* is always threatened with disappearance, being pulled too much into the ecology of relations. Subsistence and maintenance works against this threat of loss. *Zai* is a staying in place, which occurs because we are always enmeshed in relations of world. Taken together, *sonzai* marks the struggle of fighting a loss of self, trying to maintain the I one already is or has been or will be, while also remaining enmeshed in the not-I world of relations and world. Care, in this sense, is a tugging between I and not-I.

If archives are absent because an element of care is missing, then it seems reasonable to suggest that recovering or materializing those absent archives also operate from some ethic of care. Yet I would like to suggest an alternative mode of care in relation to absent archives. This alternative mode of care challenges a lopsided approach to the dialectic of I and not-I, or *son* and *zai*. This alternative mode of care does not sacrifice the pull of time to maintenance against loss. To illustrate this lopsidedness, I can't think of many better examples than my own attempts to destroy an existing archive. At age forty, when I went back to search my own personal archives from that year at the farm, I found that much had been cast out, even beyond the demons. Notes, pictures, journals, details, materials. I had so little because, long ago, I had performed my own kind of archival exorcism. I threw out everything I could, hoping to remake an identity that was apart from that time and place. Yet deliverance of that kind never works. The *daimon* will never be cast out.

To understand this alternative mode of care, however, we must be willing to engage a bit more with the world of demons. This time, it is the classical vision of the *daimon* that sheds light on archival care. Giorgio Agamben writes about the Greek notion of *daimon* in relation to the Latin god Genius. According to Agamben, Genius was the god who is with each person at the point of his birth, his godly force swirling around *genialis lectus*, the bed that inevitably serves as the scene of birth-making activity. Genius is generative, birthing us into the world every moment. As Agamben writes:

> To comprehend the concept of man which is implicit in Genius, means to understand that man is not only "I" and individual consciousness (coscienza), but that from the moment of his birth to that of his death he lives instead with an impersonal and pre-individual component. That is, man is . . . a being who is the result of the complicated dialectic between one side not (yet) singled out (individuata) and lived, and another side already marked by fate and by individual experience. (97)

The daemonic dialectic suggests another tension or friction that (imperfectly) parallels the kind of care—whether as *Sorge* or *sonzai*—that marks human involvement. On one side, there is the self-sustenance of individual experience that is always tugged between loss and maintenance. On the other side, there is the not-I of world, others, relations. This is the world of Genius, the world of the *daimon.*

The *daimon*, which Agamben reads through the Latin tradition of Genius, also appears in Hannah Arendt's account of the human condition. Arendt considers the work of disclosure before others, which is never fully graspable by us as individuals. We disclose *who* we are to others in ways that surpass our self-concepts or best attempt at self-reflection. The *daimon* is that which is disclosed to others but never to us. The *daimon* is both more than I but also that which allows I to be human at all. Arendt points to the example of Sophocles's *Oedipus Rex* and the terribly painful disclosure that is evident to the chorus though Oedipus is blind in more ways than one. "These others see," writes Arendt, "they 'have' Oedipus' *daimon* before their eyes as an example; the misery of the mortals is their blindness toward their own *daimon*" (193n18). However, while Oedipus's *daimon* marks a tragedy, this is not to say that the *daimon* is a source of misery. As both Arendt and Agamben suggest, we have no place in the world without disclosure.

The notions of possession and casting out demons take on interesting angles when we engage with these senses of the term *daimon.* In evangelical circles, Satan's evil spirits inhabit a human body and causes all kinds of turmoil that is out of the sufferer's control. These demons can be cast out in order to return the true self to her pure state, apart from the outside forces that attach to a single, individual body. Yet casting out the daemons imagined by Agamben and Arendt is an impossibility. It would mean a casting out of involvement in the world altogether: the temporality of I attempting to remain I apart from engagement with world. But no such deliverance is possible. The kind of care that involves us in the world leaves no temporal possibility of self-sustenance apart from the relations with those to whom we disclose. Casting out the daemon is the dream of every exorcist who falls back into the dream of an I whose identity is unaffected by space.

Therefore, we might consider a demon archive (or a *daimon* archive) as possessing a dialectic of care, alternating between a desire for maintenance against loss over time and the pull of disclosure toward the lived. A demon archive would be a lesser god, as it exists because of another archive's absence. Yet it is a guiding spirit, guiding the archivist and those who delve into the archive in a definite direction. It does not provide archival records of the thing itself. Instead, it leads the archivists and their users toward another place altogether. What becomes archived, then, is the disclosure of self, which can be seen as a form of maintenance, though a maintenance over which we have no control.

My Demon Archive

Twenty-five years after my father's car first drove down the gravel road in New Boston, I began to look for any archives of deliverance. My desire for such an archive emerged from my urgent need to testify to my own experiences, as well as to perhaps write the story of deliverance's effect on young women throughout this country. I also wanted to know what had become of the women who had lived at the farm and shared my experiences. But no matter where I looked, I found no such formal archive. Even so, I could not satiate my archival fever.

I began with a map of New Boston, which is in Bowie County. I contacted the Bowie County Clerk's Office by email, though I was not exactly sure how to phrase my request. To be honest, I was not sure what exactly my request was.

> Good afternoon.
>
> I'm wondering if you can help me access any records at all for some research I am doing on a property in New Boston, Texas. During the period between 1985 and 1993, it was called the Christian Gateway Farm for Girls. I am looking for anything related to property deeds, tax information, or any publicly available information relating to this property during this timespan. Can you direct me to the best possible source for locating this information?

Within a day, the chief deputy clerk of Bowie County had written me back to tell me that she could find nothing in her records that referenced Christian Gateway Farm for Girls.

Other calls turned up dead ends. I called the New Boston Public Library, hoping that it kept records of organizations or churches that had existed on this small stretch of land. The woman on the phone sounded confused before she finally gave me a friendly dismissal. Other avenues also turned up empty. I ended up at the Texas Department of Family and Protective Services, where I was told to send an open records email request for the state inspections of the home.

> From: jenny.rice@uky.edu
>
> To: openrecordsrequest@dfps.state.tx.us
>
> Good afternoon.
>
> I'm wondering if you can help me access any records at all for some research I am doing on a Girls' Home in New Boston, Texas. During the period between 1987 and 1992 (approximately), it was called the Christian Gateway Farm for Girls. I am looking for records of inspections (or any other records) for this home during this timespan.
>
> Thank you,
>
> Dr. Jenny Rice

Before hitting send, I looked over my email and considered whether to share my own relation to this place. Should I mention that I was a girl who lived in this home during my requested time span? Should I mention that I suffered nightmares for decades after leaving? Should I mention that my request was personal, emotional, painful? Should I use the term *research* at all, since these records were actually more of a search for my own comfort? Even as I was debating these questions, however, the answer came back with a disappointing result:

> Dear Ms. Rice
>
> Your request for information regarding access of any records for Christian Gateway Farm for Girls during the period between 1987 and 1992 was received. The reference number assigned to your request is 02012016UUW.
>
> Unfortunately, any documentation within that date range has already passed its retention schedule.

Strangely enough, I had not considered that official records would not be retained. Sitting in front of my laptop, I pictured all those thousands of bits— whether paper or electronic—recycling somewhere in the environment. I had no access to it, although it had perhaps never circulated more widely.

I also wrote to the girls—now women—who had also lived at the farm, all with the same experiences that have lodged in my skin. My messages vacillated constantly between a passionless request for research help and desperate pleas for engagement. My tone alternated between the professor and the survivor, depending on the person I was writing to. Sometimes, I began to wonder if they both emerged in every message.

> July 25, 2015
>
> From: jenny.rice@uky.edu
>
> To: XXXXX
>
> Hi, XXXXX. I apologize in advance for this potentially odd question. I am wondering if you're the XXXX XXXXX mentioned in this article. If so, were you ever at Gateway Christian Girls Farm? I was there from 1990–1991, and I'm finally looking to reach out to other girls who were there during this time. My online research uncovered very little, but I found this article.
>
> I apologize in advance if this is a strange question. Online research sometimes goes way wrong.
>
> Thanks in advance,
>
> Jenny (Detweiler) Rice

I checked my inbox for responses, which seldom ever arrived. I would try out different tones, strategies, phrasing—all in the hope that this would be the time that I discovered some kind of artifact trove. But it rarely happened.

Demons always say more than what a body intends. This is the case in the vision of Frank and Ida Mae Hammond's demons, or the *daimon* of Greek thought. As I search for any kind of deliverance archive, I am writing a disclosure bigger than perhaps I realize. I am writing a demon archive. A demon archive—or a *daimon* archive—does not begin from the goal of attempting to establish or find an absent archive. There are, of course, good reasons for creating such archives where none exist. We need those archives to help tell stories and make available memory for future use. But a demon archive is a different type of trawling. Instead of preservation as a guiding ethic, the demon archive haunts the absent archive in the mode of disclosure. It is a mutual moment of worlding among the demon archivist and her audience.

Whereas the search for establishing an archive may take Mnemosyne (memory's goddess) as its deity, the demon archive is guided by the lesser and undifferentiated spirits of *genius*. To create such an archive is to give the demon its due without any attempt to cast it out. Thus demon archives may be partly fictional, even fantastic. And readers are invited to search not so much for their fidelity to memory but for the demons. We may read for disclosure, which is an invitation into a worlding moment. Indeed, we might read the world of deliverance as itself a demon archive.

I thus share these accounts with my readers through an archival ethic, though not one born from a preservationist effort. This archive tells very little that mirrors useful information. Yet as a demon archive, it is *disclosive*. The disclosure here is of the archival reader who is also the archivist herself. The demon archivist can therefore only ever read to and for others. And the demon archive, living only behind our backs and never before our own eyes, lays to rest the fantasy of deliverance.

Works Cited

Agamben, Giorgio. "Genius." Translated by Laurence Simmons. *Interstices*, vol. 7, 2006, pp. 96–101.

Arendt, Hannah. *The Human Condition*. U of Chicago P, 2013.

Hammond, Frank, and Ida Mae Hammond. *Pigs in the Parlor: A Practical Guide to Deliverance*. Impact Christian Books, 1973.

Shields, James Mark. "Zange and Sorge: Two Models of 'Concern' in Comparative Philosophy of Religion." *Polyphonic Thinking and the Divine*, edited by Jim Kanaris, Rodopi, 2013, pp. 85–92.

NORTH TEXAS

Cynthia Haynes,
Clemson University

8. FORT WORTH BY DAY, COW TOWN BY NIGHT, IT'S ALL TO THE WEST OF ADIOS

J was raised in Fort Worth, Texas. I have moved away a few times, once in 1980 for a brief stint in Virginia, more recently to Denmark and Norway, and now to South Carolina. But Fort Worth is home and has been for over sixty years. The leaving is always hard, the returning always sweet. But it's the leaving that has preyed on my mind. The question of living is always a question of leaving, and not just *what* and *who* we leave behind. I think we live to leave somewhere, and somewhere along the way, the leaving gets kind of stuck in time—not frozen, but stuck the way an image gets stuck in our mind. Roland Barthes called this the *punctum* of an image, that aspect of an image that pierces us or holds our gaze in a gripping sort of way. Barthes writes that "a photograph's punctum is that accident that pricks me (but also bruises me, is poignant to me)" (27). He juxtaposes the *punctum* with what he calls the *studium* of an image, its context, its obvious meaning. The *studium* does not mean "'study,' but application to a thing, taste for someone, a kind of general, enthusiastic commitment, of course, but without special acuity" (26). The *punctum*, however, punctuates the image and its obvious meaning; there is a disturbance. We can say the same of experiences, that they possess a *punctum*. And by extension, we can say the same of experiences of place.

One particular experience serves as a metonym of Fort Worth as leaving and leaving as *punctum*. It happened sometime in the mid-1970s at the House of Pizza (HOP to the locals) near the university. The HOP was known as a mecca for amazing music and was home to some of the best musicians around: T-Bone Burnett, Stephen Bruton, Sumter Bruton, Warren and Bill Ham, Phil White, Glen Clark, Delbert McClinton, Stevie Ray Vaughan, Lou Ann Barton, Space Opera, Freddie Cisneros, Robert Ealey, Johnny Reno, and the list goes on. One night at the HOP, just before Little Whisper and the Rumors went on stage, I noticed that Stephen Bruton was wearing the best custom cowboy boots I'd ever seen. With his jeans tucked into the boots, he pivoted around to show the audience that the back of one boot said, "Adios," and the back of the other boot said, "Mother"—*Adios Mother.* And I didn't wonder which

99

mother; I wondered why the good-bye. And now . . . wherever I end up, I see those boots in my rearview mirror—as I head out to the west of adios.

I've ended up in a few other places, more or less permanent homes, over the years, but I always call Fort Worth *home*. People who don't know where it is exactly will cock their head a bit until I say, "It's thirty miles west of Dallas." But then I quickly go on to say that Dallas has *no* personality, and that Fort Worth does . . . which makes it special. You could pick Dallas up and put it down anywhere in the United States, and it would be just your ordinary megaplex (or petroplex, as we often call Dallas–Fort Worth). Its claim to fame is that it's where JFK was assassinated. Fort Worth is "where the West begins." So I say, "I live in South Carolina, but my home is Fort Worth." This generates, I hope, a Burkean identification with my audience—one that conjures up images, sounds, smells, tastes, of *home* and whatever that means to my reader. But the task of this essay is to move beyond such familiar chords and follow the "Adios Mother" to its illogical conclusion—that tug in the depths of one's being where leaving Fort Worth is a metonym for "living as leaving." Which of us is immune to such leaving, such living? Which of us is not always already "somewhere along the way"?

These questions are rhetorical and call for a rhetorical means of response. Nigel Thrift cast his response as "non-representational theory" in his work on non-representational geography and space. In their collection on *Thinking Space*, Mike Crang and Thrift put it thus: "Our intention is . . . meant to be at least indicative of the main passage points in current writing on space, all of which in one sense or the other move away from the Kantian perspective on space—as an absolute category—towards *space as process* and *in process* (that is space and time combined in becoming)" (3). In relation to what I have called "living as leaving" and Fort Worth as its metonym, Crang and Thrift offer something close. Certainly, leaving is a process, and leaving is always a leaving in space and time. They offer the example of Walter Benjamin, whose writing presents both a series of experiences of Barthes's *punctum* and a metonymic means of articulating his experiences. According to Crang and Thrift:

> At the simplest level, we can find the roots of much urban thinking in the work of those like Benjamin . . . who wrote about urban life from a Parisian context. If modernity meant the urbanisation of the mind (Schlör 1998:16) it often implied a specifically urban experience, whereby Paris came to be a metonym for both [*sic*] urban life, urbanity, and modernity. (13)

Walter Benjamin also chronicled life in Berlin, a city that (as a Jew) he most certainly had to leave. In his introduction to the collection of essays in which "A Berlin Chronicle" appears, *Reflections: Essays, Aphorisms, Autobiographical Writings*, Peter Demetz explains that "Benjamin always looked for threshold experiences" (xviii). Demetz notes that the essay's title is "a misnomer, because it actually offers a map of coexistent apartments, meeting places, elegant salons, shabby hotel rooms" (xvii–xviii). For Demetz, Benjamin's imagination suggests, "as in that of Rainer Maria Rilke, [that] space rules over time; his 'topographical consciousness' shapes experience in architectonic patterns, in neighborhoods, and in particular in urban districts the borders of which have to be crossed in trembling and sweet fear" (xvii). Benjamin explains:

> I have long, indeed for years, played with the idea of setting out the sphere of life—bios—graphically on a map. . . . He who has once begun to open the fan of memory never comes to the end of its segments; no image satisfies him, for he has seen that it can be unfolded, and only in its folds does the truth reside; that image, that taste, that touch for whose sake all this has been unfurled and dissected; and now remembrance advances from small to smallest details, from the smallest to the infinitesimal, while that which it encounters in these microcosms grows ever mightier. (5–6)

The "fan of memory never comes to the end of its segments," and *living as leaving* pays homage to such unfolding—the unfolding/leaving as microcosms of border crossings even in one's own hometown.

1968–95

It was always good to get back home to Fort Worth, until one day it wasn't. In the summer of 1968, I traveled to Europe as a wide-eyed sixteen-year-old, excited beyond my years to experience what my father had experienced in the early 1960s when he went. I remember how his suitcase smelled when he returned and opened it to find some gifts he had for me and my sister. It smelled like Europe, whatever that meant. In 1968, then, I went for three weeks on a whirlwind tour. It was sublime. I cried all the way home on the plane because I didn't want to come home. It would be another twenty-seven years before I returned, though that was not the plan. The plan was to leave Fort Worth, and I lived that leaving on a daily basis. It was my dream to live and work in Germany or Switzerland. Travel posters adorned my teenage bedroom walls. I began to study German in high school and went on to major in German in college. Somewhere along the way, the leaving dream subsided. It turned out that Fort Worth in the 1970s was, for a young woman in her twenties, quite exciting.

The music scene introduced me to a whole new world, not quite Europe, but a close second. My first job out of college was as a waitress in a downtown café popular with the county courthouse lunch bunch. I played ragtime music on their rinky-tink upright piano when I wasn't taking orders, making sandwiches, and busing tables. But soon I started booking blues bands into the place on weekend evenings. Little Whisper and the Rumors drew a huge crowd because Stephen Bruton, a local guitarist who regaled us with stories from Woodstock, was making a name for himself playing with Kris Kristofferson, Maria Muldaur, and Bonnie Raitt. He played a mean slide guitar.[1]

During those days, at the club down the street called Daddio's, I befriended another waitress. Her name was Lou Ann Barton. Turns out she was an up-and-coming blues singer who sat in with Robert Ealey and the Five Careless Lovers (among them Freddie Cisneros, Craig Simechek, and Mike Buck). Lou Ann and I soon realized we each needed a roommate, waitressing not being such a lucrative job. So we moved in together in 1976 into a tiny one-bedroom duplex on Fort Worth's East Side (not the best neighborhood, but the rent was cheap). We split the $50-a-month rent. I slept on an old pullout couch in the living room. And we stayed up until all hours of the night playing Jimmy Reed records, until the neighbor would pound on our living room walls and yell at us to turn the music down. The *punctum* of cheerful poverty was a pervasive mood in our house. We tooled around in my orange flatbed VW until it died. Then we went thrift shopping in my dad's pickup, one time spending $5 on a small vintage loveseat at Value Village. It went nicely into the back of the truck, and I kept that couch for another fifteen years. The nights were the best. We would go to Lou Ann's gigs at the New Bluebird Nightclub, or the Silver Dollar, or Daddio's, or Mable's Eat Shop (fig. 8.1). We lived the blues and lived to leave Fort Worth.

Lou Ann joined The Fabulous Thunderbirds a year or so later and moved to Austin. But she came home often and kept her stuff at our house, which was a big house a few blocks over from our first place. After about six months with the Thunderbirds, she joined Stevie Ray Vaughan's band Double Trouble, which changed into Triple Threat. We were in Austin as much as we were in Fort Worth. She took up with Keith Ferguson (eventually marrying him), the Thunderbird's bass player, and returned less frequently to Fort Worth. By the late 1970s, she left Fort Worth altogether, and I had a solid career in hotel management. I had taken a job in 1975 at the Fort Worth Hilton and worked my way up from front desk clerk to front office manager. The music scene became even more interesting because lots of big-name bands stayed at the Hilton, which was across the street from Convention Center where the concerts occurred. I checked in the Who, the Bee Gees, Elvis, the Moody Blues, Leon Russell, Boz Scaggs, and Willie Nelson, among countless others.

But the dream to work and live in Europe, and to leave Fort Worth, simmered underneath the busy days of hotel work, especially when I had the chance to check in Germans visiting Fort Worth on business. Then, in 1979, after I had moved to a better position at the DFW airport hotel, the itch to

leave Fort Worth became greater now that I was at an international airport

Figure 8.1. Author (*left*), Lou Ann Barton, Mike Buck (*seated*), Freddie Cisneros (*with guitar*), and unknown regulars of the Silver Dollar (circa 1976). Author's collection.

dealing with international guests and international languages. For two years, the leaving was a lived experience as I watched airplanes take off and land every day. I had toyed with leaving before (taking brief trips to South Texas as a guest with Leon Russell's band and to Mexico City with a trusted business client from the Hilton), but I longed to return to Europe. And one day I had the chance to move closer.

One of the executive managers at the airport hotel took a position to manage a Hilton in Williamsburg, Virginia. After arriving there, he invited five of his former assistant managers, including me, to come work for him. I was hired as front office manager. I was finally leaving Fort Worth. But it wasn't as easy as I thought it would be. The look on my mother's face was a *punctum* I'll never forget. And I wasn't able to take my three cats and my dog. That was harder than leaving my family. As I was single, the animals *were* my family. So I had to find homes for them before I left, which I did. Then off I went in my 1978 white Ford Mustang to live a slightly different version of my dream. I lasted less than a year away.

The job was fine. The colleagues were great. Williamsburg is wonderful. Checking in the Rolling Stones and attending their concert backstage was the highlight. But it turns out that Virginia had no good Tex-Mex food and *no* blues scene. I was incredibly homesick. So after four months, I started looking for a job that would move me back home. I lucked out. The Four Seasons hotel chain was building a new property in Irving, Texas, just east of the airport where I had been working. I flew to New York City for the interview, which took place at their property called the Pierre. I had never seen such a hotel in my life. I got hired as reservation manager for the Mandalay Four Seasons in Las Colinas. And in April 1982, the Four Seasons company moved me home. Rather than get a place near my job, I went straight to Fort Worth's West Side and rented a duplex one block from my best friend's house. I bought a new sky-blue Fiat convertible and started the daily commute to Las Colinas. This was the pinnacle of hotel work. Five-star facilities and five-star guests. I loved it all.

But I was beginning to realize I was intellectually starved. So in January 1984, I decided to enroll in a graduate English course at the University of Texas at Arlington (where I had received my bachelor of arts in German ten years before). But before I could register, the admissions office said I had to apply to graduate school. I wasn't prepared for that, and I had no intention of changing careers. I just wanted to read and study books in my spare time after work.

The course I ended up taking (after nixing the idea of Comparative Asian Literature) was called the Rhetoric of Reading. Perfect, I thought. I love to read! Victor Vitanza (weird name, I thought) was the professor. And the rest is history, or rather, the next ten years was all rhetoric. Three years into my part-time graduate studies, I quit working for the Four Seasons and started taking courses full-time. I temped for a while to pay the rent, often taking bizarre jobs nobody else wanted. One job was a three-week stint at the Comanche Peak Nuclear Power Plant during the final phase of its construction, working for a German company that made the turbine engines. I said yes immediately. I asked if I could bring my books to study, and my supervisors were fine with that. So I went to work at a massive construction site with five thousand men, wearing work boots, a hard hat, and safety goggles and carrying a Mr. T lunchbox and Plato's *Dialogues*. They didn't quite know what to make of me.

Eventually, because of my management experience, I was hired as writing center director at UT–Arlington. This was a much better situation because I could attend classes, study, and work at the same place. In the spring of 1994, while taking a weekend break from writing my dissertation, I decided to log in to a strange "place" called Media MOO. And there I met, by chance, a young man from Norway, Jan Holmevik, who was also taking a break from writing his master's thesis. We became good friends, virtually. So good that six months later, we created our own MOO called Lingua MOO. I had taken my first job after graduation at UT–Dallas (again not leaving the Fort Worth area). Jan helped teach me how I could use the MOO to teach writing classes. UT–Dallas allowed us to host our own educational MOO on its server, and we began customizing it to teach writing. An interesting benefit to virtual interaction in MOOs was how effective it was for language learning. Jan had perfected his English throughout the first year we spent talking and working online, and we knew this would benefit language-learning classes too. So we opened Lingua MOO to classes at Vassar and Dartmouth, as well as in Germany and France. Soon we were connected with other MOOs in Israel, Norway, and Germany. Then, in the summer of 1995, I decided to visit Jan in Norway. My dream of returning to Europe was at hand.

1995–2017

The decades are mounting up and amounting to an accumulated experience of leaving that always lurks in the rearview mirrors that populate our mobility. In 1995, it was then twenty-seven years since I had gone to Europe that first time in 1968. However, this time there was definitely a sense that I wanted very much to return to Fort Worth. Older and wiser (one hopes), I was secure in my history and in my history's location. I identify as a Texan, but more importantly, as a Fort Worthian. I was a homeowner by then. I had sixteen cats and lots of family and friends. But the lure of Norway was as powerful as the lure of northern New Mexico had been to me in the late 1970s and early 1980s, where (as a single woman) I always traveled to commune with the mountains and indigenous cultures of Taos and Santa Fe.

But since this essay is not about Norway, I intend here to *home in* on the successive "leavings" that define my life in these past two decades. The leavings are always about dying, which is not to introduce some *punctum ultima*, but to speak *into* what is our ultimate future leaving—death. Hélène Cixous writes that "the dream would be to be there, at that hour, this is the poet's dream—and getting there has always been the poem's hope" (62). What I am calling "living as leaving," Cixous describes as "our most intimate foreignness, at our last minute," which "if we could go out, and once outside, turning around, see with our own eyes the face of our own door" (63). Fort Worth doors have marked me with their faces, along with their addresses nailed above these thresholds over which my leaving Fort Worth has been played out: 1442 West Fuller Avenue, 5768 Sixth Avenue, 34 Brenton Road, 2601 Avenue G, 3926 Dexter Avenue, 2204 Western Avenue, 615 Court Street, 711 Connor, 3934 Bunting, and 3806 Clarke Avenue (my last Fort Worth address before moving to Denmark in 2005 and then South Carolina in 2006). At such addresses, I have always been what Cixous calls my "secret age":

> We, we are always interiorly our secret age, our strong-age, our preferred age, we are five years old, ten years old, the age when we were for the first time the historians or the authors of our own lives, when we left a trace,

when we were for the first time marked, struck, imprinted, we bled and signed, memory started, when we manifested ourselves as chief or queen of our own state, when we took up our own power, or else we are twenty years old or thirty-five, and on the point of surprising the universe. (64)

My secret age is the leaving age, the age for being somewhere along the way to returning to Fort Worth, where I will be buried someday in a dusty plot of earth.

When Jan and I married in 1997, we began a tradition of spending two months of each summer in Norway with his family. With each trip, I had to prepare the house at 3806 Clarke Avenue for pet sitters who lived there while caring for the cats. With each trip, there were one or two fewer cats as they began to age and die. With each trip, there were more cats buried under the big tree in the backyard: Diddle, Bugsy, Ralph, and a few others. With each trip, the hot Texas summers receded into my distant memory and the cool Norwegian summers took over. The music scene in Fort Worth began to change. They closed J & J Blues Bar. Stephen Bruton died in 2009. On *Facebook*, I am friends with a lot of folks from those heady days of leaving music clubs in the 1970s and 1980s, but one by one I see them taking their final leaving of Fort Worth and others mourning their passings. Occasionally, I post some old photos, and those of us that remember will reminisce and lament the days gone by, secretly invoking our various "interiorly secret ages."

In the photo, I am leaving the bathroom at the New Bluebird Nightclub where Robert Ealey and the Five Careless Lovers were probably playing to a lively dance floor of patrons whose cold Lone Star longneck beers were sweating on the cheap laminate tables beneath the steady thrum of the air cooler and overworked fans (fig. 8.2). Both the image and my memory of the moment evoke a *punctum* that can be read as a life lived by

Figure 8.2. Author, circa 1977, at the New Bluebird Nightclub. Author's collection.

leaving Fort Worth and leaving behind countless dance floors on which my boots shuffled to the "shuffle" and I shared a secret with the future—I would leave Fort Worth, though always returning after having lived each day as if I am on the point of surprising the universe.

Note

1. See my essay "Thinking across the Neck: Playing Slide with Fret/work Blues" for an extended riff on Bruton's work.

Works Cited

Barthes, Roland. *Camera Lucida: Reflections on Photography.* Translated by Richard Howard. Farrar, Straus, and Giroux, 1981.

Benjamin, Walter. "A Berlin Chronicle." *Reflections: Essays, Aphorisms, Autobiographical Writings*, edited by Peter Demetz, translated by Edmund Jephcott, Harcourt Brace, 1978, pp. 3–60.

Cixous, Hélène. *Stigmata: Escaping Texts.* New York: Routledge, 1998.

Demetz, Peter. Introduction. *Reflections: Essays, Aphorisms, Autobiographical Writings*, edited by Peter Demetz, translated by Edmund Jephcott, Harcourt Brace, 1978, pp. vii–xliii.

Crang, Mike, and N. J. Thrift. *Thinking Space.* Routledge, 2000.

Haynes, Cynthia. "Thinking across the Neck: Playing Slide with Fret/work Blues" *Currents in Electronic Literacy*, 2011, currents.dwrl.utexas.edu/2011/thinkingacrosstheneck.html. Accessed 20 Oct. 2017.

Doug Eskew,
Colorado State University—Pueblo

9. (WHITE-TRASH) PANTEGO

I come from a small town on the outskirts of a suburb on the outskirts of a city.[1] The city was Fort Worth—Dallas's down-home, blue-collar neighbor, hometown of Van Cliburn, Townes Van Zandt, Ornette Coleman, and Lee Harvey Oswald. Hometown to innumerable rednecks, crackers, bubbas, and bubbettes. The suburb was Arlington, destination of white-flight families, the dull anti-intellectual and religiously fundamental. The town was Pantego, a single square mile of two thousand working- and middle-class residents, their mediocre restaurants and rag-tag strip malls. Growing up in Pantego, I remember most the streets, residential streets, streets filled with folks going to and from work, parents schlepping kids to school, teenagers providing the soundtrack—the sounds of AC/DC and Judas Priest blowing from muscle cars.

My family's home in Pantego was on Country Club Lane, a name that suggests we lived on a golf course and that my mom hosted genteel lunches of cucumber sandwiches and white-wine spritzers. But my dad did not drive home each evening in a Lincoln Continental, gliding down the spacious Country Club Lane in the shade of its ancient oak and pecan trees. If the name suggests that the street was prestigious, the homes were palatial, and the residents elite, we did not live anywhere near the country club for which the street was named. We didn't even live in the same town. When I was a kid, I would sometimes ride my bike the single mile down our street into Arlington and to the country club, but riding my bike there didn't get me into the clubhouse and it didn't teach me to play golf. Riding my bike there reminded me that I did not belong there, that I lived on the ass end of Country Club Lane—literally three houses from the street's dead end in Pantego. At the other, prestigious end, Country Club Lane *was* lined with tall and abundant oaks and pecans; it did run alongside the rolling golf course. But by the time it made its way into Pantego, the homes were smaller, the lawns browner and dryer. The people had less money, less education. Some of us were white trash.

Some folks thought the people next door to us were especially white trash. The house had suffered a mysterious fire and stood empty for a while until someone bought it—a mechanic who worked out at the airport. He got it for a steal and moved in his wife and their children before he began cleaning and restoring it. He planned on doing those things, but he never got around to it. Inside, the house smelled of smoke and trash and dirty clothes. Outside, the lawn was rarely mowed and never watered. Half of the windows were shattered. That family. They were white trash, obviously white trash.

My family kept its trashiness a bit more close to the chest. We mowed our lawn most of the time and rarely let a drunken fight spill out onto the street. My mom came from a respectable family in a small, dirty oil town in far west Texas. My dad was different. He came from a long line of uneducated share-croppers. Neither my grandmother nor my great-grandmother finished the sixth grade. Both were married as teenagers, and they both married abusive men. Both became young divorcées. My grandmother and great-grandmother were kind, beautiful women who loved their families, but they were poor, untraveled, and unlettered. And regardless of how they tried to present themselves, they couldn't hide all of the trashiness. When their children married into more respectable families, everyone knew who'd gotten the better of the deal. And everyone was on the watch for the next white-trash shoe to drop.

Despite the fact that my father had gone off to Texas Tech University, that he'd met the owner of a small-town oil supply company and married his quiet daughter. Despite the fact that this odd Southern Baptist girl and the skinny boy from the wrong side of the tracks made it all the way to Country Club Lane. Despite all of the white-flight promise of "good schools" and "no busing" (1970s code for "no blacks"). Despite everything, the trashiness of our white-ness couldn't help but emerge. My parents had been aiming for membership in a country club and wanted to live in the suburb of Arlington, but they only made it to the ass end of Country Club Lane in Pantego. When, in 1979, my dad unceremoniously dumped his family for a woman he had once dated in high school, my mom's family said they had all been waiting for something like this to happen. He had come from a long line of poor white trash—the kind of trash that didn't attend a Southern Baptist church, that drank and fought and smoked. He couldn't resist. Even though he had gone to college, my dad couldn't shake his trashiness. Neither could his son.

We moved to Pantego the summer before I started the second grade. Within the first week of school, my teacher took me over to a wooden book cart and asked which of the books I had read. I went through them, pointing, one by one. "I've read this one. And this one. I really liked this one about the lion, and this other one about the family of geese." At first the teacher seemed impressed, but as I continued, pointing out book after book, her face registered skepticism and then, at some point, unease. The sheer number of books I claimed to have read made her think I couldn't have been telling the truth. "Are you sure you've read all of those books?" she asked. "Sure," I replied, feeling as if I had done something wrong. "I think I know where to put you," she said.

The point of the exercise, of interrogating a seven-year-old child, was to assess my intellectual ability. The teacher's task was to place me in one of five groups of children, ranked from smart to dumb ones. Her assessment tool was blunt—and incapable of telling her where I fit. My answers did not meet her expectations. Because her assessment tool failed, she placed me in the middle group. Not too smart, not too dumb. "We'll see how you do in this group," she told me. I guess I did fine there, because that's where I stayed, bored and unengaged, throughout my years of schooling. But since I knew nothing else, I never actually knew I was bored and unengaged. I accepted it because I was seven years old and because accepting things is what we did in our family.

And I kept accepting it, kept accepting that mediocrity and boredom I'd never thought to choose through elementary school, junior high, and into high school. Once I dropped out of school in 1985, I couldn't hold a job. My mom, seeing a bit too much of my dad in me, kicked me out of the house. Living out of my car, I continued to find my life uninteresting, uneventful, barely livable. I scarcely felt any reason to do anything at all. Certainly no reason to embrace a distant set of middle-class virtues—thrift, industry, moderation. Still, I had to find a job. A friend was a cook at a catfish restaurant, Mr. Catfish, near Six Flags, and ended up getting me a job washing dishes, which was a pretty good job for me. It was low-paying, of course, about three dollars an hour. But I didn't have to do much except show up and wash the goddamn dishes. The work took almost no thought. It was work I had been trained for for a very long time.

While many kids my age were going to high school and college, making mistakes under controlled circumstances, I was making mistakes with few protections. Instead of going to college, I washed dishes at a catfish restaurant by day and spent nights snorting pink crank, boozing, fighting, listening to heavy metal. While other kids were staying up all night studying for the next day's test, I was up all night trying to forget that we had gone to school together and they would end up in an affluent suburb. Trying to forget how my family fell apart. Trying to forget that the Southern Baptist church offered me salvation, but only if I bought into an insane worldview. I found salvation, to be sure. I found salvation in drugs, beer, and the cadences of Iron Maiden and Black Sabbath. I will never denigrate those things, the drugs, alcohol, heavy metal. Those were the options. And given the circumstances, they were largely adequate.

Thinking about how the academy has become such an important part of my life, how the pursuits of the mind now provide comfort and direction, I can't help but wonder what my life might have been like had I had academic support early on. If there were some kind of intellectually interesting program or even an unofficial intellectual clique in my junior high or high school, I didn't know about it. The University of Texas–Arlington was just blocks away from my high school. There were scholars there. The journal *Pre/Text* was founded there in the 1980s. But I had no access to that. And it wasn't until after I dropped out of high school, bored and depressed, that I even learned that I was smart. Let me restate this and let me put it in italics, because I'm white trash and unsubtle: *I was smart and no one ever told me.*

I learned that I was smart at the last possible moment. My seventy-four-year-old grandmother was worried. She knew how tough it was for a dropout, because she dropped out of sixth grade herself. Someone had told her of the GED. With my grandmother's encouragement, I took the test one day at the local community college. I went in cold—I hadn't studied for it—and yet I didn't struggle with any of the questions. When I received my scores in the mail a few weeks later, they were matched with levels of high school graduates. Oddly, my scores ranked me among the top few percentage points. That was odd because I hadn't done any schoolwork for years. Even before I left school, it was as though I had been encouraged to do the kind of work I found myself doing: washing dishes at Mr. Catfish.

For all those years, I hadn't known I was smart; yet according to the educational system of which I was part, according to that system's quantifiable definition, I was, in the end, really smart. The local institution, the one that knew me, didn't seem interested in locating a kid like me who might bring along some white-trash baggage into the smart kids' classroom. But there was that wrinkle in the system. Out of the blue, arriving at my half-empty, half-wrecked apartment in Pantego, came this dot-matrix printout, this accidental release of data that redefined who I was. Before I received the GED scores, I had been a kid who, for reasons of class and accident, couldn't be smart—that was the ideological baseline. In an instant, that reality changed. What's more, I began to realize that no one in Pantego had known this. No authorities. No caring teachers. No friends. No family. It's not that anyone was actually thinking about me, either. It's not that anyone was actively skewing their assessment. That's really the point: folks were all assuming things about my intellectual capacity that had no reference to any objective form of assessment. Folks were kind of just guessing. And it was a pretty good guess that the white-trash kid was no intellectual.

There I was, sitting in my apartment, holding that printout from the Texas Education Agency, with those scores that put much of my life to a lie. Not knowing what else to do, I returned to the scene of the crime, Tarrant County Junior College, and enrolled in some basic courses, writing, history, algebra.

After doing well enough at those, I enrolled in a few more courses, literature, sociology, philosophy. At that ugly campus (mostly a parking lot and a few one-story, brutalist buildings) on a dusty stretch of highway, I began to discover the life of the mind.

In the end, I would leave Pantego. I couldn't stop thinking about how my people had been so wrong about me for so many years. I kept thinking, If no one in Pantego knew I was smart, what else do they not know? For a long time, I kept discovering the depths of their ignorance, their immorality. Layer after ignorant, immoral layer. And I kept feeling superior to them, my white-trash people, because they believed that God was a capitalist and a Christian, that whites were superior to other races, that homosexuals were abominations. My white-trash people felt superior to others, and I felt superior to them for feeling superior to others. In the end, and this took a very long time, I found out that my people couldn't help it. They believed what everybody else in their lives believed (just as you probably believe, more or less, what the people in your life believe). I found out that everybody is bounded by ideological limitations—the common sense beyond which lies the other world of untruth, stupidity, and insanity. My white-trash people had their limitations; they were born into them, and because of class and accident, there were few ways out for them. I found out that my white-trash people weren't at fault for what they knew and what they didn't know.

In the end, I moved to Austin along with other misfit kids who couldn't get along with their Texas-hometown family and friends. While my people back in Pantego were living securely within their ethnic and ideological horizons, I was cavorting with the enemy. I even became an ivory-tower educated idiot, one of those race-mixing lefty professors. It doesn't take an education to see the calculus at work here: in embracing the life of the mind, I had rejected the life of the white-trash suburb. That doesn't mean that the academy has embraced me. Accepted me, sure. But it's been more of a begrudging acceptance. Let's be honest, when the academy strives for diversity, the categories of ethnic inclusion don't include white trash, which means that white-trash heritage is often invisible and it's often denigrated.

It's difficult, sometimes, to account for one's people. Sometimes, down in Texas, it's difficult to see what you look like to the rest of the world. You issue from a people, and you love them with everything you have, and you're so down there among them that they look perfectly natural to you. In a place like Pantego, you're so distant from the rest of the world—unless you have the money to get out and see your life from another perspective or the cultural capital that would reveal to you other ways of being, your limited common sense engulfs you. And because the whole wide world's ways of living and thinking are at odds with what seems natural and good to you, that world threatens you, threatens everything you are.

The thing about white trash is that the world really is against them. They aren't paranoid. The world, the elite world whose opinion matters, not only thinks of them as belligerent, anti-intellectual rubes, but defines itself against them, as more peaceful, rational, and sophisticated. "White trash" is what they call a white person who doesn't quite make the cut when it comes to middle-class virtues—moderation, patience, thrift, hard work. It's a racist term because it assumes the "trash" label in non-whites, at the same time that whites must be explicitly labeled as such. While there's poor white trash (PWT), there's probably more plain ol' white trash. There's rich white trash too. When tabloids published photos of Britney Spears getting drunk and running barefoot into a Jack in the Box toilet, people called her white trash. When Bill Clinton ate Big Macs in the White House and admitted to be-splattering the blue Gap dress, people called him white trash. When Sarah Palin publicly feuded with her teenage daughter's baby daddy, people called her white trash. But when it comes to white trash, spectacular white trash, it's PWT that most people think of. The bad teeth. The green-blue, blurry tattoos and hopelessly out-of-fashion hairstyles. Public intox and cheap food.

For Pierre Bourdieu, the distinction is one of taste.[2] Taste is something you get informally and early on in life. Dominant social groups determine what's tasteful—simply because they're dominant—and their ways of perceiving and acting in the world become the standard, from which all divergence is judged inferior. These valuations are unintentional, barely reflected on, so you grow up thinking they're natural. People who own other values thus seem less valuable, even less natural. To know the distinction between those who have taste and those who don't is the first step toward evaluating those with dominant values more highly—and others more lowly. Moreover, knowing what counts as taste is also the first step toward evaluating yourself less highly. Knowing these distinctions allows you to know your place. By and large, however, white trash don't know they're white trash. Not only do they not have taste; they don't know they don't have taste.

Trash, white or not, designates refuse, unbelonging—something useless, something that needs to be gotten rid of, something you throw away and are happy to have done so. When applied to place, *trash* attempts to locate a wasteland. It's a place that doesn't matter—a place you should avoid, a place the nontrashy would be better off without. Once when driving with my father through an African American ghetto in Fort Worth, he said to me, "It would be better if an enormous tornado would destroy all of this." I was shocked then by his sentiment, and I'm still shocked. It's nevertheless how you think of trash in terms of a people and their place. Google *tornado* and *white trash*   113 and you will find example after example of people making statements just like my father's, except the people are white instead of brown. Why do tornadoes hit trailer parks? God is taking out the trash.

Aristotle's word for this place of the expelled and unwanted was *apolis* (1253a). For Aristotle, a human being is a "political animal," whose natural place is the *polis*. Aristotle defined the *polis* as the place where political animals come together not only for the basic needs of defense, sustenance, and generation, but also for "the good life," for living beyond basic animal needs. The life of the human being, as distinct from the animal, is full of superfluous things like art, friendship, gastronomy, music, philosophy, gossip, theater. But even though none of these things is necessary, we consider all of them central to healthy human activity.[3] The space outside the *polis* belongs, according to Aristotle, to the beasts and the gods, for neither have need of society and the "good life." But humans are human because they need community.

Significantly, for Aristotle and other ancient Greeks, *apolis* was an adjective, not a substantive like *polis*. There was no substantive place called the *apolis*. You would never say something about "living in the *apolis*"; directions from Delphi to Thebes wouldn't include something like "Take a left at the crossroads and ride through the *apolis*." Place as a geographic category is political and social in nature; the Greeks didn't think in terms of the political where the political did not exist.

As a sociopolitical construct, to be outside the *polis* was to live without place. But in the modern era, as Giorgio Agamben argues, the placeless have been given places, and what was once indeterminate has become determinate.[4] As the modern state has charted and enclosed most of the known world, as states have done away with wildernesses and nameless expanses, they have increasingly set aside and determined the place of the placeless: the Nazi camp, Guantanamo Bay, the expanse of American prisons. Rather than sending social outcasts away into a great nowhere of seas and savannas and heaths, the modern state places the placeless in closed pseudocommunities. Moreover, I think we can now call any one of them *apolis*, keeping the term both indeterminately adjectival and determinately nominal—a definite topography with no legitimate topographic constituent. We can also add to the salient examples of Auschwitz and Camp X-Ray the American "abandoned" city centers and white-trash suburbs, pockets of humanity among the hills of Appalachia, the Rocky Mountains, and the desert expanse of the U.S. Southwest—nonplaces where people are born invisible to those who matter. White trash, black trash, brown trash, yellow trash, red trash, miscegenated trash. Wind-swept social detritus, settling in where no one would go looking

and no one would stay if they didn't have to.

It was in the *apolis* of Pantego that I was raised, among the uncaring and uncared for, taught to disbelieve the educated and to hate the nonwhite, noncitizen Other. None of us had a choice in the matter. I didn't, for instance, choose to be taught fundy religion and racism. My schoolteachers and parents and grandparents and friends didn't make those choices. Only a few escape the dominant modes of thinking. Of course, the problems with these modes of thinking are real, but such modes are made possible by the structures that support their legitimacy. You can't have an *apolis* without a *polis*. You can't have an adjective without a substantive. Complicit, then, with white-trash ideology is elite ideology. In my case, I tend to question both my white-trash past and my elite present. Caught between the two worlds, I doubt I have much choice in the matter.

As an academic, I have specialized in early modern rhetoric, with attention to the plays of Shakespeare. At one time I had intended to do something less "literary," but I received the good advice that focusing on Shakespeare would help me get a job. I did get a job—a good one, teaching working-class students. I'm deeply appreciative of this unlikely career I have developed. I like writing about Shakespeare's plays in large measure because it allows me to study class and belonging in ways that connect with my origins.

But talking about class—that is, talking about white trash like this—isn't always easy. My article "'Soldiers, Prisoners, Patrimony': *King Lear* and the Place of the Sovereign" is illustrative. The article is about how royal place is constructed and who loses in the construction of *legitimate* place—namely, the illegitimate bastard, Edmund, who is the play's villain and who is regularly ignored in academic criticism. In many ways, my article's hidden thesis is that Edmund is a white-trash hero. That's the hidden thesis—the thesis that had to be hidden to get published in an academic journal.

The quotation in the title of the essay comes from the king's villainous daughter, Regan. These are the words she says to Edmund at the moment she pledges herself to be his wife, at the moment she gives him the stuff of her sovereignty, the military power and land. Because she herself is a sovereign entity, her announcement that Edmund is now her husband ("Witness the world, that I create thee here / My lord and master" [5.3.78–79]) has full legal binding. Edmund, the most socially inferior character in the play, instantly rises to the kingdom's most socially superior status. He does all that, but in four hundred years of Shakespeare criticism, critics have rarely acknowledged it. To be sure, Edmund gets to the top by a ploy that centers on murder and seduction. He literally fucks, marries, and kills his way to the top. Critics are keen to discuss these trashy bits and how they mark him as villainous. What they do not discuss is that Edmund has no other means to improve his status.

Because he is already defined as illegitimate, Edmund has no other means than illegitimate ones to progress socially.

Edmund begins the play being out of place. He is staying at his father's castle, but the earl makes sure we know he doesn't belong there and won't be sticking around. "He hath been out nine years," Gloucester tells his colleague, Kent, "and away he shall again" (1.1.29). The precise location of this "out" is never determined. It is a placeless place, a no-place, an *apolis* that doesn't even require a name. My article describes the pair of chiasmata created, first, by Edmund's gaining of place and the king's losing of it and, second, by its reversal. Toward the beginning of the play, Lear becomes a placeless outlaw simultaneously with Edmund's rise. Toward the play's end, Edmund loses his status as Lear regains his. Indeed, as his father promised to send Edmund away, Albany makes good on that promise. As the dead bodies of all three daughters are dragged onstage to display a "proper" tragic ending, Albany sends Edmund "away" for his death. And once word comes back that Edmund has died offstage, Albany's reaction is completely predictable. "That is but a trifle here," he says (5.3.289).

Earlier versions of "'Soldiers, Prisoners, Patrimony'" featured Edmund's psychic pain and justifiable resentment. These versions were rejected by Shakespeare journals. One thing these versions pointed out was that the first thing we see in the play is Edmund's father, humiliated by the mere presence of his bastard son, attempting to cover up his shame by making Edmund the butt of an obscene and unfunny joke. Although Edmund's mother was a "whore," the earl says, she was a hot piece of ass and a great lay ("his mother fair, there was good sport at his making" [1.1.21–22]). Gloucester claims that he's over being ashamed of the bastard, but his joking betrays his claim. "I have so often blushed to acknowledge him," he says, "that now I am brazed to it" (1.1.8–10). Ultimately on the matter, Gloucester notes that Edmund "must be acknowledged." But he doesn't just say that *Edmund* must be acknowledged. He says, "The *whoreson* must be acknowledged" (1.1.22).

What is amazing to me is the way that Shakespeare scholars have defended Gloucester. The most influential defenses come from editors of the play, who have the ability to gloss the term *whoreson* so that it doesn't seem as though Gloucester is being a total dick. For instance, one of the more influential editors, David Bevington, tells readers of the play that *whoreson* means "low fellow; suggesting bastardy" but goes on to state that Gloucester uses it "with affectionate condescension." One reason, it seems to me, that scholars would be so keen to defend Gloucester is that if we see his actions as visiting real pain on his out-of-place son, we might see Edmund's resentments as justified and his father complicit in his degradation. Earlier versions of the essay made this argument about elite complicity, but I ended up suppressing those details.

Reviewers seemed unwilling to rethink the nature of Edmund's villainy and Shakespeare's critique of legitimate social order.

What I've realized over the years is that my vision of Edmund was always a vision of a white-trash hero. Like a hero, he commits a fundamental mistake that leads to a tragic downfall. Unlike the "legitimate" hero, however, our white-trash hero is out of place in elite environments, forced to swallow the denigration of his very origins, required to repress his critique of the status quo and find a solution to his predicament by illegitimate means. Finally, he is a white-trash hero because the last thing the in-place establishment will acknowledge is that he is a hero at all.

I've noticed, too, that I would never have been able to *think* about Edmund in these ways if I hadn't come from the white-trash suburb. Moreover, repressing the white-trash ethos of Shakespeare's antihero, I had mimicked my own repression of my own white-trash ethos.

One of my childhood friends also made it out. I'm not sure whether his resources were legitimate or illegitimate, probably a bit of both. I first met Darrell when we were kids. He lived a mile away from me, but his father co-owned a little cinder-block recording studio in Pantego, not half a mile from my house. The other owner lived a few doors down from me; his son was my best friend. By the time we got to high school, Darrell and I spent a lot of time together, drinking and carousing, listening to music. Darrell was a great guitar player. With his brother on drums, they formed a heavy metal band and named it after my hometown. They took the uncool-sounding word *Pantego*, dropped the -*go*, added -*ra*, and got *Pantera*. Darrell went on to become a famous guitarist, and the band he and his brother formed became one of the most successful metal bands in the 1990s. They recorded multiplatinum albums such as *Vulgar Display of Power* and *Far Beyond Driven* right there in Pantego at the shitty little Pantego Sound studio their dad and my neighbor owned.

During the 1990s, I never tried to get in touch with my old friend, never tried to go backstage, never went to a single Pantera show. I would rarely even mention to people that I had a connection to Darrell (who by that time was called "Dimebag"). I'll be honest about why I rarely mentioned it: I was ashamed. I didn't want people to know where I had come from, know of my white-trash origins. If anyone knew Darrell and I had a common background, they might know the kind of trash I hailed from. You see, Pantera didn't hide their trashiness, didn't hide the racism, the anti-intellectualism, the sexism, the idiot bigotry, the carousing and binge drinking. Darrell himself often played a Confederate flag guitar. He became friends and recorded with David Allan Coe, the ultra-outlaw country musician known, among other things, for penning some of the most racist songs imaginable. I've never listened to those songs, but the

New York Times said that in one of them, Coe "rails against white women who sleep with black men, singing that it makes him want to throw up; in another, the chorus has it that some blacks 'never die/They just smell that way'" (Strauss).

I close this essay on Pantego talking about Darrell because I no longer wish to be ashamed. I wish to make my origins and the people I hail from as clear as possible. In many ways, Darrell is a perfect representation of my people, embodying their brilliant cultural intensity that is shrouded by a wince-inducing backwardness. Because he is now dead (he was murdered onstage in 2004), I can also suggest that you watch YouTube videos of people visiting his grave. Many of these visitors are my white-trash people. You will see them smoking, drinking, crying, calling Darrell "brother," praying for God to take care of his soul. One visitor has left a picture of his pit bull. The dog, his note explains, was born the night Darrell was killed. The owner thinks his dog might be Darrell reincarnated. These are my people in some of their most intense moments, unashamedly displaying their love and grief, taking shots of whiskey, sitting around his grave, playing guitar. And if you watch these videos and chuckle at the inarticulate emotion of my people and the fantastic connection they feel with a dead, alcoholic rock star, you are not alone. I was in your shoes not long ago.

I also talk about Darrell because he displays in a profound way the relationship between belonging and unbelonging I have discussed here. Darrell owed his fame to a denigrated style of music, even more unfashionable in the 1990s than it is today. Even within this denigrated artistic form, he and his band were additionally denigrated because they were white-trash Texans. No single element of unbelonging in his narrative would have any significance without the elements of belonging. Darrell's grave stands as a final testament, standing out among the other graves in the cemetery, distinct in its gaudiness and its constant stream of white-trash devotees. It owes its significance by virtue of these differences. Much like my home of unbelonging on Country Club Lane and my place in the academy. These places and my narrative would have no significance if the unbelonging were not inexorably connected in some way to belonging. I was never completely untethered, never completely exiled. My place in the academy is always tied to my place in Pantego.

Notes

1. The author wishes to thank Don Geiss, Rodney Herring, and the editors of *Inventing Place: Writing Lone Star Rhetorics*.

2. See Bourdieu, especially 169–225 and 257–67.

3. See also Arendt 26–27.

4. Agamben's term for one of these placeless places is a "dislocating localization." See 174–76.

Works Cited

Agamben, Giorgio. *Homo Sacer: Sovereign Power and Bare Life.* Translated by Daniel Heller-Roazen, Stanford UP, 1998.

Arendt, Hannah. *The Human Condition.* 2nd ed., U of Chicago P, 1998.

Aristotle. *Politics.* Translated by H. Rackham, Harvard UP, 1932.

Bevington, David, editor. *The Complete Works of Shakespeare.* 5th ed., Pearson, 2004.

Bourdieu, Pierre. *Distinction: A Social Critique of the Judgement of Taste.* Translated by Richard Nice, Harvard UP, 1984.

Eskew, Doug. "'Soldiers, Prisoners, Patrimony': *King Lear* and the Place of the Sovereign." *Cahiers Élisabéthains*, vol. 77, no. 2, 2010, pp. 29–38.

Shakespeare, William. *The Norton Shakespeare.* Edited by Stephen Greenblatt et al., 2nd ed., Norton, 2008.

Strauss, Neil. "Songwriter's Racist Songs from 1980's Haunt Him." *New York Times*, 4 Sept. 2000, p. B1.

Jordan Frith,
University of North Texas

10. DENTON AND THE RHETORICAL
APPEAL OF AUTHENTICITY

I study space and place. Consequently, I figured it would be a fairly easy task to sit down and write a chapter about Denton as a place. I could engage with some theory from human geography, write about Denton's thriving music scene and quirky counterculture, and be done with it. But the more I thought about it, the more daunting the task became. What is Denton as a place? Is it even possible to write about a place in Texas? Or are our experiences of place—whether that place is a historical site like the Alamo or a Whataburger drive through—so partial and personal that writing about place at all requires too many caveats to be productive?

Part of what complicated my thoughts on Denton as a place was a trip I took to Sydney, Australia. Sydney had recently instituted a direct flight to Dallas, and the international terminal in Sydney's airport was filled with Texas tourism advertisements. The Texas being advertised, however, was nothing like the Texas I had come to love. The images were instead of the Texas I had imagined growing up: open prairies with a solitary cowboy framed against the huge sunset, women with big hair and even bigger cowboy boots, the bright lights and sharp spurs of the rodeo. All that was missing was a life-size statue of J. R.

This Texas of touristic appeals stood in contrast to the Texas I experienced when I moved to Denton in 2012. I had never lived anywhere but the East Coast, and I knew next to nothing about Texas. The Texas I imagined was a watered-down version of the posters I walked by in the Sydney airport, a land filled with Cowboys fans and actual cowboys. I found the Cowboys fans when I moved to Denton, but the actual cowboys . . . not so much. What I found instead was a liberal northern tip to Dallas–Fort Worth's Golden Triangle: a college town of 130,000 people with what seems like more musicians, beer gardens, and artists per capita than almost anywhere in the country. The Denton of my reality differed greatly from the Denton of my expectations.

But it is too simplistic to say that the touristic construction of Texas is just a manufactured, idealized view of a Texas that does not exist as a lived experience. Instead, thinking more about what I saw in Sydney raised some important questions: Is the Texas I love any more authentic than these touristic representations? How can I write about Denton as a place when my experience is so small? And how can I engage with those brief moments when my day-to-day experience of Texas bumps up against experiences of Denton as a place that are so foreign to me that they are almost invisible?

Those are a few of the questions I address in this essay. I am writing about Denton as a place worth engaging with, a place distinct from others in Texas. However, the main goal of my exploration of Denton as a place is to complicate what we mean when we describe *anywhere* as a place, as something authentic that can be experienced, protected, or engaged with creatively. Writing about place is productive, but it is also—by its nature—exclusionary. Any engagement with place is always partial. My experience of Denton as a place is not the Denton that votes 60 percent Republican, nor is it the 20 percent of Denton that lives below the poverty line, nor the Denton of chain restaurants on the 288 Loop. Well . . . those are all my Denton, but they are not a part of my daily experience of the city. So what is place and how can we engage with rhetorical appeals to authenticity? Those are the questions I address here.

Denton as a Place

Place is a word people use every day, but few people would likely be able to clearly define it if asked. As geographer Tim Cresswell succinctly pointed out, "Place is clearly a complicated concept" (50). After all, what do people mean when they refer to a place? In some sense, they often mean a specific geographic location But place is more than that. Telling me Denton is located at 33.2164° N, 97.1292° W tells me next to nothing. So it might help here to explain how *I* experience Denton as a place. Place, in a large sense, is subjective. Geographer Yi-Fu Tuan argued the same when he said that "place is pause" (6), a temporary cessation of movement experienced differently by each individual. So here I want to describe *my pause*, my thoughts when I stop and reflect on what I love about my city.

Denton is known colloquially as "little Austin." Austin is known nationally for its "Keep Austin Weird" slogan, thriving music scene, and strong pockets of progressive politics. Denton residents, long before I moved here, viewed their city as a smaller version of Austin that shared (and possibly exceeded) its music scene, general weirdness, and progressivism on a smaller scale. In fact, with Austin's booming growth and rising property values, some residents feel Denton has become what Austin used to be.

One can see evidence of Denton's "Austinness" throughout the city. Denton, like many Texas towns and smaller cities, is built around a central town square that serves as the city's downtown. The square features an eclectic mix of beer gardens, pubs, music venues, and independent businesses. About a mile away is the University of North Texas, with the college bars of Fry Street. Hipsters are everywhere downtown and around campus, playing music on the square, hanging out outside the coffee shops, grabbing a craft beer on a patio on a nice Texas evening. At points, it seems that 75 percent of the male population of Denton has a beard and 50 percent of the population plays an instrument. Clearly, this city of musicians, hipsters, students, and casually attired families is not the Texas of the tourism advertisements.

And for the most part, this is the Denton I experience; these characteristics are what Denton means to me. I am not alone in that. Many of the prominent city blogs, most notably *We Denton Do It*, emphasize this Denton of the downtown imaginary. The blog is a catalog of the "weird" Denton: the independent restaurants, the cool bars, the social life congregated around the downtown square and Fry Street. When I go out at night, these are the places I go, so I understand the rhetorical construction on sites like *We Denton Do It*. This is *my* Denton. A Denton of professors, students, musicians, and hipsters. A Denton of local businesses and beer gardens.

This is also the Denton many residents fight to protect. Denton has a long history as a countercultural college town, one whose social life used to be built around the Fry Street area before it began moving to the square a few years ago. Many longtime Denton residents speak nostalgically about Fry Street as a collection of cheap bars, delicious pizza, public music, and hippie sensibilities, but I never got to experience the Fry Street of their collective memory. By the time I moved to Denton, many of the old Fry Street buildings had been torn down, the businesses either moved or shuttered. These buildings were replaced by relatively high-end mixed-use apartment buildings, chain restaurants such as Chipotle and Potbelly, and even (quite controversially) a CVS.

When Fry Street began to be commercialized by chains, many residents were upset. People made documentaries preserving the history of the "old" Fry Street, residents fought development plans in city meetings, and now, more than half a decade later, one can still find animosity toward the "new" Fry Street. More recently, a Subway franchise moved onto the historic square (though it's now already closed), raising the ire of residents that franchises were damaging the "authentic" Denton. Clearly, Denton as a place is something many people see as worth fighting for.

So this is all part of the Denton I experience. Fry Street changed, but the uniqueness of the city moved downtown, and many residents still maintain an antichain ethos embraced by city council members and various city blogs. This uniqueness is what gives Denton its specificity in my experience, a place that combines the material infrastructure of the buildings, the social relations of the residents, the history as a college town devoted to its music scene, and my subject position as a thirty-four-year-old university professor. But . . . I still feel uncomfortable saying that description accurately captures what Denton *is*. I am skeptical when words like authentic are used to describe or even protect the parts of Denton I love. The next section explains why.

The Authenticity and Inauthenticity of Denton

The Denton concentrated around the town square is often presented as the "real" Denton. And that is the Denton I think of. But I am a particular subject within the larger constellation of social relations that make up the space of Denton, and part of what stands out in my experience of the "authentic" Denton is the specific kind of whiteness of the representation. Blogs like *We Denton Do It* highlight Denton's small businesses, but these businesses are mostly white. Bloggers often write about the fantastic beer gardens, but these places are seas of whiteness on a Friday night. Blogs do often touch on Denton's taquerias found on McKinney Street, less than a mile and a half from the square, but even those posts often have a certain tone of othering, writing about quick visits to the East McKinney Taco Corridor to consume "authentic" Mexican food. I do not mean this as a criticism of downtown Denton or the various city blogs. Many cities, Austin included, are socially segregated. I mention the specific type of whiteness of "authentic" Denton here to make a simple point: no representation of a place, no genuine local culture, will ever capture what a place means to everyone. Place is always, to some degree, subjectively constructed.

To explain this point, I want to move outside my experience of Denton concentrated on Fry Street and the square. Denton features a large minority population: 10 percent of the population is African American and 21 percent is Latino (U.S. Census Bureau). Like many cities, Denton features significant spatial segregation, with a disproportionate number of African Americans living in neighborhoods just southeast of downtown and majority Hispanic neighborhoods spread throughout the city. Denton also has a high poverty rate, with 20 percent of the city living below the poverty line. While many poorer neighborhoods are within a mile or two of Denton's square, these people are vastly underrepresented at the various beer gardens, patios, and quirky coffee shops that make up the "authentic" Denton of representation.

Beyond even racial or sociodemographic terms, Denton also has its share of big box stores and chain restaurants. They are located away from the city center along the 288 Loop and the Rayzor Ranch development. For all the talk on blogs of the hip new places adding to Denton's culture, many of the chains are packed with people and thriving. The idea of authenticity, then, basically refers to a square mile of the city. The Denton culture worth fighting for and protecting does not equally include the black families in the southeast, the Mexican-American neighborhoods along McKinney Street, or the chain restaurants filled with young families.

And to break down Denton even further, the culture surrounding the city as a "little Austin" is really representative of only a certain type of whiteness. I have often sat in a Denton beer garden wondering where most people hang out. After all, despite the visible number of hipsters, hippies, liberal academics, and so on, Denton is a city that votes conservative in statewide and national elections. The district's congressman is a Republican who was elected with over 60 percent of the vote. In the 2014 governor race, the city of Denton cast almost three thousand more votes for Greg Abbott than for Wendy Davis. So a lot of Republicans live in Denton. They do not seem to be centered on the downtown area, nor do they seem to be part of the "authentic" Denton culture we talk about when we write about "little Austin" or keeping Denton weird. But there certainly are rare moments when I am reminded of Denton's overall statistical demographics. For example, the annual North Texas State Fair held in Denton is filled with teens and adults in cowboy boots and cowboy hats, much more representative of the Texas of tourism posters than the Denton I experience on a daily basis. So I have no idea how to describe Denton as a place. Only in those fairly rare moments, such as the state fair or a quick taco run to a taqueria, do my experiences of Denton confront the lived reality of other residents.

The Fracking Ban and the Partiality of Place

Now I want to focus on one of those rare moments when the limitations of my understanding of Denton as a place came into stark relief. I am a political junkie. Regrettably, like so many Americans interested in politics, I focus more on national and state-wide politics than local elections. The national or statewide races I am accustomed to are accompanied by extensive polling, and the outcomes rarely surprise. That experience of politics changed for me when I got truly interested in a local issue for the first time. That issue was the proposed 2014 fracking ban in Denton. The city council had decided to put the fracking ban up for a citywide referendum, and the proposed ban was added to the 2014 ballot.

The ban sought to stop people from developing new fracking wells inside Denton's city limits, and it received a huge amount of attention from local sources and, not insignificantly, from big business outside the city as well. At one point before the vote, oil and gas companies had poured more than $700,000 into the campaign against the ban (Unger), afraid of the precedent Denton could set if the city became the first in Texas to ban new fracking wells. Clearly, the money was on the profracking side.

But in the month leading up to the vote, it became clear that popular support for the ban was growing. Lawns featured "Vote Yes" signs, events supporting the ban were packed with people, and my Facebook feed was filled with posts in support of the ban. At least from my perspective, the popular support for the ban was overwhelming. I did not know a single person who planned to vote against the ban, and I never overheard a single conversation that was profracking.

However, despite moments of certainty, the lead up to the fracking vote was also my most glaring reminder that my experience of Denton is partial and reliant on my subject position as a young (well . . . relatively young), white university professor. As I mentioned above, every single person I knew planned on voting for the ban. In *my* Denton, the ban seemed sure to pass. But I still had moments of doubt because, without the polling that accompanies larger elections, I had no way of knowing what was happening outside my self-constructed bubble. Everyone I knew was against the ban, but the vast majority of people I know in Denton are liberal and yet the city as a whole votes conservative. The people I know are mostly well off, but Denton has a high poverty rate. So ultimately, what did I really know about how the city was going to vote? Not much. It was in that moment that my experience felt so small and sheltered.

The ban did end up passing. Emphatically, with 59 percent of residents voting yes on the ban. The vote was a resounding success for Denton's counter-culture ethos. However, whether the ban passed (the Texas legislature moved immediately to overturn the ordinance) does not matter for the purposes of this chapter. What matters for this discussion was the uncertainty. Without any kind of official polling, I—and other supporters of the ban—had no idea what would happen. The "authentic" Denton focused on all-around weirdness was for the ban. But what about the white people who wear their cowboy hats and boots to the fair? The Mexican-Americans living off McKinney Street? The African Americans living in the southeast? I had no way of knowing because I do not really know *their* Denton. And importantly, when we discuss the *authentic* Denton, their Denton is not what's being discussed. So to expand on that point, I conclude with some thoughts on just what we mean when we talk about the authenticity of places.

Denton and the Strategic Rhetoric of Authenticity

It strikes me that what I have written so far may come off as overly critical. I do not mean to imply that white people in Denton are willfully blind to the experiences of other residents. Instead, I am arguing that any city has pockets of population who live their lives differently and experience place differently. And in no way is that unique to Denton. I am positing that any attempt to fully, objectively describe any city as a place is doomed to failure. Cities, even small cities, are too complex to ever be captured from one viewpoint. To further examine why, I want to turn to the thinker who has most influenced my understanding of place: the feminist geographer Doreen Massey, who back in the 1990s developed the idea of a "progressive sense of place." One of her main goals was to push back against the "authenticity" that colors so many of our discussions of place. She argues that appeals to spatial authenticity often represent a conservative, reactionary approach to place, one used to protect local culture against the influence of outsiders (read: immigrants) (*Place, Space, and Gender*).

So to Massey, place can never be fixed. It can never exist as some objective entity waiting to be experienced. But that does not mean that one place cannot be different from another. Instead, "what gives a place its specificity is not some long internalized history but the fact that it is constructed out of a particular constellation of social relations, meeting and weaving together at a particular locus" (*Place, Space, and Gender* 154). Places are ultimately nothing more (or less) than contingent, temporary collections of specific trajectories at certain geographic locations. How those trajectories converge depends on individuals' specific paths, the trajectory each followed to end up in this specific location at this specific time. That is what place is. Place is not fixed. It is not "authentic." Place is reinvented again and again as trajectories shift and flows of people, goods, information, and capital move in and out of a location.

But here is where I want to complicate this discussion because I do not think it is enough to simply make the point that we need to be careful when we write about place. Of course we do. Critical reflections should acknowledge that rhetorical appeals to spatial authenticity and essentialism often exclude huge swaths of the population, and any rhetorical interventions into place will be necessarily subjective. But I argue that—even as we recognize those limitations—we must be willing to make value judgments and critically intervene in moments in which the rhetorical appeal to authenticity is productive. Authenticity, in itself, is a rhetorical invention. The term is squishy and deployed strategically. But that does not mean authenticity is an inherently bad appeal. Some experiences of place are worth fighting for.

Most of this chapter has dealt with the problems with the idea of authentic places through an examination of Denton. Denton is known for certain things, but those certain things are not shared equally by all its residents. When *We Denton Do It* authors say a restaurant has failed to become a part of the "collective Denton consciousness" (Milne), what they generally mean is that it has not become part of a certain segment of Denton culture, the dominant cultural narrative of "weird" counterculture. But . . . is it fair or even productive to criticize appeals to authenticity? After all, I bet most anyone reading this can think of an aspect of a place he or she wants to be preserved. Many Austinites sympathize with the overall message of "Keep Austin Weird," which is an appeal to an innate "Austinness" that is damaged by outsiders moving to the city, rising property values, and the homogenization of national chains. I cannot say that I would not prefer that Austin remain weird and do not have sympathy for those appeals. But even with that sympathy, I must also recognize that any similar appeal also is inherently conservative and exclusionary. A certain Austin is preserved in "Keep Austin Weird" campaigns, an Austin enjoyed by a certain type of resident.

And the same points apply to Denton. When people fought in the mid-2000s to preserve Fry Street, they were fighting to preserve not only history but also authenticity. Denton culture was supposedly perverted by the fancy new apartments and the chains that moved in near campus. When people were enraged that a Subway temporarily opened on the square, the rhetorical appeals often focused on an innate "Dentonness" that was being polluted. And when blogs talk about valuable additions to Denton culture, they are not talking about the new Panda Express on 288, even if that Panda Express draws more Dentonites than the new restaurant near the square.

So what to do with the rhetorical appeals of authenticity? To work through my thoughts, I want to return to Doreen Massey. As mentioned above, she criticized closed-off conceptualizations of place as reactionary. However, in a later work, *For Space*, she left room for strategic appeals to essentialism in regards to place. Her work features a discussion of the Deni Indian lands in western Brazil. The campaign to protect the Deni lands against logging focused mostly on authenticity of culture and the closed-off nature of their space. The arguments boiled down to "This is a place worth protecting from outside interests." In many other cases, such as debates in Hamburg (or Texas, for that matter), nearly identical appeals to authenticity of local culture are deployed in often xenophobic terms to push back against immigration. In essence, the fight to preserve Deni lands from outside interests and the fight against immigration in so many industrialized cities have used the same rhetorical appeals. Does that mean we must judge them the same way? Massey argues no: "'Defence of a local way of life' can likewise cut both ways. The question cannot be whether demarcation (boundary building) is simply good or bad. Perhaps Hamburg should indeed open up, while the Deni are allowed their protective borderlands" (165).

Ultimately, whether appeals to authenticity—to a "local" culture—are ethically defensible depends on how one feels about what is being preserved. By their very nature, these appeals leave someone and something out. Each time we define the culture of a place, we are excluding other voices that may not be a part of that culture or that hope to someday be part of that culture. However, just as an appeal to pathos may be a good thing in a commercial raising money for animal shelters and a bad thing in a demagogue's stump speech, rhetorical appeals to authenticity are deployed strategically and are not inherently good or bad. *We Denton Do It*'s appeals to Denton culture are fine with me when they are used to fight off chain restaurants from opening branches downtown. An appeal to "authentic" Denton would not be fine with me if it focused on protesting a Mosque or enacting citywide English-only policies.

What this discussion has built to is the possibly unexciting, but I think important, conclusion that when we ask the question "What *is* this place?" we should always answer with "It depends." It makes sense rhetorically to write about places, to try to get at some essential thing that makes a place specific. But even as we do so, we must recognize that place specificity is contingent on the temporary coming together of multiple trajectories and is experienced differently depending on subject position. There is no "authentic" Denton that can encapsulate everyone's experience. The vigor to pass the fracking ban ended up working, but it just as easily could have failed because we had little idea how people outside our bubble would vote. Many of Denton's Mexican-American residents likely have never been to any of the bars, restaurants, or music venues that make up *We Denton Do It*'s Denton culture, and many of the white Christian families who form the reliable Republican voting bloc likely have not been either.

Any narrative of a place by necessity ignores other narratives. We can strive to make depictions of place as polyvocal as possible, but that makes it difficult to get at any kind of specificity necessary for rhetorical placemaking. We must acknowledge that fact even while recognizing that appeals to local culture and authenticity can be productive even as they are exclusionary. I love *my* Denton. I think it is a better place because of its weirdness, music, and craft beer. I would fight and donate money to keep *my* Denton weird. I have no problems when people appeal to these things as "essential" Denton, even as I recognize that those appeals are strategic and not ontological. But I hope I have shown why we must at least recognize the limitations of discussions of place even as we recognize their usefulness. After all, *my* Denton is not *the* Denton. My Denton is a partial, fragmented experience of a place too complex for a single person to ever capture.

Works Cited

Cresswell, Tim. *Place: A Short Introduction*. Malden, MA: Blackwell, 2004.

Massey, Doreen. *For Space*. Sage, 2005.

———. *Place, Space, and Gender*. U of Minnesota P, 1994.

Milne, Will. "Now Open: Hickory and Fry." *We Denton Do It*, 26 Feb. 2015, wedentondoit.com/blog/2015/2/15/now-open-hickory-and-fry. Accessed 3 Apr. 2015.

Roden, Kevin. "How Denton Voted on Nov 4 by Council District." *Roden for Denton*, 14 Nov. 2014, rodenfordenton.com/2014/11/how-denton-voted-on -nov-4-by-council-district/. Accessed 3 Apr. 2015.

Tuan, Yi-Fu. *Space and Place: The Perspective of Experience.* U of Minnesota P, 1977.

Unger, Todd. "Outside Money Flows into Denton Fracking Debate." *WFAA*, 2014, web.archive.org/web/20150103142231/http://www.wfaa.com:80/story /news/local/denton-county/2014/10/29/outside-money-flows-into-denton -anti-fracking-measure/18088991/. Accessed 3 Apr. 2015.

U.S. Census Bureau. "Denton city, Texas." *American Fact Finder*, 2015, fact-finder.census.gov/faces/nav/jsf/pages/community_facts.xhtml?src=bkmk#. Accessed 12 Apr. 2015.

We Denton Do It. wedentondoit.com/. Accessed 3 Apr. 2015.

Michael Odom,
Texas A&M University—Commerce

11. *WALNUT HILL STORY*: MEMORY, HISTORY, AND THE BUILT ENVIRONMENT IN THE EXPERIENCE OF A PLACE

*I*n late summer 2014, I made a number of visits to the area around the intersection of Walnut Hill Lane and North Central Expressway in Dallas. I went there to take notes on the neighborhood and record video snippets of the urban environment. I edited the video into a fifteen-minute piece and wrote a first-person narrative script for it. The words crawl across the screen from right to left at various speeds. That fall, I reworked the video, shortening its run time to ten minutes and adding voice-over work read by an actress. The result became *Walnut Hill Story*, the fourth video in a series begun in 2011.[1] In this essay, I examine why I made such things.

Each video addresses the psychogeography of a node along Central, forming a project I've named *Psycho Central*. The word *psychogeography* was first used by the situationist Guy Debord in a 1953 essay on urban geography. He wrote:

> Psychogeography sets for itself the study of the precise laws and specific effects of the geographical environment, whether consciously organized or not, on the emotions and behavior of individuals. The charmingly vague adjective *psychogeographical* can be applied to the findings arrived at by this type of investigation, to their influence on human feelings, and more generally to any situation or conduct that seems to reflect the same spirit of discovery. (8)

In one video, I trimmed Debord's definition down to "the intersection of consciousness and place," which has the benefit of brevity, even if it ignores the unconscious and is thus incomplete.

I came to video as an attempt to integrate the two channels of my aesthetic practice. I am trained as a painter, a maker of images. But for more than thirty years, I have also written critically about art. Painting and writing are very different activities, of course. At times I tried to bring them together by making paintings that incorporated oil paint and digital prints of rough drafts of art reviews. Using stencils cut from weather maps and details of corrected text, I shuffled isobars and rewrites together to make images that look like the one in fig. 11.1.

But it was video that offered me the visual and verbal melding that I needed. The *Psycho Central* project has afforded me the opportunity to apply art critical ideas and methods to the experience of the urban environment. The version of psychogeography I've developed enables me to approach a place both as a source of images to be juxtaposed (sequentially and in split-screen simultaneity) and as an already-formed aesthetic event—a found-art, sculptural installation that I can engage in critique.

North Central Expressway runs mostly north and south, connecting downtown Dallas with the northern suburbs where my family moved in 1959. The sequence of the *Psycho Central* videos follows the highway north from Deep Ellum to the Freedman's Memorial at Lemmon Avenue to the intersection of Knox Street and Henderson Avenue with the freeway and most recently to Walnut Hill Lane. As the project has evolved, the videos have become more personal. The scripts are all first-person narratives, but increasingly my memories of the places blend with the history of the highway and its current realities. This is likely because I'm approaching my boyhood home as I follow the highway north.

Figure 11.1. *F Word*, by Michael Odom. Oil and digital print on canvas, 20 × 16 inches, 2005.

But memories can be treacherous. Nowadays a mosaic mural designed by Miguel Covarrubias graces the front drive at the Dallas Museum of Art. I clearly recall seeing (and loving) it when we drove past its original place on Central Expressway in the 1960s. Research provided the original address: a mile away from what I remembered and on the other side of the road. The same was true for memories associated with *Walnut Hill Story*.

Important as it is, memory forms only part of the engagement with the place. Associations of visuals and judgments—the idea of art criticism—also enter into the mix. I worked my way along the street in an intuitive way, photographing what presented itself to be photographed. Debord and his fellow situationists (and the lettrists who preceded them) called this a *dérive*, meaning "a drift." The idea of a dérive actually dates from before the official founding of the Situationist International in 1957. Ivan Chtcheglov in his 1953 essay "Formulary for a New Urbanism" wrote of an imaginary city with districts that "correspond to the whole spectrum of diverse feelings that one encounters *by chance* in everyday life." (6). There would be a "Bizarre Quarter—Happy Quarter (specially reserved for habitation)—Noble and Tragic Quarter (for good children)—Historical Quarter (museum, schools)—Useful Quarter (hospital, tool shops)—Sinister Quarter, etc. . . . The main activity of the inhabitants will be CONTINUOUS DRIFTING" (7). He posits that drifting through the city facilitates the interaction of consciousness and place. Walking can be an emotional, contemplative, and intellectual event.

Dérive is a remarkable word for a remarkable concept. McKenzie Wark writes:

> Its Latin root "derivare" means to draw off a stream, to divert a flow. Its English descendants include the word "derive" and also "river." Its whole field of meaning is aquatic, conjuring up flows, channels, eddies, currents, and also drifting, sailing, or tacking against the wind. (22)

The practice of a dérive can serve to renew and enrich one's consciousness of the urban surroundings. Wark again:

> They [the Lettrist International] discovered a new city via a calculated drifting (*dérive*) through the old. Theirs would be a city of play, love, adventure, made for arousing new passions, a city that might finally justify the conceit that this is a civilization worthy of its predecessors. (17)

In 1958, an essay by Debord titled "Theory of the Dérive" appeared in the second issue of *Situationist International*. After describing the "playful-constructive behavior" involved in consciously drifting, he writes:

> The lessons drawn from dérives enable us to draft the first surveys of the psychogeographical articulations of a modern city. Beyond the discovery

of unities of ambience, of their main components and their spatial localization, one comes to perceive their principle axes of passage, their exits and their defenses. One arrives at the central hypothesis of the existence of psychogeographical pivot points. One measures the distances that actually separate two regions of a city, distances that may have little relation with the physical distance between them. (66)

Dallas's Central Expressway offers a psychogeographer scores of such pivot points. The highway overpass at Walnut Hill Lane is one of them. This is an encounter with urban space that seeks to complicate the relationships of citizens with the space of their city.

Before I was really aware of it, the dérive became my method. Visual and auditory cues, the enticement of water crossing a concrete barrier, a branch swaying in the near foreground, the huge culverts that pass under the always busy roadways, and the endless traffic noise—all these directed my drifting attention. Collecting them in the camera was the proper response to the place. And the video became an artwork, enough of an artwork to be exhibited in art galleries, at least. In the same essay in which he introduces the term *psychogeography*, Debord links the need for such urban awareness to understanding aesthetic experiences:

> The sudden change of ambience in a street within the space of a few meters; the evident division of the city into zones of distinct psychic atmospheres; the path of least resistance that is automatically followed in aimless strolls (and which has no relation to the physical contour of the terrain); the appealing or repelling character of certain places—these phenomena all seem to be neglected. In any case they are never envisaged as depending on causes that can be uncovered by careful analysis and turned to account. . . . In fact, the variety of possible combinations of ambiences, analogous to the blending of pure chemicals in an infinite number of mixtures, gives rise to feelings as differentiated and complex as any other form of spectacle can evoke. ("Introduction to a Critique of Urban Geography" 10)

He then turns to a brief discussion of paintings by the Italian master of the uncanny, Georgio de Chirico, and the French baroque painter Claude Lorrain, whose landscapes make use of architectural ruins (11). The traditions of visual art are intimately blended with the city. So artists can and do use cities to enrich visual expression. This is possible only because viewers of their work can read (consciously or not) the visual cues artists employ. All of us are part of the game.

The associative nature of the dérive also has value for the work of an art critic seeking to evaluate and explicate a work of art more conventionally conceived and produced than an urban neighborhood. Consider, for example, a sculpture by the German artist Joseph Beuys titled *Capri Battery*. It consists of a yellow lightbulb screwed into a socket made to plug into a wall outlet, but is plugged into a lemon instead. If one wanders through the material semiotics of the thing, certain ordinary associations arise. The bulb and the lemon are similar in color and shape: they rhyme. But one is brittle and made in a factory; it's technological. The other is food. It grew on a tree. It contains seeds that could produce more lemons. It contains life. The bulb offers the possibility of light and all that the idea of illumination might imply. The acids in the lemon's juice probably do react with the metals in the wall plug, but any reaction is too feeble to light the bulb. But the technological bulb *is* plugged into the organic lemon as though it seeks power there, and this leads to further associations about the relationship of our technology to the natural world. Beuys's materials have these meanings and many more besides. Such associations are foundational to my art writing.

As I shot video images along the street, I was most often the only pedestrian among hundreds of cars. My method was to choose an image, set up my tripod, and record the event, item, or scene in thirty- to sixty-second segments. And then I walked a little before setting up the camera again. Traffic figures prominently in the imagery and especially the soundtrack. On both sides of the highway and on the highway itself, the landscape is carved and reshaped by cars and the needs of cars, by the planning required to make them move with efficiency. That efficiency is an economic imperative. Drivers and highways are engaged in the functioning of the city's business. As I practiced my dérive, I was not. Wark writes:

> The dérive cuts across the division of the space of the city into work, rest and leisure zones. By wandering about in the space of the city according to their own sense of time, those undertaking a dérive find other uses for space besides functional. The time of the dérive is no longer divided between productive time and leisure time. It is time that plays in between the useful and the gratuitous. (25)

Wark calls this a critical practice, doing something by observing.

It is important to note that this critique identifies resting and leisure as participants in an economic conception of the space of the city that has no room for the useless. In *Wanderlust*, Rebecca Solnit writes, "Most American cities and towns, however, are organized around consumption and production, as were the dire industrial cities of England, and public space is merely the void between workplaces, shops and dwellings" (176). The car culture of Dallas (or almost any city) serves to deliver people to and from work and economically productive places of leisure such as bars, theaters, restaurants.

The place I studied was largely one of the voids Solnit writes about—a non-place for transient people going places and getting things done that I tried to experience as a place, to read it like a lemon and a lightbulb.

In this practice, walking is very helpful. Slowing down alters the experience of the time it takes to move through space, of course, but it also alters the awareness one has of the space and time of the experience. Solnit writes, "Walking shares with making and working that crucial element of engagement of the body and the mind with the world, of knowing the world through the body and the body through the world" (29). The textures of a place, its material being, are made more corporeal in the act of walking. This involves more than simply noticing things one can't easily see while driving, though that is certainly involved too. Walking through a place encourages an awareness of the physical space one passes through.

One night in the early summer of 1963, my father and I walked along a creek near Walnut Hill Lane and Central. We had lights strapped to our heads and twelve-volt batteries at our waists. Dad had a grabber, a spring-loaded steel trap on a ten-foot aluminum pole. We were after bullfrogs. It was not a dérive; it was a hunt. But this memory prompted me to revisit the place five decades later. It led me to walk there with my camera. And this memory informs my present-day experience of the place, its psychogeography.

In *Civilization and Its Discontents*, Freud writes:

> Now let us, by a flight of imagination, suppose that Rome is not a human habitation but psychical entity with a similarly long and copious past—an entity, that is to say, in which nothing that has once come into existence will have passed away and all the earlier phases of development continue to exist alongside the latest one. This would mean that in Rome the palaces of the Caesars and the Septizonium of Septimius Severus would still be rising to their old heights on the Palatine and that the castle of S. Angelo would still be carrying on its battlements the beautiful statues which graced it until the siege by the Goths, and so on. (18)

This passage is not intended to be a psychogeographic text, and almost immediately, Freud dismisses the historical, urban geography conceit as unhelpful to his argument. But the passage helps describe some parts of my experience of the place in my video. The area is built up today. Parts have been rebuilt more than once. Medical offices, apartments, condos, water treatments, restaurants, strip malls are the local ecology now. The street has grown many lanes since that summer. The number of cars and trucks has grown to fill all those lanes. Today geographic information systems (GIS) report on the relative wealth of the two sides of Central, the earning, buying, and spending power of residents. But that night in 1963, we were alone in the weeds that lined a sluggish stream. 135

I recall no development at all. My time in the place in the 1960s haunts my time there today, haunts it irrationally.

When you hunt frogs, you shine a light along the banks of a stream or pond. Frogs' bellies shine white in the dark. My father stepped into the water to catch a frog, and the water under his feet boiled. It was a snake. To my child's eye, it was many snakes. Dad drew a big knife and hacked the snake to pieces.

This story was present when I shot my video. It enriched the place I photographed, as it also embodied a masculinized substrate to the urban environment. Hunting, killing, violence, phallic objects—these and other (conscious and unconscious) echoes of maleness are not there only in my faulty memory. They hum in the public spaces of Dallas like background radiation. The public space is itself largely gendered. And so the script I wrote for the video folds the snake story into the experience of the present-day place. And so I asked a woman to read my script.

The dérive informed my approach to the place and shaped my response to its psychogeography. It also informed the structure of the video I made of the place. The video wanders the neighborhood and associates memories with observations about public space. It connects GIS data about the differing economic levels on either side of the highway with imagery of plants, construction, and traffic, and stories of present-day Dallas with stories of the summer of 1963.

Walnut Hill Story Script

Walnut Hill Lane crosses Central Expressway a few miles north of Henderson Avenue.

I parked in a garage shared by a dialysis clinic, a glaucoma center, and several other healthcare-related businesses.

The east side of Central at Walnut Hill is thick with medical outfits.

There's a hospital complex up the hill beyond the light rail station.

A few years back, I walked the area, revisiting a memory.

A battered man holding a bag connected to his catheter approached me.

His head had numerous cuts and abrasions.

He asked for a cigarette.

Once when I was 11 or 12 my father and I hunted bullfrogs along the water there.

Dad used a grabber, a spring-loaded trap on the business end of a 10-foot aluminum pole.

You hunt frogs in the dark with a 12-volt light strapped to your head.

The frogs' bellies shine white when the light hits them.

If you see something shiny on the bank, it's either a frog or a beer can.

There were no medical offices along the street back then.

There was almost no development.

After I parked, I walked up towards the light rail station and got lunch at a mediocre Lebanese place.

Suspiciously flavorless lamb kebabs.

Dad's grabber had a trigger in the center of the trap, so he could jab it at the bullfrogs and catch them.

He was good at it.

He was also brutal when he caught them, chopping their legs off with a big knife his father had made from a worn-out saw.

Without first killing them—you only eat their legs, you see.

I've found a couple of aerial photos of the intersection that date from February 1959, when my family moved to Texas.

Nobody hunts frogs near that part of Central anymore.

But the water is still there—Jenkins Branch, a dammed up minor tributary of White Rock Creek, presenting a raggedy water treatment for apartments and medical office east of Central.

Turtles and carp live in the green water on the east side of Central.

Trash seems to flourish as you approach the highway, as well.

Central passes over Walnut Hill and also over the stream, which is channeled through an impressive system of culverts beneath the big highway.

Very few use them, but a couple of walkways pass beneath Central.

Parts of the walk are encrusted with grackle and pigeon shit.

The afternoon traffic roared above me and around me as I crossed to the west.

I saw a number of eggshells on the walk.

We wore wader boots when we went frogging that summer night in the early 1960s.

Dad stepped from the bank to grab a frog.

The water beneath him boiled with snakes.

He hacked at them with his big knife.

Pieces of bloody snake flew about.

The culvert and dam system now in place controls the flow of water from the west and fills a well maintained pond that doubtless improves the property value of a big, gated condo complex west of Central.

It's deeply privatized space.

The offices of the Dallas County Republican Party are located in the strip mall between the pond and Central.

Across Walnut Hill north of the condos is a major construction site where 40 acres of what the Dallas Morning News called "aging apartments" were torn down right before the Great Recession seven years ago.

The apartments weren't there the night Dad killed the snakes.

The News reported last year that a big retail/office/residential complex was to be built on the site.

One version of the site's design was said to have a "European feel."

It was apparently rejected.

In my child's eye, Dad killed many snakes that night back in the 60s.

I have imagined as many as 5 of them dead in the water and weeds.

I recall blood and death and much chopping.

And being afraid.

But my memory is almost certainly wrong.

I remember a stream, but the aerial photos clearly show the stream was dammed before February 1959.

And Dad said it was only one snake.

My smartphone tells me that median income for the neighborhood east of Central is 20% below the national average.

It's 15% higher than average west of the highway.

Retail spending by residents east of Central: 23% below average.

West of Central: 10% above.

Restaurant spending by residents east of Central: 11% below the national average.

West of Central: 21% above.

I inherited the knife when my father died.

Note

1. The video is online at https://vimeo.com/116840545.

Works Cited

Chtcheglov, Ivan. "Formulary for a New Urbanism." Knabb, pp. 1–8.

Debord, Guy. "Introduction to a Critique of Urban Geography." Knabb, pp. 8–12.

———. "Theory of the Derive." Knabb, pp. 62–66.

Freud, Sigmund. *Civilization and Its Discontents.* W. W. Norton, 1962.

Knabb, Ken, editor and translator. *Situationist International Anthology.* Bureau of Public Secrets, 2006.

Solnit, Rebecca. *Wanderlust: A History of Walking.* Viking, 2000.

Wark, McKenzie. *The Beach beneath the Street: The Everyday Life and Glorious Times of the Situationist International.* Verso, 2011.

Ryan Skinnell,
San José State University

12. RECONCILING TEXAS; OR, INVENTING (A) PLACE OUT OF PLACE

An invention of what is possible is not an invention.
—Jacques Derrida, "Deconstruction in America"

In the words of one commentator, "Reconciliation, in essence, represents a place, the point of encounter where concerns about both the past and the future can meet." . . . Reconciliation represents a *topos* of potential, a place for becoming that is equally a coming into place.
—Eric Doxtader, "Reconciliation: A Rhetorical Concept/ion"

*T*here's a bumper sticker gracing an untold number of bumpers, tailgates, and rear windows in Texas that reads, "I wasn't born in Texas, but I got here as fast as I could." Based on the prevalence of this sentiment and the spectacles of prominently displayed Texas pride—state flags, decorative Lone Stars, and colloquial injunctions against messing with the state—plastered on seemingly every available surface, it is not hard to conclude Texas is a place many people desire to be. It was not, however, a place I desired to be.

In January 2011, I booked a flight to the Dallas–Fort Worth (DFW) area. I was on the job market that year, and I was eager and excited to be going on a campus interview at the University of North Texas (UNT). As much as I wanted a job like UNT's, however, my eagerness and excitement were hardly unconditional. I viscerally hated the thought of visiting Texas, to say nothing of contemplating moving there. I am not exaggerating. Before the campus visit—even before submitting my application materials—I had an anxiety dream about being lost and wandering around in a vast, unforgiving desert that I knew (in my dream) to be Texas. In the months between when I applied for the job and when I eventually visited Texas, the dream reoccurred periodically. It was the only such dream I had about any place to which I applied. Texas looms large in the public imaginary, and no more so than for people who want nothing to do with it. It loomed very large in my imaginary,

139

and I was not at all eager or excited about Texas, whatever my feelings about gainful employment or the job itself may have been.

This reflection on my feelings about Texas is not (just) a retroactive attempt at catharsis. Rather, it is the beginning of an attempt to unpack the effects of my reluctance to Texas (or "Texas") as a more general consideration of rhetorical invention's relationship to place. In rhetorical studies, it is common to think of place and placemaking in terms of positive inventive potential— place provides the constitutive grounds (*topos*) for inventive practice because places are distinctive, affective, and evocative. As well, places are material and occupied (embodied). They enable presence and propinquity, and therefore meaningful engagement (relational). They are available for invocation, iteration, and productive redefinition (symbolic). And sometimes they represent untapped rhetorical potential (modifiable).

In any case, there is a certain romance about place in rhetorical studies that is nicely encapsulated in Michael Hyde's introduction to *The* Ethos *of Rhetoric*, subtitled "Rhetorically, We Dwell." Hyde begins by reinvigorating a "'primordial' meaning" of the term *ethos* "to refer to the way discourse is used to transform space and time into 'dwelling places' where people can deliberate about and 'know together' some matter of interest" (xiii). By recuperating the ancient sense of place underwriting ethos, Hyde reconstructs a concept that is often radically individualized into something more inviting, hospitable, and communal. In Hyde's formulation, place plays a productive, even idealized, role in rhetorical action because it is grounded and shared. Used in this "architectural" sense, he writes, "The *ethos* of rhetoric makes use of our inventive and symbolic capacity to construct dwelling places that are stimulating and aesthetically, psychologically, socially, and perhaps theologically, instructive" (xiii).

Hyde's interest is in ethos, so his opening paean is perhaps more eulogistic than some other rhetoricians' theoretical engagements with place. Nevertheless, in rhetorical studies broadly, Hyde's sense of place is all but interchangeable with rhetorical possibility, which we are ideally meant to inhabit and therefore realize (see, e.g., Blair et al.; Endres and Senda-Cook; Poirot and Watson). Moreover, this optimistic sensibility is an interdisciplinary phenomenon. In "Listening to the City: Oral History and Place in the Digital Era," digital humanist and historian Mark Tebeau briefly surveys "two decades of scholarship premised on the argument that 'place' matters" (27) across a number of fields. No doubt owing to attempts to demonstrate that place matters, the terms used to give emphasis to place generally have a positive valence. Even in acknowledging that places can be bad or sites of negative affect, rhetoric's orientation to place is almost always rendered as positive potentiality. We might even say place is *utopic* in rhetorical studies.[1]

Given the abiding belief in the potentiality of place, we might ask how different places/locations invite inhabitants to create and explore the multiplicity of potential meanings. We might ask how Texas more specifically constitutes a *topos* for generating or inventing the multiple meanings of place, which then invite further inventive practices. I submit that a reasonable answer to these questions is that place does not necessarily invite positive attachments and situated meaning-making. If the promise of place is that it provides the kind of referential specificity and simultaneous differentiation necessary to invent place and to place invention, my totalizing reluctance to "Texas" suggests the promise is hardly a guarantee.

It is through this lens that I look back at my arrival in Texas. On the same day UNT's search committee interviewed me in Los Angeles, the department chair invited me to Denton, about forty miles north of Dallas, for a campus visit. Within a couple of days, I was making plans to do so. Within two weeks, I landed at the DFW airport and was shuttled off to UNT.

My sense of Texas as a potential home, however, was rather cynical. As I prepared for the trip, I joked with friends about being greeted off the plane by a dusty personified mustache, drowning in a ten-gallon hat, crossed with bandoliers, jingling with spurs, and smelling vaguely of chewing tobacco—Yosemite Sam with a Sam Elliott drawl. I was halfway prepared to be whisked away to the nearest megachurch and assigned membership in a high school football booster club. Although I recognized I was reducing and oversimplifying a complex place, I also knew that Texas was big, it was cattle, and it was conservative, and I was suspicious of all of it.

☆ ☆ ☆ ☆ ☆

"I Wasn't Born in Texas, but I Came Here Kicking and Screaming."

☆ ☆ ☆ ☆ ☆

If invention can be understood, in Aristotle's terms, as a form of willful encounter—as the practice of finding available means—then it requires at least some level of motivation. The necessity of motivated action is reinforced by Hyde's contention that place allows people to construct dwelling places and "'know together' some matter of interest." Potential must be intentionally, if not necessarily consciously, exploited. In fact, motivation is the unstated premise of most theories of invention—invention is a practice and requires a motivated practitioner (though motivation may take many forms). Likewise, inventing requires vulnerability. Even in the instrumental way some versions of invention get rendered, it still implies the possibility—and even necessity—of exposing something new, which may result in fundamental change. Absent motivation and vulnerability, there is no place for invention, whatever other potential exists.

In Hyde's panegyric, place's positive potentiality runs cover for the motivation necessary to dwell and undergo change. This is the case in most theories of rhetorical place, and it certainly makes good sense for thinking of possibilities that place makes available. I have no interest in suggesting that positive, productive concepts of rhetorical place are wrong. But I do wonder how we can make sense of place's relationship to invention when potential inventors are *ectopic* (from the Greek ἐκ, "out" + τόπος, "place," *ektopos* = "out of place"). Or otherwise, what inventive possibilities exist in places for people who are reluctant to inhabit them? Or still otherwise, is it possible to invent place for someone who is emplaced out of place?

I want to defer answers to these questions for the time being so that I might first return to Texas.

When I landed at the airport for my campus interview, I collected my luggage and called the person who was responsible for picking me up. He arrived about twenty minutes after I landed, and as we were loading my luggage into his SUV, he apologized for his tardiness: "I was teaching, and everyone else from the search committee is attending the African American candidate's job talk."

I later learned that UNT's English Department had a second job opening, for an African American literature specialist. Candidates for the rhetoric and writing position and candidates for the African American literature position were visiting on overlapping dates. Other members of the department were attending the African American (literature specialist) candidate's talk, which coincided with my flight's arrival. This kind of shorthand, abbreviating "African American literature specialist" to "African Americanist" or "African American candidate" for example, is common in academia. But I didn't know another position was being filled in the department, so I did not make that connection. When my host referred to the "African American candidate," I thought he was informing me they had brought a token "diversity" candidate to campus. Consequently, I spent much of the drive from the airport to the hotel genuinely distressed by the apparent actualization of my earlier (anxious) joke about being greeted at the airport by an unabashed Texas stereotype.

My point in recounting this story is twofold. First, it should be clear my reluctance about being in Texas was considerably amplified in that moment. Texas was a place to which I traveled. It was potentially a place I would inhabit with my family. But I patently did not want to be there. I wanted nothing to do with it. That initial encounter with what I assumed to be an openly racist potential colleague crystallized my animosity toward Texas as a place, which had been to that point nebulous. The fact that my misunderstanding about the other candidate was quickly cleared up did not magically end my animosity, though it dampened it. But even without that catalyst, my animosity toward the place would not have ceased to exist.

Second, there was very little room for (re)inventing Texas under those circumstances. Without any particular motivation to search for Texas's available means, whatever that may mean, I had little reason to invent Texas as anything other than "Texas." In other words, my initial reluctance to the ideograph of "Texas" made the actual place of Texas (and any locale within it) unavailable to me as a place of positive potentiality. For me, Texas was not a "dwelling place" of the sort Hyde conjures. I had no intention of "dwelling" there, even if I lived there. It was a location, certainly—place as a physical fact. But the looming, hulking, imaginary "place" of "Texas" is really no place at all— it is an uncomplicated, streamlined, ideological placeholder. Additionally, UNT's campus, the city of Denton, and DFW airport were no less "Texas" for being geographically specific. In more familiar rhetorico-academic terms, I constructed "Texas" as the (hated) other against which to concretize my own (righteous) sense of self/s, effectively ruling out any inventive potential for placemaking.

☆ ☆ ☆ ☆ ☆

"I Wasn't Born in Texas, and I'll Be Damned If I'm Going to Stay."

☆ ☆ ☆ ☆ ☆

I believe this is the immediate answer to my earlier question, Is it possible to invent place for someone emplaced out of place? One answer, it seems to me, is that it is possible to live in a place, be in a place, physically inhabit a place, and nevertheless fail (or refuse) to encounter it as a place of specificity, differentiation, and potential invention. Place may enable invention, but absent motivation and vulnerability, place does not compel invention. As such, rhetorical theories of place are not very instructive for a rhetorical subject who is out of place, because theories of placemaking generally posit a subject with some form of (positive) connection to the place they're inventing or inventing in. Even in negatively constructed places, there is commonly an impetus for reclaiming the right to invent (in) a place—that is, rhetorical placemaking is an act of (positive) attachment and even (potential) ownership. For a rhetorical subject who wants no part of a place, who lacks the motivation to encounter place in a way that doesn't confirm ideological biases, there is only division, which leaves anyone emplaced out of place at an impasse. I want to suggest preliminarily that the relationship I'm describing is a rather common experience of place, especially in a period of globalized mobility.

But while I think this is potentially a right answer, it is also an unsatisfying answer given the innumerable people who are emplaced out of place—whether as a result of occupations or natural disasters or wars, or even for people who feel out of place where they have always been. In those circumstances, I think people who are emplaced out of place eventually begin the process of inventing place. Invention is not forever blocked for people emplaced out of place. So the question shifts slightly, from How does place enable invention? to How does place become available for invention within hostile conditions?

There is, I think, an answer to my second question, which is superficially apparent in the colloquialism "Go to your happy place." A "happy place" allows a person in some form of distress to retreat to a place of mental comfort even while he or she remains physically emplaced out of place. In popular culture, the happy place is an escape into a fully interiorized hallucination. If it is a dwelling place, it is available to each individual only on his or her own terms. A "happy place" is not a shared, communal, habitable place. What I have in mind instead is the discovery (invention) of an exterior place within a place. For people who cannot live their lives in constant hallucination, I suggest we might productively theorize a practice of inventing a "place out of place"—a practice that allows for someone emplaced out of place to recuperate the positive potentiality of rhetorical place even while living in a place that he or she is otherwise unmotivated to reinvent. What is needed here is a theory for encountering and remaking animosity that can clear the way for (re)inventing place—for reinventing Texas, in this case. For this, I turn to rhetorical reconciliation.

In "Reconciliation: A Rhetorical Concept/ion," Erik Doxtader investigates the "definitional puzzle" of reconciliation as a rhetorical concept/ion (see also Hatch). As he maps the definitional terrain of the term, Doxtader also unpacks the central work of reconciliation, which "entails the transformation of a thing, state of mind, event, or relationship into something that it is not" (269). For Doxtader, reconciliation is a form of conflict resolution that confronts violence by destabilizing identitarian certainty. It is a movement between violence and mutual understanding "that both enacts and opens the potential for rhetorical invention" (268). As such, reconciliation fundamentally transforms relationships by clearing room for productive disagreement and negotiation. As Doxtader puts it, "Reconciliation's rhetorical production marks not the resolution of conflict but the inauguration of a struggle" (282).

Doxtader's theory of reconciliation is too complex and detailed for a full treatment here, but I want to briefly tease out certain aspects of the concept.

At its base, reconciliation is a mode of transformation that becomes available when all parties agree only to the fact that current conditions are unsustainable—when something has to change, but there are no other shared grounds for engagement. As Doxtader indicates when discussing Paul the Apostle's theory of reconciliation, "[It] follows from deep disagreement with and distrust of the other" (272). When deep disagreement and distrust have reached a (violent) fever pitch, reconciliation becomes possible. Reconciliation is therefore kairotic.

In the kairotic moment, reconciliation introduces a moment of exception to the current state of affairs during which all agree to suspend the laws by which they are inexorably opposed in order to engage with one another. The moment of exception occasioned by reconciliation "brings the release of identity in the name of creating channels for identification" (276). An important point, however, is that reconciliation does not compel actors to forget, erase, or ignore the historical conditions from which they are attempting to break. What is entailed in reconciliation is neither forgiveness nor amnesia, but rather willing destabilization of self-certainty to remake the terms for collective existence. Actors agree to engage without agreeing to disregard the circumstances that made such engagement necessary. The parties involved "retain their animosity but come to stand *as they are not* with respect to the historical reasons for their conflict" (279). In this temporary state of exception, new norms for rhetorical and human interaction are invented and negotiated among people who are otherwise members of hostile factions.

The stakes of reconciliation as Doxtader elaborates them are rather more consequential than was my experience of landing in Texas, and I would suggest they are more consequential than the experiences of most people who are emplaced out of place. I want to proceed carefully so as not to reduce the gravity of Doxtader's concept/ion. Nevertheless, rhetorical reconciliation suggests a modality for engaging amid hostility that allows me to chart a course for inventing place out of place.

☆ ☆ ☆ ☆ ☆

A curious thing happened on my first full day on campus at UNT. In the course of my campus interview, which included the standard routine of meals, meetings, presentations, and formal and informal introductions, I began to notice what I want to call a recurring performance of emplaced out of place. A number of people, from faculty to graduate students to deans, both Texas natives and transplants alike, subtly acknowledged my resistance to visiting Texas. Many of the transplants had come to Texas reluctantly as well, and many of the Texas natives seemed to empathize. One way they demonstrated their empathy was by inventing a place out of place.

☆ ☆ ☆ ☆ ☆

"Don't Worry, Denton Is Not Texas."

☆ ☆ ☆ ☆ ☆

No fewer than six people, without provocation, assured me during my campus interview that I would be okay moving to Denton because Denton was patently (and ostensibly uniquely) not Texas. The reasons proffered for such a claim were a wonderful assortment. To name a few:

1. Denton is the home of Brave Combo, a multiple Grammy award–winning band formed in 1979 by UNT alumni. Brave Combo is world renowned, having been namechecked by Bob Dylan (Flanagan) and immortalized in a 2004 episode of *The Simpsons*. The band is a reminder that Denton plays host to a diverse and thriving music scene, including semiregular appearances by Denton's favorite sons and daughters in Brave Combo, and UNT has one of the top-rated jazz programs in the country, which attracts aspiring musicians from around the world. Although Brave Combo is from Denton, one significant detail for reluctant Texans is that the band's music is a combination of polka, jazz, world beat, and Latin influences. In other words, the iconic Denton band is not identifiably a "Texas" band.

2. Although Denton is still a relatively small city, with only about 120,000 residents, including nonpermanent college students, it offers many of the cosmopolitan affordances of bigger cities because of its proximity to Dallas and Fort Worth. It has regular farmers' markets, two universities within a few miles of each other (UNT and Texas Woman's University), and a culturally diverse population, as evidenced by the variety of culinary options in the area. At the same time, Denton maintains a small-town feel by limiting the number of corporate-owned businesses within city limits, supporting local businesses, and encouraging local artists and artisans to hawk their wares. In many ways, Denton is "weird" like Austin to the south, but Denton doesn't have the dubious distinction as the seat of state government tethering it to "Texas." Denton is too weird to be Texas.[2]

3. Every year, a local newspaper produces a "Best of Denton" list, which includes restaurants, book stores, and so on. The recipients get a handsome plaque so patrons know they're getting "the best" Denton has to offer. It is no small source of amusement to reluctant Texans that the "Best Steakhouse in Denton" was Outback Steakhouse several years running. Ironically, for years the only other restaurant in serious contention was Texas Roadhouse. But the salient point is that no place in actual-Texas would name an Australian-themed chain, famed for its deep-fried onion appetizer, as the local "Best Steakhouse."

"Don't Worry, Denton Is Not-Texas."

When I first started to recognize the invocation of not-Texas, frankly, I was charmed. For one, no one who cast Denton as not-Texas attempted to persuade me I was wrong about "Texas." They seemed perfectly willing to concede, at least implicitly, that any hostility I felt toward "Texas" was understandable, even warranted. In fact, it was on the grounds of shared opposition to "Texas" that assertions about Denton as not-Texas were generally offered. And the localization of Denton as not-Texas reinforced the exclusivity of the claim. That is, I suppose it was easier for me to believe that Denton was not-Texas than it would have been for me to imagine somehow that Texas is not really "Texas."

At a glance, not-Texas seems like a clever bit of trickery designed to allow reluctant residents to imagine themselves as separate from "Texas," existing apart in a sort of exiles' community. Not-Texas, then, might be understood as the invention of a *utopic* place that allows inhabitants to delude themselves— not-Texas as an island of virtue adrift in a sea of unspeakable awfulness. But not-Texas is not romantically utopic. The people who advance claims about not-Texas are not naive or unaware of the ways Denton is stereotypically "Texas." Not-Texas is *not* some magical invented place that exists as a hallucinatory happy place apart from reality. Rather, not-Texas is a place out of place. It is a performative enactment of the kind of rhetorical reconciliation that makes invention possible in otherwise hostile circumstances.

The invention of not-Texas creates a space of exception in which unmotivated actors (in this case, me and other people emplaced out of place in Texas) become motivated to undertake the willing destabilization of self-certainty necessary to create channels for identification. In the simplest terms, such spaces of exception make being emplaced out of place negotiable. Not-Texas makes inventive motivation and vulnerability possible, not by excising hostility or obscuring antagonisms—neither forgiveness nor amnesia—but by setting them aside to invent new norms for rhetorical and human interaction.

To recall Doxtader, "Reconciliation's rhetorical production marks not the resolution of conflict but the inauguration of a struggle" (282). In this sense, not-Texas is the postulation of a temporary space of exception in which the rules of "Texas" are suspended to clear the way for (re)inventing Denton and by proxy (re)inventing Texas. Not-Texas is therefore the antecedent to a struggle over what Denton, and ultimately Texas, can mean. This is because not-Texas is simultaneously incorporated by and exterior to the physical place of Texas. Perhaps paradoxically, the invention of place out of place creates the possibility for reinventing the actual place by holding the two in tension.

The postulation of not-Texas does not imbue it with positive rhetorical potential supposedly endemic to place. Rather, Not-Texas is a space of exception that reorients the grounds of engagement to make hostility less self-evident and less self-righteous. As such, it invites deeper engagement, not detachment. It invites the emplaced out of place to inhabit a contested space and take responsibility for inquiring into and negotiating the terms of collective existence. To make it slightly less abstract, the invitation extended to me during my campus interview by the inhabitants of Not-Texas was equally an invitation to engage with, to struggle over, and to (re)invent Denton.

There can be no doubt that for many people, Texas and specifically Denton bear exploration as generative or inventional places in the sense evoked by Hyde's "dwelling places." For all the people I met who self-identified as fellow exiles, a far greater number imagined Denton and Texas as places of positive potentiality. Nevertheless, at the time of this writing, I had lived in Texas for four years and had discovered that the "Denton is not Texas" trope is common in conversations where at least one person is not a Texas native. Not-Texas is reinvented daily among the emplaced out of place, as well as by people who empathize. Not-Texas is a common, even routine, way to encourage the motivation and vulnerability necessary to encounter and (re)invent Texas and Denton.

The localized practice of inventing not-Texas in Denton tells rhetoricians something about the limits of considering place strictly, or even primarily, in terms of positive inventive potential. But I want to stretch the concept further and briefly observe that not-Texas is, in fact, not localized to Denton. It is a common trope in other places in Texas as well. Depending on whom you talk to, Austin, El Paso, Galveston, and San Antonio are not Texas either. But the trope travels farther still. As I wrote this essay, I discovered that Iowa City is not really Iowa, Shanghai is not really China, and Orange County is not really California. No doubt locales around the world are invented and reinvented in exceptional places out of place. Wherever people are emplaced out of place, spaces of exception are likely to be invented. The sort of rhetorical reconciliation that makes Denton available as a site of productive engagement and struggle is a necessary corollary to rhetorical theories of place for the same reasons rhetorical theories of place are

appealing to begin with.

Notes

1. The etymology of *utopia* is rather interesting, if tangential to my purposes, for considering ways rhetoricians think about place: from the Greek *οὐ*, "no, not" + τόπος, "place," *eutopos* = "not a place."

2. At Denton's annual Arts and Jazz Festival in 2014, I overheard a woman tell some friends she'd "forgotten how many fucking hippies there are in Denton." As someone raised near Hollywood, California, I find this characterization pretty laughable, but it nevertheless rehearses, from a different angle, the claim that Denton is not Texas.

Works Cited

Blair, Carole, et al., eds. *Places of Public Memory: The Rhetoric of Museums and Memorials*. Tuscaloosa: U of Alabama P, 2010.

Derrida, Jacques, et al. "Deconstruction in America: An Interview with Jacques Derrida." *Critical Exchange*, vol. 17, 1985, pp. 1–33.

Doxtader, Erik. "Reconciliation: A Rhetorical Concept/ion." *Quarterly Journal of Speech*, vol. 89, no. 4, 2003, 267–92.

Endres, Danielle, and Samantha Senda-Cook. "Location Matters: The Rhetoric of Place in Protest." *Quarterly Journal of Speech*, vol. 97, no. 3, 2011, 257–82.

Flanagan, Bill. "Bob Dylan Discusses Holiday Music, Christmas and Feeding the Hungry." *Street News Service*, 23 Nov. 2009. Accessed 27 May 2015.

Hatch, John B. "Between Religious Visions and Secular Realities: (Dia)logology and the Rhetoric of Reconciliation." Coming to Terms with Reconciliation symposium, 10–11 Nov. 2006, University of Wisconsin–Madison.

Hyde, Michael J. "Introduction: Rhetorically, We Dwell." *The Ethos of Rhetoric*, edited by Hyde, U of South Carolina P, 2004, pp. xiii–xxviii.

Poirot, Kristan, and Shevaun E. Watson. "Memories of Freedom and White Resilience: Place, Tourism, and Urban Slavery." *Rhetoric Society Quarterly*, vol. 45, no. 2, 2015, pp. 91–116.

Tebeau, Mark. "Listening to the City: Oral History and Place in the Digital Era." *The Oral History Review*, vol. 40, no. 1, 2013, pp. 25–35.

SOUTH TEXAS

William T. Burdette,
University of Texas–Austin

13. FROM BESPOKE TO BAROQUE: FOLDING AND UNFOLDING THE BURRITO IN SAN ANTONIO

Remembering the Alamo

As a child, I went with my grandparents to the Alamo in San Antonio. I had a memorable breakfast burrito (which has become my madeleine) at an interchangeable Tex-Mex place on the River Walk. My grandparents traveled a lot; their livelihood came from the airlines. Like his father, my father worked for the airlines. Over the years, we all settled in Texas, but I still feel unsettled, like a tourist. I have a complicated relationship with tourism. As Dean MacCannell writes, "The term 'tourist' is increasingly used as a derisive label for someone who seems content with his obviously inauthentic experiences" (592). On subsequent trips to San Antonio, I found the nontourist pose difficult to strike. Staying on or near the River Walk is enough to force anyone into touristic behaviors, such as eating whatever is available—though it may be contrived and mass produced—or walking farther from the hotel portal in search of an experience that is somehow more real.

Tourism is problematic, not just for people and cultures, but for whole ecosystems. Take, for example, the Alamo as a convergence of both tourism and colonialism that epitomizes the commoditization of memorialization, which tends to go along with capitalism. Vital to discussions of tourism, colonialism, commoditization, and memorialization is the A-word. *Authentic* has become a locus of attention in rhetorics of food and place. In this essay, I outline some examples of these discussions and read them against the Deleuzian folds that induce the baroque. I juxtapose this with a discussion of the relationship among "authenticity," burritos, and baroque architecture of tourist destinations such as San Antonio's missions. Finally, I lean toward a processual hospitality that involves many parties wrestling with authenticity simultaneously and over time.

The construction of authenticity is not only a rhetorical problem for tourists. It is part of our everyday lives. In "Joe's Rhetoric: Finding Authenticity at Starbucks," Greg Dickinson writes about authenticity in terms of everyday life. 153

We do not have to travel to a foreign land to experience authenticity tension; we can experience it over coffee or lunch. Writing about burritos in "An 'A' Word Production: Authentic Design," Douglas Walls says, "The word 'authentic' kind of drives me crazy." *Authentic* troubles Walls because of the way some attempt to construct authenticity with poor design. Walls continues, "Burritos plus pictures of banditos plus green white and red equals authentic burrito and the trope becomes invisible at a certain point." That is, after enough repetition in the same context, the word *authentic* is taken for granted, gets overused by corporate marketing, and takes on conflicting meanings. As it becomes over-determined, *authentic* can be applied to anything, even its opposite.

The frustration that some feel with the idea of authenticity likely stems from discomfort at the way phenomena are reconstructed in and through public memory. In *Distant Publics*, Jenny Rice writes about authenticity in Branson, Missouri, a place that is, like the Alamo, (re)constructed for, and popular among, tourists. Rice notes, "Nestled in the Ozarks, Branson is home to Old West theme parks, family-friendly music shows, and plenty of stores that feature authentic products like handmade soap and woodcarvings." The handmade soap is authentic to the "Old West," but the "Old West" is authentic to late twentieth-century Branson, not the American West of the late 1870s. In Rice's words, "As the Branson example shows, the horizon of memory may not even be real." Building on the work of Bradford Vivian, she points out that "public memory is not a perfect copy of authentic or original events. Public memory is not a vertical line that attaches its memorializers to the authentic point of origination." In other words, authenticity is produced by the same rhetorical tools that create memorials.

Vivian, in "Jefferson's Other," writes, "The ethos of authenticity plays a vital role in the production of public memory. . . . Rather than constituting the model on which all likenesses are based, authentic memory is the consummate artifice, the one whose ethos of authenticity is most convincing." And memory changes with each reiteration. "The connective tissue of remembrance is not an essence preserved, but memory's ephemeral and imperfect recollection of itself" (299). The tackiest tourist trap produces some amount of authenticity just by referencing the past, and the classiest, most staid memorial or lovingly restored building still constructs and reconstructs the conditions for an authentic experience for visitors. This work in rhetoric suggests that when it comes to authenticity, remembering the Alamo might be more complicated than initially thought.

Gazing into the Deleuzian Fold

Given the complications involved with memory and authenticity, it is helpful to weave a warp and woof that loosely bind ideas constituted by conflicting meanings. In *The Fold*, Gilles Deleuze explains how the idea of the fold imbues things with coherence even though they can be deconstructed. "A flexible or an elastic body still has cohering parts that form a fold, such that they are not separated into parts of parts but are rather divided to infinity in smaller and smaller folds that always retain a certain cohesion" (6). We can make things and take them apart, but we can never get them out of their contextual en-foldedness. Deleuze writes, "A fold is always folded within a fold, like a cavern in a cavern. The unit of matter, the smallest element of the labyrinth, is the fold, not the point which is never a part, but a simple extremity of the line" (6). As things crumble and decay, they are enfolded in new ways, as swirling folds of dust or colonies of organisms. When we unfold things, we are not eliminating folds, but rather finding other folds. "Unfolding is thus not the contrary of folding, but follows the fold up to the following fold. Particles are 'turned into folds,' that a 'contrary effort changes over and again'" (6). Out of the fold comes complexity.

The idea of the fold gives rise to the baroque, which refers not only to a moment in time, a style of architecture, or a kind of cooking, but also to a kind of activity. Baroque activity is sustained attunement to the contours of matter in a particular location over a period of time. It is not just human attunement, but the attunement of multiple cultures (in all senses of that word) that converge on and in the folds of the baroque. Deleuze writes, "Fold after fold: if the Baroque can be stretched beyond its precise historical limits, it appears to us that it is always by virtue of this criterion" (33). Deleuze articulates six qualities of the baroque: the fold, textures, the inside and the outside, the high and the low, the unfold, and the paradigm. Of the fold, he explains that "the Baroque invents the infinite work or process. The problem is not how to finish a fold, but how to continue it, to have it go through the ceiling, how to bring it to infinity" (34).

Baroque Burritos?

As we quest for "authenticity" in the traces of the baroque in San Antonio, we can look to these qualities—folds, textures, insides and outsides, highs and lows, unfolds, and paradigms—as focal points. Understanding the burrito's connection to the baroque requires some creative food history. Certainly there are important distinctions between seventeenth-century interior Mexican food and twentieth-century Tex-Mex. But we can say that the same forces that brought baroque architecture to the missions of San Antonio also brought the ingredients for the burrito. Is the Tex-Mex burrito baroque?

Probably not. But working in the realm of the Deleuzian baroque, which is "stretched beyond its precise historical limits," we can see a connection between the burrito and the baroque. It is possible to read the mother sauces of Tex-Mex—chili sauce, enchilada sauce, chili gravy, chili—as descendants of mole, which is baroque cuisine. On this, Tex-Mex cookbook author Robb Walsh and interior Mexican food promoter Diana Kennedy can agree. And mole was a kind of generic term at first. As Rachel Laudan writes in *Cuisine and Empire*, "Mole had multiple resonances in the Mexican kitchen. In the Aztec Nahuatl spoken by many servants, *molli* meant sauce. In Portuguese, *mollo* (pronounced something like "molio" in English) meant sauce.... *Moler* means to grind in Spanish, the crucial technique used in preparing these sauces." This is not to say that chili or enchilada sauce emerged from the same periods or places as mole in Mexico, but that they share a genealogy. Jeffrey Pilcher admits that mole's Tex-Mex cousin, chili, is a kind of distant relation when he calls William Gebhardt's 1896 development of mass market Eagle Chili Powder "a pale industrial copy of moles" ("'Montezuma's Revenge'"). There is no one mole, only moles. Walsh explains that "'mole' in Puebla isn't the same as 'mole' in Oaxaca, and in Mérida, there isn't any mole at all." What makes mole baroque is the way cultures are folded into it.

Laudan writes about the making of the national dish of Mexico:

> On 12 December 1926, the national newspaper Excelsior ran a story on how Sor Andrea de la Asunción had created mole poblano, the national dish, in the Dominican Santa Rosa convent in Puebla by combining European nuts, cloves, and pepper with Mexican chiles and chocolate.

Already we have a postrevolution Mexican newspaper retelling the sauce's backstory to highlight the blending of indigenous and Spanish influences going back to the late 1680s. Laudan notes, "Thus a dish that derived from Islam and was the high cuisine of Mexican-born Spaniards, sharply distinguished from the cuisine of the indigenous peoples, was reinterpreted as a result of the seamless mixing of races." If there is a noningredient component that makes mole "holy mole," it might be the mix. So if you sauce a burrito—whether with chili, enchilada sauce, or mole—you "baroquen" it with a concoction that would have been unthinkable before a mixing of cultures.

Searching for Authentic Food in the Tourist Trap

Even on a municipal level, one can use burritos to talk about real estate and borders. San Antonio has at least three zones of burritos. The regional and national chains such as Freebirds World Burrito and Chipotle Mexican Grill occupy the suburbs north of Midtown, churning out contemporary bespoke burritos customized by the customer. Less visible are the burritos served in mom-and-pop restaurants between the tourist traps along the River Walk and the exurbs that ring the city. Better burritos might be found there, but I am a tourist. My interest here is in the places closest to the Alamo that cluster along the River Walk and serve Tex-Mex-style wet burritos and breakfast burritos to tourists: Rita's on the River, Rio Rio, the Original, Barriba Cantina, and Guadalajara Grill. Some use the word *authentic*, but all of them textually construct a touristic tradition for their foods on menus and websites. The notion of the tourist trap provides a context in which to read those menus and websites.

In *The Lawless Roads*, Graham Greene coins the term "tourist trap," and food has been part of the trap from the beginning:

> At every station, the food-sellers came by, bearing the best food in Mexico —legs of hot fried chicken to be eaten in the fingers and tortillas wrapped round dark rich anonymous scraps of meat; and different stations had their different tourist traps—at Apizaco, hideous little painted clubs and walking-sticks, at Rinconada little grey stone mortars for pounding out corn. (88)

For Greene, the food is enticing, but the souvenirs—those most obvious of revenue units—are not. However, as foods and drinks increasingly become the revenue units, they take on qualities similar to souvenirs. This can be disenchanting. Tortillas or chips coming off a conveyor belt are like bric-a-brac stamped out of a mold. The architecture, even if original, is made to seem ersatz by the surrounding key chains and tchotchkes that replicate its forms. This is what Deleuze calls the "façade": "The façade-matter goes down below, while the soul-room goes up above." He writes, "The infinite fold then moves between the two levels. But by being divided, it greatly expands on either side: the fold is divided into folds, which are tucked inside and which spill onto the outside, thus connected as are the high and the low" (35). As with the Deleuzian fold, in the tourist trap, the high and low are connected through the movement that occurs in the search for authenticity.

Tourist destinations like those along San Antonio's River Walk are sites of what MacCannell calls "staged authenticity." MacCannell's notion of staged authenticity requires a front region and a back region that correspond to Deleuze's high and low. The front region, the façade, is where the performance happens. The back region, which is "closed to audiences and outsiders, allows concealment of props and activities that might discredit the performance out front" (590–91). "In other words," MacCannell notes, "sustaining a firm sense of social reality requires some mystification" (591). This mystification can go both ways. It can be used to trap and trick, but it can also be used to give people a more "authentic" experience. "Social reality that is sustained through mystification may be a 'false' reality as occurs in conning. Equally interesting is the case wherein mystification is required to create a sense of 'real' reality" (591).

Suspecting this, some tourists quest for authenticity. In her foreword to *Culinary Tourism*, Barbara Kirshenblatt-Gimblett states that "the question of authenticity" is central to tourism. Why, she wonders, "if we do not debate the authenticity of the toast and coffee of our daily breakfast, do we become anxious about the authenticity of an ethnic restaurant or gastronomic travel experience?" This anxiety, she concludes, comes from "our inability to experience the coalescence" of the familiar and the unfamiliar. What makes a quest a quest, however, is the transformative power of experience. The anxiety comes from the fact that we believe travel should be transformative. As Erik Cohen points out in "Authenticity and Commoditization in Tourism," there are many different types of tourists. Cohen's five tourist types range from existential tourists, who only want to get off the beaten track and consume the "other," to diversionary tourists, who never want to leave the resort. Some may be able to experience Kirshenblatt-Gimblett's coalescence of the familiar and unfamiliar, but others may not. Travel may transform tourists to varying degrees.

To Cohen's typology, we might add culinary tourists, who focus on authenticity as it relates to food, and this discussion almost always involves what is made and grows in the region. Scholars such as Jeff Rice (Detweiler) and Thomas Rickert have adopted the term *terroir* from oenophile and craft beer rhetorics to talk about the ways food moves through places and gets rooted in place. A culinary tourism perspective adds to this discussion by amplifying the human exploration of the place. In *Culinary Tourism*, Lucy Long situates "culinary tourism" as "the intentional, exploratory participation in the foodways of an other." As Jeffrey Pilcher writes in *Planet Taco*, culinary tourism has become an industry precisely to address authenticity issues related to food. "Culinary tourism, the intentional exploration of the foods of another group, has become a rapidly growing industry. The ideal of authenticity, of getting food prepared the way it is supposed to be, is central to the experience."

But authenticity is always rhetorically constructed. Whoever constructs the experience determines the labeling ("original," "authentic," "classic") or lack thereof. Robb Walsh explains in *The Tex-Mex Cookbook*, "There had never been any reason for the chili queens or the Tejano fondas on San Antonio's West Side to guarantee 'genuine Mexican food.'" According to Walsh, "After Anglos got into the business, it became mandatory. Texas-Mexican restaurants forever after promised authenticity and delivered whatever their audience actually wanted." Labeling Tex-Mex food "authentic Mexican" is now a tradition going back more than a century despite the presence of the burrito, which is, to some, out of place. Walsh says burritos are Cal-Mex, while the "embodiment of Tex-Mex is a cheese enchilada with gravy" (Drape).

Walsh writes in *The Tex-Mex Cookbook*, "Burritos are often categorized as

Tex-Mex by those who use the term to mean Americanized Mexican food. But while burritos have long been popular in Arizona and California, they weren't seen in Texas until very recently." Even if it is a recent transplant in historical terms, the burrito has a decades-long history on the River Walk. A quick tour of burritos on the menus of River Walk restaurants can help build a lexicon for the rhetoric of authenticity and identify the tension inherent in defining the original.

The most classic of the Tex-Mex burritos on the River Walk can be illustrated by Rita's on the River's El Burrito (fig. 13.1). The sauce and presentation are what distinguish the Tex-Mex-style burrito from the Mission-style burrito. El Burrito is served like an enchilada: on a plate, smothered with enchilada sauce, to be eaten with utensils, with a side of rice and beans. The restaurant's website states that "Rita's on the River is known by many as the place 'Where we take our friends from out of town.'" It is a place for tourists, highlighting "handmade tortillas," "colorful Tex-Mex flavors of San Antonio," and "many local dishes."

Rio Rio serves a breakfast burrito, notable for its size (three eggs) and its mix of ingredients from California cuisine (avocado) and Tex-Mex (American cheese). It uses the word *authentic*, saying, "When your agenda specifies authentic Mexican flavor in a bright festive atmosphere, Rio Rio handles it all in the most enthusiastic manner." Also on the menu are Signature Burritos, with beef or chicken fajitas, carnitas, barbacoa. If burritos authenticate the restaurant, they do so—as flour tortilla–wrapped foods always do—in the

Figure 13.1. El Burrito, classic tourist fare at Rita's on the River. It is served like an enchilada with enchilada sauce, but the flour tortilla makes it a burrito. That golden cheese makes it classic Tex-Mex. "El Burrito." *Rita's on the River*, 2015.

tradition of visitors to town. If the restaurant authenticates the burritos, it does so in a Derridean sense: "In order to function, that is, to be readable, a signature must have a repeatable, iterable, imitable form" (20). The flour tortilla—what, in part, differentiates a Tex-Mex burrito from an enchilada—is an instantiation of repetition, mechanized long before the corn tortilla.

The Original that opened in 1988 in San Antonio is not the Original that opened in 1900 in San Antonio, but the current Original was granted the rights to the name by the family of Chicagoan Otis M. Farnsworth, who opened the first Original in San Antonio. Farnsworth's first Original restaurant was also the first restaurant on the River Walk, according to Walsh in *The Tex-Mex Cookbook*, and all the other Originals were "copies of the original Original—the granddaddy of the genre." The current Original has a breakfast burrito on the menu alongside "3 buttermilk pancakes, served with butter, syrup, and 2 strips of bacon for $8.99." If one tends to think that pancakes are not traditionally served at authentic Mexican restaurants, consider that, according to Pilcher, Sanborns in Mexico City served them: "The chefs at Sanborns . . . greeted American travelers with familiar hotcakes and ice cream sodas in addition to a nonthreatening selection of Mexican cuisine, including their signature dish, enchiladas suizas" ("'Montezuma's Revenge'").

A Barriba Burrito at Barriba Cantina in San Antonio ("EST 1975," according to its menu) consists of ingredients from several locations and uses the word *traditional* several times. The cantina notes that its chips and tortillas are made with "a vintage tortilla maker brought to San Antonio from Mexico in the 1920s." According to its website, "A new spin on an old tradition awaits you at Barriba Cantina." The words *tradition*, *vintage*, *old world*, and *classic* are clearly part of the touristic lexicon.

Guadalajara Grill describes nothing about its Burrito Dinner but lists it not far from the Guadalajara Favorites section, which includes Chicken in Oaxacan Mole Sauce. Its website states, "After more than two decades our team continues to serve locals and tourists with attentive service, authentic, freshly prepared dishes." It also notes that in 2009, the "second floor of our historic building [was renovated] to create an elegant private dining room for weddings, parties and events." This was done as part of the effort to make "customers' dining experience special and memorable." *Memorable* is key here. Historic buildings with event spaces at places like Guadalajara Grill and Barriba Cantina can be understood as spaces where the ritual and historic are performed alongside mundane events. The missions are not all that different.

Authenticities in Ruins: Inside and Outside the "Baroquen" Window

We began at the Alamo, but for all its popularity, it is not a great example of the baroque, except in the way that it is enfolded in a system of missions.

Let us conclude by traveling away from the Alamo and its throngs of tourists in search of more authentic (re)constructions. South of the Alamo, we find the church at the Mission San José y San Miguel de Aguayo (fig. 13.2). The mission's façade and its Rose Window have been a locus of baroque attention for groups of sculptors, churchgoers, historians, and tourists since the new cornerstone was laid in 1768 (Quirarte 65). Deleuze writes, "The infinite fold separates or moves between matter and soul, the façade and the closed room, the outside and the inside . . . the outer façade of reception and inner rooms of action" (35). Arriving at this new harmony has been a long process. The baroque is a repeated gathering of people and things. Deleuze notes, "A Baroque line would move exactly according to the fold, and that would bring together architects, painters, musicians, poets, and philosophers" (34).

The Rose Window at the San José Mission is a striking example of baroque architecture that has served as a gathering point (fig. 13.3). What is striking about the Rose Window example is how the baroque is framed and reframed. The fence surrounding the window suggests that this has been a focal point, for some time, of what John Urry and Jonas Larsen have called "the tourist gaze." Some tourists have apparently done more than just gaze, as the fence implies. Bits have been broken off the baroque frame of the window. In many places on the façade, graffiti has been etched in the walls, adding another layer of scratches and swirls to the spot (figs. 13.2, 13.4).

Figure 13.2. Façade of the church at the Mission San José y San Miguel de Aguayo and detail of the restored left statue and niche. Photograph by Will Burdette, June 4, 2015.

The choice of material here is key. Limestone allowed for easy sculpting (Quirarte 73). In the ensuing years, this material encouraged "writers" with few skills and crude tools. "Known commonly as writing," Jenny Edbauer (Rice) notes in "(Meta)physical Graffiti," graffiti "exists within a particular cultural-historical scene" (137). The scene includes, among other things, the material that is written on, surveillance of the surface (another layer of baroque attention), and the exigency or call to write. Rice explains, "According

Figure 13.3. Rose Window at the mission. Photograph by Will Burdette, June 4, 2015.

Figure 13.4. Statue on the right side of the façade at the mission and detail of graffiti. Photograph by Will Burdette, June 4, 2015.

to some of our most familiar composition models, writing reacts to a call; it is an act of participation within a discourse community. We can certainly read the scene of graffiti through this rhetorical lens" (137). Diane Davis, building on Avital Ronell's take on Gustave Flaubert's letter quoted in Jonathan Culler's *Flaubert: The Uses of Uncertainty*, retells the story of Thompson, the bad tourist who carved his name in large letters into another monument and tourist attraction, Pompey's Pillar in Egypt. Davis meditates on the certitude of this act, calling it the "rhetoric of assertion" and contrasting it with a communitarian "rhetoric of exposition." "Rigorous inquiry leads one, again and again, precisely to the unsettling of certitude—and so to the continual exposition of what 'we' share" (141). Setting aside for a minute whether graffiti is good or bad, one thing we can say about it is that it is part of the baroque experience. The rhetorics of assertion are overlaid atop reverential flourishes. The marks may be cleaned and the façade restored, but other assertions are likely to mar it.

Graffiti is not even the most violent form of desecration at the mission site. The bodies of the statues of the front façade were shot up by visiting troops. "According to eyewitness accounts, some of the soldiers quartered at the mission from 1841 to 1850 used the church facade sculptures for target practice" (Quirarte 75). In a personal narrative, John Russell Bartlett wrote about the unfolding of the façade:

> The action of the weather has done much to destroy the figures; and the work of ruin has been assisted by the numerous military companies near here, who, finding in the hands and features of the statues convenient marks for rifle and pistol shots, did not fail to improve the opportunity for showing at the same time their skill in arms and their contempt for the Mexican belief.

Photographs from before 1890 show the façade in total disrepair, with missing heads, arms, and torsos of the statues nearest the hole where the front door once stood. In 1868, the north wall started to fall. By 1874, most of the wall was gone, along with the roof (Quirarte 81).

Lest we assume humans are the only actants on the structure, Bartlett reminds us that the weather, which brings together all manner of swirling, flowing, and blowing baroque forces, is also implicated in the deconstruction of the church. Deleuze writes, "Folds of winds, of waters, of fire and earth, and subterranean folds of veins of ore in a mine. In a system of complex interactions, the solid pleats of 'natural geography' refer to the effect first of fire, and then of waters and winds on the earth" (6). For Deleuze, the fold "is not only in clothing, but includes the body, rocks, waters, earth, and line" (34). Parts of the mission were unfolded by weather and time. Arms, torsos, robes, and the body of the baby Virgin Mary were re-created in the twentieth century to restore the building to its former glory. From 1933 to 1937, the portal to the church was partially restored. More of it was restored in 1949. Many restorations have been done over the almost 250 years that the church has been standing. It is a process of continual reconstruction. A wrought iron gate was added in 1935. The front door is from 1937. And we know all this because of the tons of sketches, paintings, lithographs, photographs, diaries, and books that chronicle the ever-changing state of the façade, a tradition in which this work participates. These traditions are financed by corporate entities and authenticated with other kinds of tags such as signatures and plaques (fig. 13.5). The Rose Window is baroque but also broken over time. As recently as December 2014, the Rose Window was again under repair (fig. 13.6). What we experience as authentic constructions are possible only if our understanding of authenticity involves processes as recently as today.

Figure 13.5. Exhibit acknowledgment, a plaque, and a woodcarver's inscription at the mission. Photograph by Will Burdette, June 4, 2015.

Figure 13.6. Inside of the Rose Window at the mission and a sign noting that it is under repair. Again. Photograph by Will Burdette, June 4, 2015.

Toward a Rhetoric of Processual Authenticity

Both Tex-Mex cuisine and the missions of San Antonio have complicated histories with rich nodes of activity during Spanish colonialism and again during the tourist colonization of the twentieth century. These are just two nodes in a baroque network of folds within folds and also unfolds. Most important for the purposes of theorizing a processual hospitality is the activation of the fold and the unfold. According to Deleuze, "When the fold ceases being represented in order to become a 'method,' a process, an act, the unfold becomes the result of the act that is expressed exactly in this fashion" (35–36). As we unfold, we could choose a different word or invent a new word to avoid stumbling into *authenticity*. But sidestepping that word because of its baggage is a missed opportunity. We can unhinge authenticity from origins and unhinge origins from narrative requirements. Rather than "Authentic or not?" the question now becomes "Authentic to whom and when?" Questions spin off from there.

In "Authenticity as a Concept in Tourism Research," Kjell Olsen writes of a "processual approach" to authenticity. Building on that, I want to gesture toward a processual hospitality that turns on the study of processes to regenerate authenticity. In this processual hospitality, the baroque would be understood as a kind of attention that imagines the reiteration of tourist spaces not as traps, but as historic-but-dynamic parts of authenti-cities where mutually beneficial cultural exchange takes place. Food is an indispensable part of that exchange. In a discussion of how ethnic foods can lead to positive cultural contact, food historian Jeffrey Pilcher finds it "heartening that in the United States, for example, Tex-Mex burritos and Vietnamese spring rolls have gained legitimacy, a form of cultural citizenship, just as in earlier times hot dogs and spaghetti helped win acceptance for German and Italian Americans" (*Food in World History*). Despite their problematic provenance, burritos have, for decades, been on authentic-yet-already-hybrid Tex-Mex menus along the River Walk, a stone's throw from the Ripley's Believe It or Not! Odditorium, just across from the Alamo. How we remember this scene is, in part, how we reiterate it.

Works Cited

Barriba Cantina, County Line Restaurants, www.barribacantina.com/food
    .html. Accessed 5 June 2015.

Bartlett, John Russell. *Personal Narrative of Explorations & Incidents in Texas,*
    New Mexico, California, Sonora, and Chihuahua: Connected with the United
    States and Mexican Boundary Commission, during the Years 1850, '51, '52,
    and '53. Google Play Book ed., D Appleton, 1854.

Cohen, Erik. "Authenticity and Commoditization in Tourism." *Annals of Tourism Research*, vol. 15, no. 3, 1988, pp. 371–86.

Davis, D. Diane. "Finitude's Clamor; or, Notes toward a Communitarian Literacy." *College Composition and Communication*, vol. 53, no. 1, 2001, pp. 119–45.

Deleuze, Gilles. *The Fold: Leibniz and the Baroque*. Athlone, 1993.

Derrida, Jacques. "Signature Event Context." *Limited Inc*, edited by Gerald Graff, translated by Jeffrey Mehlman and Samuel Weber, Northwestern UP, 1988, pp. 1–23.

Detweiler, Eric. Interview with Jeff Rice. *Zeugma*, Digital Writing and Research Lab, 14 July 2014, zeugma.dwrl.utexas.edu/episodes/interview-jeff-rice. Accessed 16 Dec. 2014.

Dickinson, Greg. "Joe's Rhetoric: Finding Authenticity at Starbucks." *Rhetoric Society Quarterly*, vol. 32, no. 4, 2002, pp. 5–27.

Drape, Joe. "A Celebration of Tex-Mex, without Apology." *The New York Times*, 24 Oct. 2007. www.nytimes.com/2007/10/24/dining/24texm.html?pagewanted =all&_r=1&. Accessed 5 June 2015.

Edbauer, Jennifer H. "(Meta)Physical Graffiti: 'Getting Up' as Affective Writing Model." *JAC*, vol. 25, no. 1, 2005, pp. 131–59.

"El Burrito." *Rita's on the River*, 2015, ritasontheriver.com/menu/el-burrito/. Accessed 5 June 2015.

Greene, Graham. *The Lawless Roads*. Penguin, 2006.

Guadalajara Grill, www.guadalajaragrill.us/menu. Accessed 5 June 2015.

Kennedy, Diana. Introduction. *The Essential Cuisines of Mexico*, by Kennedy, Random House, 2000, pp. xii–xv.

Kirshenblatt-Gimblett, Barbara. Foreword. Long.

Laudan, Rachel. *Cuisine and Empire: Cooking in World History*. Kindle ed., U of California P, 2013.

Long, Lucy M., editor. *Culinary Tourism*. Kindle ed., U of Kentucky P, 2010.

———. Introduction. Long.

MacCannell, Dean. "Staged Authenticity: Arrangements of Social Space in Tourist Settings." *American Journal of Sociology*, vol. 79, no. 3, 1973, pp. 589–603.

Olsen, Kjell. "Authenticity as a Concept in Tourism Research: The Social Organization of the Experience of Authenticity." *Tourist Studies*, vol. 2, no. 2, 2002, pp. 159–82.

The Original Mexican Restaurant and Bar, 2014, originalmexican.com/breakfast/. Accessed 5 June 2015.

Pilcher, Jeffrey M. *Food in World History*. Kindle ed., Routledge, 2006. Theme in World History.

———. "From 'Montezuma's Revenge' to 'Mexican Truffles': Culinary Tourism across the Rio Grande." Long.

———. *Planet Taco: A Global History of Mexican Food*. Kindle ed., Oxford UP, 2012.

Quirarte, Jacinto. *The Art and Architecture of the Texas Missions*. U of Texas P, 2002.

Rice, Jenny. *Distant Publics: Development Rhetoric and the Subject of Crisis*. Google Play Book ed., U of Pittsburgh P, 2012.

Rickert, Thomas. *Ambient Rhetoric: The Attunements of Rhetorical Being*. U of Pittsburgh P, 2013.

Rio Rio Cantina Fresh Tex-Mex, Paesanos Restaurant Group, 2013, riorioriver walk.com/menus/. Accessed 5 June 2015.

Urry, John, and Jonas Larsen. *The Tourist Gaze 3.0*. ePub ed., Sage, 2011.

Vivian, Bradford. "Jefferson's Other." *Quarterly Journal of Speech*, vol. 88, no. 3, 2002, pp. 284–302.

Walls, Douglas. "An 'A' Word Production: Authentic Design." *Kairos*, vol. 13, no. 1, 2008, kairos.technorhetoric.net/13.1/disputatio/walls/. Accessed 5 June 2015.

Walsh, Robb. *The Tex-Mex Cookbook: A History in Recipes and Photos*. Kindle ed., Ten Speed, 2004.

Victor J. Vitanza,
Clemson University

14. TEXAS WITHOUT TEXAS: THE SEPTIC TANK *WHERE HOUSTON* BECAME MODERN . . . IN *PARIS, TEXAS*

DEDICATION: *For the community without a community*
(Jean-Luc Nancy and Claire Denis)

How to re-begin without Notes (if not Knots) . . . of Thoughts . . .

"I cannot keep my subject still. It goes along befuddled and staggering, with a natural drunkenness. I take it in this condition, just as it is at the moment I give my attention to it. I do not portray being: I portray passing. . . . If my mind could gain a firm footing, I would not make essays, I would make decisions; but it is always in apprenticeship and on trial."—Michel de Montaigne, "Of Repentance," 610–11

"An 'acceptance' of the universe . . . may also be roundabout way of 'making peace with the faeces.'"—Kenneth Burke, *A Grammar of Motives*, 23

"Spontaneously, without any theological training, I, a child, grasped the incompatibility of God and shit and thus came to question the basic thesis of Christian anthropology, namely that man was created in God's image. Either/ or: either man was created in God's image—and has intestines!—or God lacks intestines and man is not like him."—Milan Kundera, *The Unbearable Lightness of Being*, 245 (see also 246–48)

"No good opera plot can be sensible, for people do not sing when they are feeling sensible."—W. H. Auden, "Notes on Music and Opera," 472

What is "it" (Id?) that motivates and qualifies me for peacemaking in place-making.[1] Or for displacing Texas in terms of myself? My families? My heritages? My genealogies? My understandings? My pleasures? Yes, my pleasures! Being all Sicilian! And yet, being a citizen of the world. Being Cosmopolitan. Which is to be, as Nietzsche suggests, *human, all so human*. My inference, therefore, is that I am motivated to perpetually rebegin with a focus on places (*topoi*, conceptual starting places, here, there, anywhere, everywhere). Perhaps I might add, *Stasis* and *Enstasis*. That is, in a State of being-born, or being-legitimized. In my case, being-born in Houston. St. Joseph's Hospital, downtown. Hence, my legal *Status*. As a Texan! Once upon a time, however, many Sicilians left mother Sicily, far left, for New York, California, and Texas. My Sicilian DNA—specifically, from Palermo and Corleone—is traced to TX and beyond.

However, thereafter, through an Event (*Ereignis*)—I cannot but tell you all—I encountered being-thrown into /\/\ a statelessness of *Exstatis,* not Ecstasy, yet a bit of the etymology of the word to form, given Martin Heidegger, Ecstasy. Or as many say, a trancelike state of mind. Thrown outside oneself. My cells. My selves. In a word, *syncopic*. A loss of time. A loss of proper language.

Avital Ronell has made much of this matter in *Crack Wars*. But I am, whoever I am along the way, going in various directions of statelessness. Creating a *trace* without end. I was born by wa*yves* of electricity.

The text reflexively asks: Vito, don't you think that the word *Texas* has a ring in it of TexASS? *Vito*: Possibly! Words resonate with words, like keys struck on a piano. TexASS? If you think so! "TexASS our TexASS, All hail the mighty state." Have you read Freud's discussion of the five stages? His psychosexual stage theory? Supposedly, KB did.

Okay, I will give you the originating anecdote: When I was three or five months old, I was crawling on the carpet—now, in my mind, a magic carpet— in my grandmother's house. My mother and my grandmother were taking turns arching their eyebrows. Then there was *the moment*: I discovered on the floor a bobby pin. I inserted it into a wall socket. I was shocked. Thrown. In darkness. Night terrors. Awaking, I saw my hand-arm all black. Covered with carbon soot. My Sicilian grandmother, Lillie, excited, made much of "the black hand." She said I was a sign, an electric sign. Today she would say a gram. *An emblem of wide scope.* For my grandmother, I was born for a major task to perform. She alluded to This Thing of Ours. My grandmother was without literacy, but with orality. She spun stories of *this Event*, unbeknownst, preparing me for a *trace*, for electracy. Our Thing. . . . To echo Augustine as well as Barthes, my black arm was *a puncture of recognition*. With *traces*.

Let's Start again and again: I *reely* don't know how many times I have attempted to write this script that desires to become a crypt. Becoming-Cryptic. One time, several times, I had to set this attempt aside and return to the seedplot of my thinking: Dominique Laporte's *Histoire de la merde*.

The genre of the essay here will become a *screenplay* mixed with an attempt, a trial (*essayer*). At times, the essay will be taken over by text itself (language reflexivity), saying what desires to be said. No one is to edit it or to become addicted to it, for it is *as it is not*. I, Vito, will *place* my thoughts in the *filmic* (in a lure). As for what sense it might communicate, I would say, or plan, to *reelize* Barthes's third meaning (*sens*): "obtuse" (55; see also Burgin 25–26). I will have written in a montage throughout the scripts as Michel de Montaigne would have accomplished if he had been brought into the world of Houston, Texas, rather than Guyenne, France. We have our special credentials. *Come si dice in famiglia, noi siamo cittadini del mondo. Ci sono da Siclily e, quindi, siamo cosmopoliti.* And yet there are other resources in the good book/s.

Vito's ex-stasis for reinventing my, at times his, credentials: Further testaments: Joyce's *Finnegans Wake*: Yes. You will discover/find a reference to my name: **"Victa Nyanza"** (558) . . .

Recall: my name, Victor (Conqueror) + Vita (Life) + Anza or Inza (Against). In translation: *Conqueror of Death*! Also, the *Nyanza* of the *Wake* is No (definitive) Answer to any question. But keeping the question open for all impossible possibilities. . . .

After all has been said and undone, "I am a son of Michel de *montaggio*."

Who said that? Who said that?

There's more: In Mircea Eliade's novella *Youth without Youth*, Eliade makes clear that the hero of the novel is "destined to fame" (117), for his name is found, like mine, in *Finnegans Wake*.

I refer now to Francis Ford Coppola's film with the same title as the novella, and with the potential for scripts that are time-traveling events. Cousin Francis released the film as a gift to me just a few days before my annual birthday, December 14, 2007 (USA).

The Text "it"self Interrupts Vito: Are you not being Silly!!! Now?
Vito responds: Trust your ear of the other: I am (a) *Siciliana*!
The Text: You are referring to the genre in music?
Vito: Of course! And more. All *wayves* more.

Here, a plot summary of Eliade's/Coppola's novella/film: "In Romania in the late 1930s, Dominic (Tim Roth) is an old man who has sacrificed everything—including the love of his life, Laura (Alexandra Maria Lara)—in his study of the origin of language. He is planning his suicide when a bolt of lightning reduces his age and magnifies his brain power."

Now you ask, what does this have to do with Re-thinking/re-placing Texas, etc.? . . . My **nyanza**: Nothing. To stand on Nothing. That is, Nothing exists. Hints, all exists. I, of course, take this mis-reading from my *paisan* Gorgias.

The text interrupts Vito (who is not veto) and tells the readers: After this preface of unfoundedness (i.e., of the Event, *Ereignis*), Vito will sketch out the toc-with-tics, more-and-more tics, for the writings. Here are the sections that will include images, B/W. Including a pic of Vito's aunt Mary's having fallen into a septic tank, as well as other pix of Vito's growing and suffering-learning, and of his family leaving for the city limits. Understand: The great shift in our filmic *reel*ality occurs when the value of the *septic tank* becomes a *skeptic tank*. With Montaigne, Vito shares a "scar" and a healthy relationship with language (see Hallie).

This making of the film will be performed, anachronistically, in a set of filmic, syncopated, obtuse scenes—as the above might suggest to a reader of Roland Barthes's notion of *a third sense*. These scenes will vary once the St. Vitus Pictures production crew begins to produce the film.[2] Here is a list of titles, a throw of the dice, for each section of the film and its screenplay. Or, rather, "film stills." From Houston, TX, yet to *Paris, TX.* . . . Which is a mere photograph! In reading/thinking stay in (yet out of) tune.

After this series of anecdotes-cum-antidotes, Vito will now especially further open the inventional antidotes expressed above, that he called upon in a dialogue several years ago at the European Graduate School (Saas-Fee, Switzerland) in discussions with Claire Denis (assistant director of Wim Wender's film *Paris, Texas* [1984], as well as *Wings of Desire* [1987]). Claire of course has many wonderful films of her own (see Wenders, Foreword).

Reading (shooting) Scripts: Notes toward *The Septic Tank Where Houston Became Modern.*

Fold: Darkness of the outskirts city of light

1. Opening (at least 3 minutes): Black screen. Sound of a lawn mower. And then, a minute later, another lawn mower. Back and forth. As if in a conversation.

2. Cut: Primordial Setting: A voice-over (as if the pagan gods' voices): "Seven days after the bombing of Pearl Harbor (December 7, 1941), the young Vito Vitanza celebrated his *first birthday* with his extended family (December 17, 1941). Through the years and places, Vito, from time to times, looks carefully at the faces of his parents, of his grandmother Mary, of his cousins. All in a set of photographs. He has yet, over the years, to see any anxiety in their dispositions. None.

[insert a photo of Dad and Mom holding me up]

3. Cut: Setting: A voice-over (a man's voice): With the so-called end of WW II, Vito's parents left Harrisburg, Texas, which was and remains in Houston, Texas. With the beginning of the war, Vito's parents had moved into a duplex that was established on a huge beautiful boulevard. Vito's dad, an electrician, was drafted to work on battleships, wiring them.

4. Cut: Vito's mom to his dad: "You bought . . . What! Where!"

5. Cut: Black screen. *A voice-over:* After the war, they moved *outside the city limits,* where there was no electricity, no water, or other public services. A new war had begun.

6. Cut: Vito's dad to his mom: "I bought a small grocery store on Golf Drive, outside city limits. Near a train track. You know . . . *the other side of the tracks* is Garden Oaks."

7. Cut: Mom to Dad: "No, I didn't and don't want to know!"

8. Cut: Dad: "The house and store are separate from each other. The house is not as large as you might want. (Pause with hesitations.) There is a porch, two rooms, and a lean-to where the kitchen will be."

9. Cut: Vito's mom screams out: "And when will that be!"

10. Cut: A disconcerting face. For Vito.

11. Cut: Black screen: A voice-over: The interaction between parents becomes—not that you or I can know—*an opera*. Virtually a Sicilian opera, moving from a *Burletta* to a *Farsa*. It must be understood, however, that transalpine people often think that a Sicilian (okay, perhaps also an Italian) speaks loudly and with a full body statement and, therefore, is *angry*. Nothing could be further from the truth of the matter. Transalpine people confuse PASSION with anger.

12. Cut: voice-over: Delivered as by mechanical reproductions: "Oh, yes, the question is where to place this remembrance lost so as not to remain lost forever." Vito remembers his dad saying: "Do not forget Sacco and Vanzetti."

Fold: Enchanted wrong side of the tracks

13. Cut: The times lost: The camcorder is broken for the day. The camera, however, steps in and fosters the rhythms. Photographs. Syncopated. Flowing. Cameras, like camcorders, love all things that flow. The remembrances of the times lost often hide themselves in photographers' images. Or in Freud's "Screen Memories." In the obtuse angles of the twisted photographs. We will think of a photograph of Paris, Texas, eventually.

[**Note to the photographer**: The Test Drive, below, is to determine whether the photographs help recall and support, one on one, the memories of times lost or found anew. Or Destroyed. For the child. (See also Agamben.)]

[*Again,* **Note to the photographer**: Given the differences between Vito's mom/ dad and dad/mom, let us now study what Vito has dealt to us to play with.]:

At last: A voice-over Narration spoken in a calm voice /tone: The child pretends or the child becomes . . . a hero. He has read the comics. With his dad. But perhaps more and more of what might become strange is necessary. The child does not know. In this case, he tries to entertain . . . perhaps tame . . . parents. Sentimentality, however, may not, if ever, be enough to continue with the St. Ranger. Of the situation. With his loving pet to play with.[3]

Narration: Let us recognize: *The Lone Ranger*, in comic books, but more so after being shot and cut, making a film, is never enough. Let us call on his partner.

Tonto? Okay, it's not the case— Tonto is simply old school just, or unjust so, as the Lone Ranger itself has repeatedly become a mere myth at best. And further revised recently.[4] Anyway, Tonto, supposedly, was not that nice when he refers to the masked man as "kemo sabe." But then, who knows and who else is available? Our hero? Respelling a word to recognize or call on another for help is doubtful. So let's bring in the modern stick-them-up character:

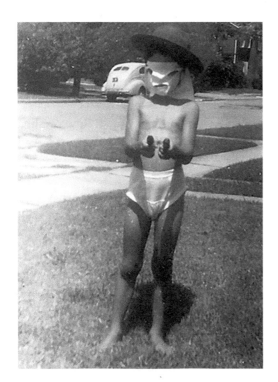

14. Cut: A voice asks: Vito, does this work? Your thoughts? ... No! ... No! ... No! Forget Sacco and Vanzetti! ... *impossibile!*

Fold: City Limits Open

15. Cut: voice-over, this time, as if the Voice of God: When Vito was about four years old, his dad dug a big, wide hole in the ground and put in a tank, what he called SEPTIC tank. Vito's dad and he are hunched down and looking into the tank:

Vito: "Dad, what is that stuff in there floating around?"

Dad: "Victor, that's *shit*!"

Mom: "No, no, no! Do not use that word around our son! Do you understand!"

16. Cut: voice-over: Vito's mom had Father Phillip, from St. Rose of Lima Church, bless their tank. He blessed it with Holy Water. Enough said. And then, the cover was placed over the tank and sealed.

17. Cut: voice-over: A month or so later, Vito's mom and dad heard that Aunt Mary had fallen in her family's septic tank. Vito's aunt and her family had dug a deep and wide hole like his dad did. The extra problem with this fall: Vito's aunt was a little over 350 pounds. While her family called for help to lift her out, one of the kids took her picture.

[The image should be floating in various directions, turning here and turning there, while the voice-over speaks the above.]

While the image is floating and the voice-over, above, is slowly being spoken: Vito remembers—silently, for himself—his aunt Mary . . .

The Text: Wait a minute, Vito! You are writing this as a screenplay and so who will hear it? See it? In the film?

Vito: . . . remembers—silently, for himself—his aunt Mary, who traditionally created *a table* for *St. Joseph's Day*. It was a feast once a year (March 19). Simply put: it's a feast. Vito's aunt would invite select children in the extended family as well as kids in the neighborhood to sit at the dining table and to sample the foods (including wines), everything on the St. Joseph table. Again:

One sample at a time. Favorites for the kids or not. The kids must clean their plates. Oh, the red Sicilian wines were added to a glass of Coke. To dilute the wines. The motto in the Vitanza Family, among grandmothers, was (still is) "Red wines make for strong blood."

Vito: . . . remembers his aunt inviting him to be Baby Jesus. Vito was four years old. He sat at the front of the dining table. He recalls a large vase filled with water and with four stalks of celery, with their leaves turned upside down into the water. When all was ready, the priest blessed the water after having blessed everything on the St. Joseph's table.

Vito: . . . recalls having been helped by his aunt to take the stalks in both hands and to shake the stalks-leaves with holy water on everyone at the table. In this act he had blessed the other children at the table.

Fold: City of crawling and darkness: Limited City that further transformed Vito's life

18. Cut: voice-over for transition (Gray, early morning, raining puddles, Mom is gone with Iola, her friend during the War):

Vito (in the family store, at a window): "Dad can I go outside? My friends are jumping up and down in the rain."

Dad: "Yes."

Vito (Leaves the store and joins all the kids, outside, wading through the ditches, screaming and laughing): "Look at me. I'm jumping up and down in this water as it splashes and carries all kinds of floating objects. This water is getting in my face and head. My eyes are burning!"

19. Cut: It's been about 45 minutes since Vito and friends stopped playing in the ditches. Vito returns to the store):

Vito: "I'm really dizzy. Can I have a Coke?"

20. Cut: voice-over, black screen: Vito's mother and Iola return home. They give Vito three aspirins. Vito becomes terribly sick. Finally, two days later, Vito's mother takes him to a doctor in town, Houston. The doctor tells Vito's mother to take him to Jefferson Davis Hospital. Vito is admitted. He is in a ward with three other boys, all orphans and thus from the orphanage.

21. Cut, a day later: Four nurses and a doctor come in, turn Vito over, and with a brush they paint his spine with a brown substance. The doctor, then, cuts (taps) into Vito's spine for spinal fluid.

22. Cut, another day passes: Vito has polio (bacterial meningitis), nonparalytic polio.

23. Cut: At nights, when others were a sleep, a young black woman, a nurse, visits Vito. She pretends to be a wild horse and carries Vito on her back, all up and down the hallway. He pretends to be the Lone Ranger. She is a godsend.

The Text: The time spent day to day seemed empty except for special attention given to Vito. He was fed each morning with an IV in an arm to nourish and medicate him.

24. Cut, three weeks later: Vito leaves the hospital. Now at home, Vito's mother wraps his arms and legs with "hot packs." (The treatment: slices of rubber sheets and wool sheets prepared in boiling hot water and in layers placed on arms and legs.) For weeks and weeks. Finally, he improves his walk and his body in general. People in the neighborhood begin to return to Vito's family grocery store. Finally, Vito returns to being the kid who wants to accommodate everyone.

But then again, Ronnie, one of the kids across the dirt road, comes down with polio.

Shortly after, Vito's mom has Vito take Jonas Salk's sugar cube with the vaccine. Just in case.

Fold: Capitale de la Commode

25. Cut: There is progress, or steps in making progress:

Vito: "Dad, we have had a septic tank now for a year or so. And we have electricity now. When are you going to give us a commode? The outhouse with the seat that opens up a view of the maggots eating our droppings is too much for me now."

Dad: "Soon, Vito. First we have to dig for—I mean drill for—water and then purchase a pump so that we can have water in the house. And then a commode. But also your mom can wash the dishes as well in a sink. But we will continue to use the galvanized tub for bathing. Your mom can boil the water hot and pour it in the tub. Then we can take a bath from time to time."

Vito: "Dad, where are you going to put the kitchen in our house and then a commode?"

Dad: "I will rebuild the lean-to and *on one side* put in a sink, with running water, and a place for an oven and on *the other side* put in a commode, linking it with the septic tank. I will put up a shower curtain to separate the kitchen, cooking, from the commode, pooping."

Vito: "Dad, what are you going to do with the old outhouse?" . . .

Fold: City Limits of poverty—City of dreams . . . Nightmares . . .

26. Cut: The times to forget: voice-over: On improper proper occasions, later in his lives, Vito expresses how he experienced "poverty." He knew, however, that he had no understanding of the word or of poverty itself. The kids on the other side of the train tracks who were his playmates spoke of poverty. Like later mates who spoke of it. . . . And then later there was Sister Patrice, who spoke of Diogenes of Sinope.

27. Cut: Vito's dad rented the grocery store and the house . . . Hallelujah!

28. Cut: The family—not able to fully liberate themselves to the other, better side of the tracks—moves adjacent to the railway tracks: When the trains pass, the three rooms, built above a two-car garage, shake, tremble. The trains scream. At first, Vito is troubled by the trains. So close, so threatening. After a while, however, Vito walks, trying to balance himself, on the train tracks. For Vito, living is a joy. An adventure.

29. Cut: Vito starts school, Houston ISD: public, first grade, Cooley School. Later, Catholic, third grade, St. Rose of Lima. . . . Time passes. Vito could not quite understand what is expected of him in terms of the alphabet and counting: 1, 2, 3; A, B, C. . . . Vito has chicken pox, measles, mumps, etc. . . . Sister Rosario quotes Benjamin Franklin: "Lost time is never found again." Vito differs with Ben by thinking that *time flushed eternally returns*. But Vito keeps this thought to himself.

30. Cuts: Vito's initiations: First confession. First communion. First confirmation. First gun. First tornado. First kiss. And unexpectedly, Vito's first

sequential nightmares: Waking up screaming: "Something terrible is going to happen. The Blessed Virgin Mary told me so!" Vito's mom speaks with Sister Rosario.

Sister Rosario: "Victor, your mom tells me you are having nightmares. About our Blessed Virgin Mary. Victor, are you afraid of God?"

Vito: "I don't think so. But then, sometimes, I guess I do. Tell me, Sister, what should I feel?"

Sister Rosario: "Okay, Victor. I want you to leave the room, take a recess, a time off, when we have Catechism class. Just for a few days, okay?"

Fold: Re-placemaking of the City Limits: Filming and Mapping the transformation of Houston City Limits . . .

31. Cut: voice-over: In time, Vito's mom studied with Ms. David, a survivor of the Holocaust, to become an electrologist, one who removes for women unwanted hair.

32. Cut: voice-over: Unwanted.

33. Cuts: voice-over: In time everything breaks up. . . . Tic-Toc, Tic-Toc, Tic-Toc. Etc. Vito thinks the trick is to discover the reversible of time: Toc to Tic, jumping across nothing. And yet, eventually Toc without, only with: Toc /\/\ Toc /\/\ Toc /\/\ and the beat goes on and on. Syncope. Syncopation. . . . Elimination. . . . EXcreation. . . .

Fold: In—*Paris, Texas* (1984)

34. Cut: Takes from the film, not the city a.k.a. Paris, TX, but the film. Itself. Takes from the film's various versions of visualizations.

35. Cut: Vito's voice-over: "We have arrived, so to speak. Well, not to speak as Travis does. About this film of films. Keep in mind that I viewed the film when it first appeared. Certainly I remain moved with the film. But it was not until I had a chance to discuss the film further with *Claire Denis*—not to reminisce about the discussion here—that I began *to live* in the film. Then I was moved, on the move. Movies. First: some simple facts that bear repeating: The primary one being the film was never shot in Paris, Texas, at all."

The film is not about Paris, Texas. Rather, it's about Travis's *photograph.*

The opening scenes of the film focus on Travis walking across the desert, later walking on the train tracks, and then walking next to the power lines—all, perhaps, are attempts to follow the signs of the modes of communication. Without language. The script says of Travis: "Language is useless to Travis." The power of the film, which is a given, is that Travis for miles and minutes in motion never speaks. Travis loses consciousness. The doctor who finds and helps Travis calls Travis's brother, Walt, who lives in LA, California. Walt flies to Texas and finds Travis. When Travis hears Walt referring to his son's name, Hunter, Travis begins to cry. The first word Travis speaks to his brother, Walt, is "Paris." There's of course confusion with Paris, France.

Finally, Travis shows Walt a Polaroid of a vacant lot. "Travis stares at the photo and then tries to locate 'Paris' [TX] on the map again. Walt is watching him the whole time through the rear view mirror." Pages of the script, and of the filmic conversation, are immense. The photograph:

"A plot of land in Paris, Texas. As the viewers are told, Travis believes that his mom and dad conceived him on this stretch of land. Travis buys the land. Perhaps in an attempt to legitimize the land. But it remains a photograph of a place never visited in the film, nor apparently visited by Travis. This photograph, however, is useful to Travis."

36. Cut: Travis, after finding Walt and Hunter, finds Jane: Walt tells Travis that a woman deposits a check every month for Hunter in a Houston bank account. Hunter and Travis find Jane, making a drive-by deposit at the bank. (Travis has found his child, now his wife.) A day later, Travis follows her to the striptease place where she works. It's a striptease place with peepholes that are one-way mirrors. With a telephone that allows the client to speak with the stripper. While the client can look in, the stripper cannot look out. (Vito thinks: Is this arrangement not a confession box?) The second time around visiting Jane, Travis confesses to Jane his deep-rooted jealousy and his attempt to control her. And how he began to hate himself. And why he left her. Minutes later, Travis turns the one-sided mirrors so that Jane can see him. Face-to-face. An exceptionally emotional moment! Jane wants Travis to stay with her and Hunter. But Travis retreats once again to depart for a place "without language or streets."[5]

37. Cut: Years ago, during a summertime on the calendar, I read / studied / stuttered Immanuel Kant's three critiques (Pure reason, Practical reason, Judgment, Aesthetics, and then, the mathematical sublime, the uncountable or unaccountable). While Kant is rolling out these three attempts, the third (turd) backs up, like a septic tank backing up, in the house of Kant. The SUBLIME, the uncountable, *one, two, some more.* Backs up into the so-called pure and practical (see also Deleuze 46–67). Hence, the metaphysics of shit.

Fold: In Again—Yet another Reopening of the Cinema

38. Cut: The recognition of affirmation of all. A Prayer is put forth:

Let us pray:

"'I love everything that flows,' said the great blind Milton of our times [J. Joyce] . . . Yes, I said to myself, I too love everything that flows: rivers, sewers, lava, semen, blood, bile, words, sentences. I love the amniotic fluid when it spills out of the bag. I love the kidney with its painful gall-stones, its gravel and what-not; I love the urine that pours out scalding and the clap that runs endlessly; I love the words of hysterics and the sentences that flow on like dysentery and mirror all the sick images of the soul. . . . I love everything that flows, even the menstrual flow that carries away the seed unfecund. I love scripts that flow, be they hieratic, esoteric, perverse, polymorph, or unilateral. . . . I love everything that flows . . . the violence of the prophets, the obscenity that is ecstasy, the wisdom of the fanatic, the priest with his rubber litany, the foul words of the whore, the spittle that floats away in the gutter, the milk of the breast and the bitter honey that pours from the womb, all that is fluid, melting, dissolute and dissolvent, all the pus and dirt that in flowing is purified, that loses its sense of origin, that makes the great circuit toward death and dissolution" (Miller 257–58).

Notes

1. Placemaking (all one word) is a movement to think about public and pubic places. See www.pps.org/reference/what_is_placemaking/.

2. St. Vitus Pictures is a nonprofit (status) film production company that Vito established 2013.

3. It happens! A couple who bought groceries from my parents told my mom that Duke had been run over by a car a few blocks from the store.

4. The most recent Disney filmic version of *The Lone Ranger* (Johnny Depp and Armie Hammer) presents the impossibility of any hope for a child as well as an adult. However, Alexie's book might lighten the severity of impossibility for all of us.

5. See the plot summary for *Paris, Texas* at *Wikipedia*, last modified 7 Sept. 2017, http://en.wikipedia.org/wiki/Paris,_Texas_%28film%29#Plot. There is the possibility of hope for a child and an adult (in this case, a mother in presence; and not yet, a father).

Works Cited and Consulted

Agamben, Giorgio. *Infancy and History: Essays on the Destruction of Experience*. Translated by Liz Heron. Verso. 1993.

Alexie, Sherman. *The Lone Ranger and Tonto Fistfight in Heaven*. Grove Press, 2005.

Auden, W. H. "Notes on Music and Opera." *The Dyer's Hand and Other Essays*, edited by Auden, Random House, 1968, pp. 465–74.

Barthes, Roland. "The Third Meaning: Research Notes on Some Eisenstein Stills." *Image-Music-Text*, selected and translated by Stephen Heath, Hill and Wang, 1977, pp. 52–68.

Burgin, Victor. "Barthes's Discretion." *Writing the Image after Roland Barthes*, edited by Jean-Michel Rabaté, U of Pennsylvania P, 1997, pp. 19–31.

Burke, Kenneth. *A Grammar of Motives*. U of California P, 1969.

Coppola, Francis Ford, director. *Youth without Youth*. American Zoetrope, Sony Pictures Classics, 2007.

Deleuze, Gilles. *Kant's Critical Philosophy*. Translated by Hugh Tomlinson and Barbara Habberjam. U of Minnesota P, 1984.

Eliade, Mircea. *Youth without Youth*. Translated by Mac Linscott Ricketts. U of Chicago P, 2007.

Freud, Sigmund. "Screen Memories." *Standard Edition of the Complete Psychological Works of Sigmund Freud*, vol. 3, Hogarth Press, 1962, pp. 301–22.

———. "Three Essays on the Theory of Sexuality." *Standard Edition of the Complete Psychological Works of Sigmund Freud*, vol. 7, Hogarth Press, 1953, pp. 135–243.

Hallie, Philip P. *The Scar of Montaigne: An Essay in Personal Philosophy*. Wesleyan UP, 1966.

Harris, Aisha. "What Do You Mean 'Kemosabe,' Kemosabe?" *Slate*, 26 June 2013, www.slate.com/blogs/browbeat/2013/06/26/kemosabe_meaning_origin _and_history_of_tonto_s_word_in_lone_ranger.html. Accessed 3 Oct. 2017.

Joyce, James. *Finnegans Wake*. Penguin Books, 1976.

Kundera, Milan. *The Unbearable Lightness of Being*. Translated by Michael Henry Heim. Harper and Row, 1987.

Laporte, Dominique. *History of Shit*. Translated by Nadia Benabid and Rodolphe el-Khoury. MIT P, 2000.

Miller, Henry. *Tropic of Cancer*. Grove Weidenfeld, 1961.

Montaigne, Michel de. "Of Repentance." *The Complete Essays of Montaigne*, translated by Donald M. Frame, Stanford UP, 1976, 610–20.

Nietzsche, Friedrich. *Human, All Too Human*. Translated by R. J. Hollingdale. Cambridge UP, 1996.

Ronell, Avital. *Crack Wars: Literature, Addiction, Mania*. U of Nebraska P, 1992.

Verbinski, Gore, director. *The Lone Ranger*. Produced by Jerry Bruckheimer. Walt Disney Pictures, 2013.

Wenders, Wim. Foreword. *The Films of Claire Denis: Intimacy on the Border*, edited by Marjorie Vecchio, I. B. Tauris, 2014, xix–xxiii.

———, director. *Paris, Texas*. Tobis and Argos, 1984.

Wooten, Heather Green. *The Polio Years in Texas: Battling a Terrifying Unknown*. A&M UP, 2009.

Jennifer D. Carlson,
Rice University

15. EAGLEVILLE

"*They* call it Eagleville." It was 2010 and my father had called to say that a seismic scan had revealed oil nine thousand feet beneath the rusted Airstream trailer where my grandparents used to spend the winter holidays. Within a year, he had agreed to lease our land in a "package" with several adjacent tracts, which together would be leased out to the highest-bidding oil company, drilled, and fracked. In environmental studies, hydraulic fracturing, or fracking, was already a hotly debated issue; Josh Fox's *Gasland* was making its way around the country, and the Sierra Club had begun to back down from its initial support of the technology. But fracking was news to many in the counties at the heart of South Texas's Brush Country, which has since been transformed into the most productive oilfield in the most fossil-fuel-producing nation in the world (EIA 2015). Hydraulic fracturing and horizontal drilling have opened up vast reservoirs of oil and gas trapped in shale deposits from the Late Cretaceous period, when much of the American Midwest was covered in marine waters. The Eagle Ford Shale formation spans over four hundred miles from the Texas-Mexico border east toward Louisiana and north into the Dallas–Fort Worth metroplex, sloping upward to where its outcroppings were first spotted near the erstwhile town of Eagle Ford (Railroad Commission). Most drilling in the play takes place in South Texas's Brush Country, where Petrohawk Energy Corporation drilled the first frac well in La Salle County in 2008.

This essay offers an ethnographic perspective on the Eagle Ford Shale's unfolding, aimed at bringing some of its singular aspects into greater relief among a growing literature on unconventional oil, its social repercussions, and its environmental impact. The Eagle Ford Shale has been frequently cited in news coverage for its surplus of hydrocarbons, but its social and physical terrain is less popularly known than other areas transformed through fracking, such as the Bakken Shale communities of the Smithsonian Channel's *Boomtowners* or the areas of Pennsylvania, Colorado, Wyoming, and North Texas featured in Josh Fox's *Gasland* films. Energy humanities scholars have explored cultural dynamics in areas such as the Barnett and Marcellus Shale plays in North Texas and Pennsylvania, respectively, as well as the dizzying transformations taking place across the Bakken Shale, particularly in North Dakota. The Eagle Ford Shale has yet to be so studied, perhaps because the Brush Country is so sparsely populated, and protest against shale oil and gas drilling has been negligible in comparison to popular outcry elsewhere.

In what follows, the study of a place (or, as framed below, a "taking-place") absent in existing narratives opens up new perspectives in the cultural study of oil and gas exploration, as well as new views on Texas. Grounded in my own history with the Brush Country, the work also enfolds personal experience into the mapping of place. Drawing on things that "really happened," I write the shale play as a virtual object and, in so doing, offer new views to its actual unfolding. This work is productively haunted by unfixed but forceful fantasies of selfhood and time, as people in the shale play "sense out" (Carlson and Stewart 114) their personal possibilities in a changing landscape.

Placing the Eagle Ford Shale

Eagleville is amorphous, its location shifting according to the technologies through which it is sensed out. The shale play is inextricably connected to the geographic terrain of South Texas at the same time that it exceeds that physical space, composed of vectors of bodies, information and capital that move beyond those sites where land is leased and wells are drilled. The shifting flows of the play include familiar elements of petrochemical colonization—oil workers and freight drivers; rigs, pipelines, and water wells; power lines and digital infrastructure; capital manifested in bank transfers, freshly inked paychecks, money orders, new cars, and other markers of sudden wealth among landowners and roughnecks alike. But the play is also composed of things with little obvious connection to the oil industry, such as the more-than-human social infrastructures that existed prior to the fracking boom: the communities of "critters" (Haraway 5) glimpsed in abandoned owls' nests, sloughed-off snakeskins, or coyote and javelina tracks; the patronage networks linking overlapping groups of landowners, ranchers, workers, truckers and cattle, shifting according to who owns the land where and who's always run cows on it; the three-table restaurant where people have been eating lunch for years when they come in from working the cattle pens; the trails that Central Americans have used to cross into Texas from the Mexican states of Coahuila and Nuevo León; the movements of human coyotes, Latino immigrants (some of whom now use the pipelines as paths to avoid detection), and the Border Patrol. The region's transformation continues, bringing with it a dizzying array of sensations, concerns, and capital promises in communities sparsely populated but densely fabulated by those who live there. Eagleville's composition is ongoing, worlded through the movements of an ever-changing multiplicity.

How, then, might an ethnographer study the place that is the Eagle Ford Shale? Geographer Doreen Massey has suggested that scholars approach places as "moments in networks of social relations and understandings, . . . where a larger proportion of those relations, experiences and understandings are constructed on a far larger scale than what we happen to define as the place itself" (Massey 154). Later work in cultural geography considers place not only as a site, but as an event—a "taking-place" (Anderson and Harrison) that is ontologically "multiple" (Hinchcliffe), continually composed by distinct yet overlapping and interpenetrating social assemblages. Place is not only compositional but also contingently known through "experience and experiment" (McCormack, "Thinking in Transition"; see also Carlson and Stewart 114).

Additionally, by framing place as an affective composition, it is possible to gain a sense of how places become public—or, in other words, how places become matters of concern for a given population. Anthropological scholarship on senses and placemaking—particularly the work of Kathleen Stewart—explores place as the piling up of affective experience, indexed by discourse but always exceeding representation. This piling up of experience constitutes a politics apart from liberal expectations as to how public participation might look, sound, and feel. In rhetoric, similarly, Jenny Rice draws on the nexus of sentiment, discourse, and place to theorize how affectively charged discourse practices inform the kinds of political actions that people take (or not) in regard to place (*Distant Publics*). These texts move the question of how to conceive of politics in spaces such as Brush Country, where overt protest against fracking has been negligible while ambivalence about it abounds.

Here I write through some of the quotidian ways people on the Eagle Ford Shale—particularly those who made their lives here before the boom began—sense out this emerging place and the possibilities for acting in it. Repurposing the name of the oilfield, "Eagleville" is the taking-place that occurs as people live out fossil fuel development in South Texas and mark space and time by its promises. Neither a fixed location nor a fluid imaginary, Eagleville is a site where imagination is coterminous with physical terrain, worlded through the ways corporeal actors index these social transformations and their implications. To be "in" Eagleville is to stitch sensory impressions together along a warp of petrochemical exploration. Eagleville "happens" in the moment of recognition that things have changed and the sense that this change is connected to petrochemical development. Such moments of recognition are not simply realizations of what has happened, but predications of causality with ongoing effects. Below, I juxtapose several of these moments in an effort to flesh out Eagleville's taking-place among those who claim the South Texas Brush Country as their home place. The moments are drawn from my own observations in communities on the

Eagle Ford Shale, particularly in McMullen County, which I have visited since childhood.

Together, this work charts a "spectral geography" (McCormack, "Remotely Sensing") of the Eagle Ford Shale. Geographer Derek McCormack developed this concept to describe the cultural afterlife of Salomon August Andrée's ill-fated expedition to the North Pole. After Andrée's hot air balloon vanished from Norway's Svalbard archipelago shortly after its departure in 1897, widespread "rumor and speculation" (644) as to the balloon's whereabouts, further animated by the 1930 discovery of the expedition's "artefactual" (641) remains, ensured that the expedition persisted in spectral form decades after its physical end. In the thrall of Eagleville as in the aftermath of the Andrée Expedition, everyday speculation about technoscientific projects and their possible outworkings produces new cultural terrains that are affectively sensed and socially consequential. In McMullen County and other areas of South Texas, this speculation creates the parameters by which the shale play is alternately and simultaneously named and felt.

Development itself—or as people gloss it, "the fracking"—is a spectral object attached to the changes happening in the Brush Country. Yet by mapping the spectral geography of Eagleville, I also posit a speculative ontology of that which exists in the Eagle Ford Shale. As in Stuart McLean's "speculative poetic ontology" (592) of European wetlands—a novel juxtaposition of ethnographic accounts, historical observations, and philosophical writings, intended to generate new ways of looking at bogs, fens, and swamps—my writing is ontogenetic, inevitably giving rise to the sense of how life "is" in the shale play, however partial this sense may be. It invites new attunements to the poetics of everyday life at sites of petrochemical development and their implications, both for Texas and for the larger "fold" (Rice "From Architectonic to Tectonics") of shale oil and gas drilling across the United States.

Entering Eagleville

Until recently, drilling had never been as lucrative in South Texas as it was on the Gulf Coast or in the Permian Basin. Moving inland, there is (or was, not long ago) the immediate sense of a divide between Texas's south central rangelands and the oil country to the east and west, with its fields of rusting derricks. Drilling in the Brush Country was piecemeal, reflecting the diverse geology of surface formations that span South Texas.

Consider the case of McMullen County. From the late 1800s onward, oil and gas boomlets came and went. For a while, Anglo settlers herded sheep here, and numerous *Mexicanos* arrived to help with the shearing (many of their descendants went on to become ranch hands for the large landowners in the area); settlers cultivated the grasslands that once spanned the region to plant sorghum, cotton, and corn; and developers attempted to build several towns. The railroad arrived in 1912, creeping eastward from an existing line that linked farming villages in in the Rio Grande Valley, ultimately turning north toward San Antonio and, later, south to Corpus Christi. Colonizers poured in, hoping to profit from cheap farmland and continued growth. One of these schemes attracted a number of Czech immigrant families, including my great-grandparents. The town the Czechs hoped to found never materialized, however. By the time the stock market crashed in 1929, Brush Country farmers were choked by drought, and the cattle industry was soon devastated by a tick fever quarantine. Ranching rebounded within a decade, but farming never did. Farmland became rangeland as ranching families bought out the majority of the Czechs, consolidating their lands. Many smaller landowners who held on to their property did so by leasing out their land for ranching, as my own grandparents and parents have. By 1986, the *Handbook of Texas* attests, cattle ranching accounted for 90 percent of the county's income; other area industries included kitty litter production; tourism, primarily from hunting; and natural gas processing. In the midst of this, unconventional carbon cracked open historical time in South Texas, shifting the terms by which people placed themselves regarding capital and possibility.

The Mayor of Eagleville

As my father began detailing possibilities for drilling beneath our land, we were pulled into the orbit of an increasingly familiar narrative: the story of the rural landowner in the thrall of unconventional oil who receives a wildcatter's letter asking for an oil and gas lease. The landowner hopes that the lease will enable him or her to maintain the property without developing it further, as small landowners find it increasingly difficult to keep their land and save money at the same time, even if—and sometimes especially if—they work the land themselves. The landowner signs the lease and may or may not secure a fair price for the company's initial use of the land. After the well is drilled and fracked, monthly checks arrive, provided the landowner successfully secured a share of the royalties. Many landowners agree to an oil lease only to have their property devalued with pipeline construction, their water supply contaminated by frac chemicals, or their sensorium otherwise disrupted with potentially toxic sights, sounds, and smells.

As elsewhere in the United States where people signed oil and gas leases simply because they felt that the land would be ruined no matter what they did (Gold 10–11), many South Texans with whom I've spoken had little hope that their land would remain unchanged by the drilling. But stopping the drilling was "impossible," they said; one had to ensure that drilling took place in the most responsible way. Resource lawyers suggested that even if you didn't agree to sign a lease, there was no way to guarantee that the companies wouldn't take the oil beneath your land. If you didn't sign the lease, you would never be made whole again for the inevitable damage done to your land. The only way to cut your losses was to lease the land at as high a price as you could get, with royalty payments and environmental protections where possible. Such logic underpinned my father's rationale for allowing a North Texas oil company access to our property.

Writing on rhetoric and petrocolonialism in the Marcellus Shale, Brian Cope notes that some areas of Pennsylvania are seen as worth saving, while others are already damned and thus conducive to drilling (29). The experiences of Brush Country residents and workers illuminate the intricate ways people view land as an object of care and concern even as they move to profit from its exploitation. Some people dreaded the potential for ecological destruction and some did not. (One woman laughed at the thought that the land her late husband had cherished—land that she'd resented all their marriage—finally paid off after all.) But all expressed incredulity at the amounts of money thrown around during negotiations. Telephones lit up as neighbors called neighbors to find out how much money they'd been promised. Some were forthright with their concerns, others more circumspect, depending on how well they got on with the people next door. The air sizzled with nervous elation, edged with promises of early retirement and the hum of new car engines. Maybe that man who worked two jobs to hang on to his land would be able to retire after all. My father ramped up his visits to the land, driving around the drill pad and inspecting the rigs coming on- and offline around the area. "He's the mayor of Eagleville," commented one of our neighbors, an old cattle baron who was rapidly becoming a new oil baron. South Texas became unhinged as specters of capital promise swirled on the horizon, yet nobody knew how long the money would actually last. "Sign the lease now," people said, "before it's too late."

Petrohenge

We watched the clearing of spiny hackberry and cactus at the site of the drill pad, the construction of the rig, the drilling and the fracking, and the aftermath, when the rig was packed up and the crew moved on, leaving only a series of pipes at the site. Horizontal drilling has enabled companies to "stack production" by digging multiple wells from one location, a fact often cited in arguments that fracking is cleaner and less invasive than previous technologies. The rigs number only one or so per tract on average and stand for just a few weeks at each site, leaving a small array of pipes at the site of drill pad. Pastures full of rusting derricks pumping away—one derrick for each well over a particular oil deposit—are a thing of the past. But while

South Texas's horizon may be uncluttered by rigs in the long term, the oil industry's footprint will remain visible at other angles. Some frac wells are already dry, exhausted, but the petrohenges will persist into the future, a stratum above the Archaic Age arrowheads that wash up whenever it rains. As remote sensing technology shrinks the globe, Texans use Google Earth to view their home places at increasing orders of magnitude, staggered by the sight of once-uninterrupted rangelands dotted with gravel clearings and water reservoirs. The impression is dizzying: old landmarks such as water tanks and ranch roads are muted next to the stark white of the pads.

For those familiar with the terrain, such images are as provocative as the images of nighttime drilling activity as it is visible from space: a Milky Way of rig lights and gas flares arcing from the Rio Grande to the Guadalupe River. Before the fracking, South Texan skies were capped with a dome of stars invisible in cities. But now drill pads light the horizon with an endless dusk, rendering invisible the galaxy of stars that spanned the sky before the boom began. Passing them at a distance, one sees the rigs looking like Tinkertoys wrapped in Christmas lights, each accompanied by the flicker of a natural gas flare. While their glow seems constant, the sites are in constant transformation, winking out when the crews dismantle the rig for transport to the next destination.

Traffic to and from the drill pads is ceaseless. There have always been cars on the road in the Brush Country—eighteen-wheelers have been driving the backroads here since before NAFTA was passed, and the hum of passing trucks, overlaid with intermittent bursts of coyote song, is characteristic of the area. The problem with the frac traffic, according to those who live there, is the sheer number of trucks on the road and the speed at which they move. Consider that each well requires over ninety eighteen-wheelers of sand to frac the shale. Then imagine a two-lane highway dotted with wells on either side, constantly inundated with trucks carrying rig parts, chemicals, sand, wastewater, and other materials. The trucks won't stop for you, and there's no passing them—not that you'd want to. They'd only ride your bumper, forcing you to the shoulder. The light of the trucks on the roads blends with the light of the rigs on the horizon, the whine of the eighteen-wheelers merging with the whir of the machinery. All register as a crescendo of something you didn't realize you'd always been listening to. Every day junk falls off the rigs, the plastics and alu-silvers glistening against the drought-yellowed grass.

As unconventional oil encroached on the Brush Country, new kinds of toxics, capital, and infrastructure refigured the everyday lives of those who lived there. Watching workers drill into our property and pump it full of water, sand, and unknown chemicals (at that time, the state had not yet required the disclosure of frac chemicals), we noticed certain things that stuck out:

the shiny cerulean drill bit, its diamond edging pointed out by the on-site manager who palmed it across both of his hands; the impeccably tidy rig in bright shades of red, white, and yellow; the unnaturally clear water sluicing into the well in preparation for fracking; the fluorescent glow of the computer monitors under continuous observation in the control room on the rig. Rather than the absence of toxics, the cleanliness evoked their constant presence, which necessitated an endless array of practices, controls, inspections.

Several acres of a neighboring ranch had been cleared to make way for the freight trucks and well assembly. Rising out of a gravel clearing, the gated rig humming with activity and anticipation. Trailers and a doghouse evinced the constant presence of oil industry representatives, human or canine. Yet there was a banality to this securitization. The dog, Katy, barked and yowled until you petted her. The entrance to the drill pad was guarded by a retired couple from another state who were paid to park at various gates and sign in the visitors. They drove their RV from site to site. The fracking became real for my father when he drove up to visit the drill pad one day to find hazmat suits lying around the site, casually available in the event of an emergency.

Felt Areas

Nonhuman actors also make Eagleville and make themselves known there, and humans come to know Eagleville with them and through them. Consider two stories of seismic activity and humans' awareness of it in the Eagle Ford Shale.

In October 2011, a 4.6-magnitude earthquake rattled windows and cracked walls in Peggy, a small community in Atascosa County, sixty miles southeast of San Antonio. The earthquake's "felt area" spanned from the southern edge of San Antonio to the Mexican border, one of sixty-two seismic events that took place across South Texas from 2009 to 2011 (Frohlich and Brunt 59). The Peggy earthquake trended in the national and local news but hardly made waves at the same magnitude as the earthquakes that have rattled North Texas with the expansion of the Barnett Shale play. Geologists had already established a correlation between injection wells—used to dispose of spent frac water—and seismic activity. But the Peggy earthquake compelled closer study of tremors in the Eagle Ford Shale play too, so Eagleville took form yet again—in a map of seismic activity rendered by seismographs in the region.

That such a mapping was possible at all was due to a fortuitous coincidence of sensor placement and the commencement of fracking activity. The USArray project is a traveling network of four hundred seismographs intended to ground the integrated study of the earth's lithosphere on a continental scale, and twenty-five of those seismographs happened to be located in Texas from

2009 to 2011. Based on the data from USArray, maps of drilling activity, and reports from residents, geologists concluded that seismic activity can be triggered by extraction as well as injection, whether that extraction stems from the removal of water or of hydrocarbons (Frohlich and Brunt 62). These results have not made waves in the Brush Country; for those with whom I've spoken, it's a no-brainer that fracking triggers seismic activity.

But in Eagleville, awareness of this seismic activity takes a different form than scientific papers or petitions in protest. Ten months after our land was fracked and one month after the Peggy earthquake, I was driving an all-terrain vehicle down a gravel road half a mile from the nearest drill pad when a sibilant racket rose above the whine of the old Kawasaki motor, an improbable chorus of cicadas in the heart of the rangeland. I knew without looking that I was in the presence of a rattlesnake—in the absence of locusts, only rattlers could make that kind of racket—and a quick glance backward revealed a six-foot viper uncoiling angrily, rearing up to strike at the ATV's retreating tailgate. Although Brush Country rattlesnakes were usually brumating by this time of year, this one was unseasonably awake.

At camp, the story of my encounter triggered a long retelling of the more memorable rattlesnake sightings we'd had over the past fifty years. My father added that there had been an inordinate amount of rattlesnake sightings in the area recently. A bulldozer driver had spotted more than five in a single day's work not far from the camp. Neighbors speculated that vibrations from the fracking—or, more plausibly, the drilling—had disturbed the snakes' hibernacula, leading them to strike out of season.

Could we say that, of those who fabulate the Eagle Ford Shale play, the people who use snakes and the people who use seismographs represent two different kinds of geological "publics," each marshaling a different array of knowledge, materials, and movement? Where, if anywhere, do these publics overlap beyond surveys that report an earthquake's felt area? Which came first: the recognition that animals were upset or the knowledge that unusual seismic activity was taking place? All the while, seismic stories pile up in any number of areas, making Eagleville in the moment that a snake's "anger" is connected to real and imagined rattlings of the earth.

Right-of-Way

The sense that landowners are the primary stakeholders in development projects pervades contemporary coverage of fracking debates, with troublesome implications for social policy. In Texas, the 2015 passage of House Bill 20 nullified municipal bans on fracking and established the state as the sole arbiter of drilling projects, enshrining landowners' rights to sell their minerals regardless of how populated the area in question was. The fetishization of the "landowner" as an idealized bourgeois self reinforces the sense that subjectivity is contingent on the ownership of property, thus denying the possibility of speech or action to those who do not possess recognizable forms of capital. Landowners are a disparate group of actors spanning multiple socioeconomic strata, in terms of both income and accrued social capital. The pressures of maintaining property rights relative to those who have more (or less) lead to contagious senses of promise, threat, failure, and success, played out in large and small ways in interactions among neighbors.

Before the Brush Country was fracked, most of the land in the area was used for ranching and deer hunting. Ranchers leased out multiple tracts in a common area, many yet to be fenced in or divided only by rusting barbed wire. Landowners negotiated hunting leases with outfitters or the hunters themselves. In the mid-twentieth century, most of the hunters wintered in primitive camps, old RVs, or portable buildings with no electricity or plumbing. As hunting became more of a leisure sport, many of the camps sported flat-screen TVs, running water, and even wet bars. Land management in the Brush Country grew out of a series of mundane negotiations among owners, ranchers, ranch hands, hunters, game wardens, and in some cases, the utility workers who might need access to power lines or infrastructure that crisscrossed a given property. Some landowners owned multiple tracts of land and leased land they didn't own, shifting roles according to the tracts, the people who worked on them, and any neighbors who bordered them.

The importance of strong social ties becomes clear when relations fall apart, as they did when one landowning family negotiated with a wastewater transfer company to install a brine disposal well on their land. Their neighbors found out about the injection well only when the Texas Railroad Commission sent out notices informing them of their right to protest the project. As the permitting process began, landowners' frac-induced highs turned to dread as they scrambled to find lawyers who might help them stop the well, saving their water supply from a permanent influx of volatile organic compounds. The threat that oil companies had promised to keep at bay during drilling suddenly became real, the toxics spilling forth in hurried phone calls, sweaty palms, and fear-fueled tirades triggered by the sense that the inevitable had indeed come to pass—the land *would* be ruined, but not in the terms they had agreed on when they signed their oil and gas leases. The landowners prepared for a protest hearing at the Railroad Commission with no real hope that anything could be done, since state officials showed no inclination to recognize the potentially harmful effects of frac water injection.

Yet the hearing never came to pass. A concerned rancher bought up the long-forgotten easements from the defunct San Antonio railroad, a line that had once crossed all the properties on the western side of Highway 97, running parallel to the highway. Constructed around 1912, the rail line had been abandoned in the 1930s, its tracks dismantled in 1959. When I was little, my mother and I would go look at the morning dew glistening on the spiderwebs that grew in the clearing left over from the tracks. The old rail line once connected the Rio Grande Valley with the town of Pleasanton, where it forked northward to San Antonio and eventually made its way to the Gulf via Corpus Christi. Today the Gulf line is the only one that still runs, but in other areas, South Texas rail has risen anew to meet the demands posed by the shale play: several railyards have opened across the Brush Country for the export of hydrocarbons and the import of frac sand, with plans to install chemical production facilities on site for processing fossil fuels. But the story about the failed injection well points to another way old infrastructure is made to serve new purposes, retrenching ranchers' power in a new milieu. By buying up the railroad easements, the rancher gained the right to restrict any traffic that might cross the old railroad's still-extant right-of-way, since anyone who wished to access their land from the highway inevitably had to cross the rise in the ground that once supported the railroad tracks. The threat of the injection well was suddenly, strikingly, neutralized.

Whereas small landowners were left to appeal to the Railroad Commission, a bureaucratic apparatus likely to rule in favor of the injection well, large landowners had the ability to reactivate long-forgotten rights-of-way from a past that few people realized was still present. For the smaller landowners in the area, the rancher's purchase of the easements edged the windfall of petrochemical profit with new uncertainty. In the end, having effectively shut down the injection well project, the rancher returned the easements to those in the path of the dispute. Yet their move to stop the injection well blunted the neighbors' optimism about oil and gas exploration. It brought into relief the sense that while Eagleville is marked by the idea that anyone can get rich and anything can happen, some people will always have more wealth than others and thus more freedom in choosing how their land is to be affected by fracking.

While all the land is subject to contamination at the hands of Big Oil, some kinds of contamination are considered less undesirable than others for any number of reasons. The move to allow drilling that makes money for multiple stakeholders (fracking) while protesting drilling that will profit only one stakeholder (wastewater injection) results from place-specific logics of acceptable contamination and contagious concern. Meanwhile, those who do *not* own land, but who make their lives here—however temporarily—are equally part of Eagleville's multiple making, but their part in this taking-place goes unrecognized by laws that privilege the figure of the landowner as the primary citizens of an emerging petrostate.

Conclusion

Driving through the Brush Country in 2017, you can see signs along the road placing you in Eagleville: Eagleford Seafood & Steak, Eagle Ford Urgent Care, Eagle Ford Lodge, Eagle Ford Waste Water Recycling. "Frac Water Sold Here," say hand-lettered posterboards staked along the highways. Despite the recent oil price collapse, drilling persists; operators are ramping up their use of frac sand to loosen as many hydrocarbons as possible in one go. Elected officials in Brush Country counties say they're "still blessed" (Baker). The idiom of petrochemical promise persists. Tracing out quotidian aspects of everyday life at sites of petrochemical development offers newfound perspective on the cultural dynamics through which consent is manufactured, agreements are reached, protests are quelled, and development unfolds.

Thus the Brush Country becomes Eagleville, a taking-place in the thrall of petrochemical development, its possibilities, and its vicissitudes. Placing these moments into concrete yet idiosyncratic historical contexts furnishes a "deep map" (Heat-Moon) of social terrains that constitute the Eagle Ford Shale. Here deeply situated interplays of sensibilities and interests swarm at sites of oil and gas extraction. In a space where development is a foregone conclusion, people attend to geological shifts not in the language of ecological concern or environmental audits, but as conversation pieces that enable certain statements about development while foreclosing others. Invoking the inevitability of development, they create the infrastructures by which such development unfolds. Statements that change is necessary, inevitable, or happening because of the fracking conjure Eagleville's quantum world. A "distributed field of affective materials" (McCormack, "Remotely Sensing" 642), Eagleville is nonetheless connective for being diffuse—tethered, in the case of the stories here, to those who make their lives on, with, and through the land that they would frac.

Works Cited and Consulted

Anderson, Ben, and Paul Harrison, editors. *Taking-Place: Non-representational Theories and Geography*. Ashgate, 2010.

Baker, Joe. "'Blessing': South Texas County Judges Thankful for Economic Impact of Eagle Ford Shale Oil and Gas Production." *Beeville Bee-Picayune*, June 2015, www.mysoutex.com/view/full_story/26720501/article--Blessing ---South-Texas-county-judges-thankful-for-economic-impact-of-Eagle -Ford-Shale-oil-and-gas-production? Accessed 25 June 2015.

Callister, Deborah Cox. "Land Community Participation: A New 'Public' Participation Model." *Environmental Communication*, vol. 7, no. 4, 2013, pp. 435–55.

Carlson, Jennifer, and Kathleen Stewart. "The Legibilities of Mood Work." *New Formations*, vol. 82, 2014, pp. 114–33.

Chapa, Sergio. "Demand for Sand: Frac Sand Use per Well Goes Up Amid Low Prices." *Houston Business Journal*, 1 July 2015, www.bizjournals.com /houston/morning_call/2015/07/demand-for-sand-frac-sand-use-per-well -goes-up.html. Accessed 2 July 2015.

Cope, Brian. "Eço-Seeing a Tradition of Colonization: Revealing Shadow Realities of Marcellus Drilling." *Environmental Rhetoric and Ecologies of Place*, edited by Peter Goggin, Routledge, 2013, pp. 28–41.

Energy Information Administration (EIA). *Top 100 U.S. Oil and Gas Fields*. EIA, US Department of Energy, 2015.

———. *Updates to the EIA Eagle Ford Play Maps*. EIA, US Department of Energy, 2014.

Frohlich, Cliff, and Michael Brunt. Two-Year Survey of Earthquakes and Injection/ Production Wells in the Eagle Ford Shale, Texas, prior to the MW4.8 20 October 2011 Earthquake. *Earth and Planetary Science Letters*, vol. 379, 2013, pp. 56–83.

Gold, Russell. *The Boom: How Fracking Ignited the American Energy Revolution and Changed the World*. Simon & Schuster, 2014.

Haraway, Donna. *When Species Meet*. U of Minnesota P, 2008.

Hawhee, Debra. "Rhetoric's Sensorium." *Quarterly Journal of Speech*, vol. 101, no. 1, 2015, pp. 2–17.

Heat-Moon, William Least. *PrairyErth: A Deep Map*. Mariner Books, 1999.

Hinchcliffe, Steve. "Working with Multiples: A Non-representational Approach." Anderson and Harrison, pp. 303–20.

Long, Sonny. "Earthquake Shakes South Texas." *Victoria Advocate*, 20 October 2011. www.victoriaadvocate.com/news/2011/oct/20/sl_earthquake_102111 _155884/. Accessed 21 June 2015.

Massey, Doreen. *Space, Place, and Gender*. U of Minnesota P, 1994.

McCormack, Derek P. "Remotely Sensing Affective Afterlives: The Spectral Geographies of Material Remains." *Annals of the Association of American Geographers*, vol. 100, no. 3, 2010, pp. 640–54.

———. "Thinking in Transition: The Affirmative Refrain of Experience/Experiment." Anderson and Harrison, pp. 201–20.

McLean, Stuart. "Black Goo: Forceful Encounters with Matter in Europe's Muddy Margins." *Cultural Anthropology*, vol. 26, no. 4, 2011, pp. 589–619.

Railroad Commission of Texas. "Eagle Ford Shale Information." *Railroad Commission of Texas*. 13 Sept. 2017. http://www.rrc.state.tx.us/oil-gas/major-oil -and-gas-formations/eagle-ford-shale-information/. Accessed 19 Oct. 2017

Rice, Jenny. *Distant Publics: Development Rhetorics and the Subject of Crisis*. U of Pittsburgh P, 2012.

———. "From Architectonic to Tectonics: Introducing Regional Rhetorics." *Rhetoric Society Quarterly*, vol. 42, no. 3, 2012, pp. 201–13.

Stewart, Kathleen C. *Ordinary Affects*. Duke UP, 2007.

Donna Dunbar-Odom,
Texas A&M University—Commerce

16. WE ALL REMEMBER THE ALAMO: MATERIALIZING THE PERSONAL

A Personal Connection/Reflection

At the 2014 Thomas R. Watson Conference on Rhetoric and Composition, I presented a paper on a panel titled "What We Do with the Anger." I was first, focusing on two memoirs by women who had suffered as a result of the environmental degradation of their hometowns; the remaining papers were much more clearly about the other two panelists' personal local experiences: the recent water contamination in West Virginia (the speaker is a native West Virginian) and environmental racism in Commerce, Texas. When I introduced myself and my paper, I mentioned that mine was the only one that was not personal or local, but after I sat down and listened to the other papers, I saw the personal connections, connections that had completely escaped me until I took the time to reflect.

I was writing about environmental and nuclear pollution experienced by strangers. But I vividly recall funerals of family members who died of cancers possibly related to their use of chemicals on my grandparents' cotton farm near Greenville, Texas. My half-sister spent her adolescence exposed to nuclear radiation when she lived in occupied Japan with her mother and stepfather. She died of cancer at the age of fifty, cancer that kept re-forming and returning beginning in her late thirties. It turns out that I had indeed written personally about texts that connect to my own life on a deep personal level.

Arguing for the Personal

I begin with this example to help me make a larger argument about scholarship and research. Too many scholars dismiss personal writing as hopelessly mired in identity politics or as weakly relying on limited and particular experience. However, the rhetorical power of that experience, rather than being banished, should become a potent supplemental strategy providing a sense of the writer's investedness in the project as well as providing pleasure to a reading audience. That is, scholarly writers should foreground personal and material connections to their subject matter and their positions. I am arguing that scholarly writing is enlivened and made more relevant to larger audiences if we meld personal lived experience with the scholarly arguments being made. Rather than ignoring the writer's material existence, such an interweaving uses the writer's material body and location as integral and vital to the work being done.

A seminal text that makes passionate and clear use of the personal to fuel a larger argument is Mike Rose's *Lives on the Boundary*. In the last sentence of his preface, he writes, "The stories of my work with literacy interweave with the story of my own engagement with language. *Lives on the Boundary* is both vignette and commentary, reflection and analysis. I didn't know how else to get it right" (xii). Rose's 1989 book argues for a much more nuanced and complex look at and approach to "remedial" education, an argument made all the more powerful by his personal experiences as a member of "America's educational underclass" saved by a caring teacher. Without the narratives of his experiences with inner-city public schooling, the force of his critique would be weakened; it is the interweaving of the personal with the big issue that provides the impact and is likely what has given his book continued relevance.

Inventing Place: Writing Lone Star Rhetorics explores Texas's multiple meanings and significations, as well as our personal relationships to these meanings and significations. As a fourth-generation Texan, I cannot write about Texas if I cannot write in the first person about the state that shaped me in profound ways and still has the power to surprise me. My arguments are placed and personal.

Remembering the Alamo

On a late afternoon in the early 1960s, my father did something radically out of character; suddenly appalled to realize that I, at the age of nine or so, had never seen the Alamo, he loaded my mother and me in the car and drove from Dallas to San Antonio for a twenty-hour "vacation." I had to visit the shrine.

It was a hot, sticky Friday, and my parents and I were sitting in the front yard in the shade of our cottonwood trees. It was probably around 4 P.M. because my dad had been home from work for a while and he was into his second or third beer. He was a milkman, so he left for work around 4 A.M. and was home by early afternoon, depending on how deliveries had gone and how long it had taken him to unload his truck.

Dad was at that sweet spot right after relaxed but before drunk and was uncharacteristically talkative. How did the Alamo come up in our conversation? I have no recollection. But as a Texas-born kid, I had already absorbed the fact of its existence and quite a bit of its significance. Davy Crockett was a big deal, and we could all sing, "Davy, Davy Crockett, king of the wild frontier." Possibly I said something like "I wish I could see the Alamo," but that seems unlikely because, as a working-class kid in a working-class family with limited means, it would never have occurred to me that it could happen. Our vacations were always and only trips to Abilene to see my dad's sister and her family.

So while I can't recall how the trip came about, I do recall my father deciding that he had to take me to see the Alamo *right then*. In those days, my mother, a stay-at-home wife and mother, didn't argue with him although I'm sure she wasn't happy about this sudden call to action. She grabbed changes of clothes for the three of us, slapped together bologna sandwiches, and got me ready. My dad sat in the car with the rest of his six-pack and honked the horn for us to hurry.

It was hot. The car was un-air-conditioned. (Was it the yellow 1951 Studebaker? I hope so.) When we hit the highway, I know Dad was driving fast because Mom kept telling him to slow down. We must have driven Interstate 35, which at that time was only a few years old. I remember dead grass on the verge, and I remember darkness, and I remember a long drive with only one stop for a bathroom break and a drink of water. Sandwiches were eaten in the car on the move.

By the time we reached San Antonio, it was late and we were dehydrated and sticky. My dad then did something else utterly out of character: he got us a room in a motel. I had never stayed in a motel before and knew pretty much nothing about what a motel *should* be like, but even I knew this motel was a dump. We couldn't have been in our room long before Dad declared we couldn't sleep there (I vaguely remember that the air-conditioning wasn't working), so out we shambled. I can only assume my dad had procured and consumed more beer because I'm pretty sure his shouting match with the desk clerk was fueled by alcohol, as was his announcement that we were going to sleep in the motel's little lobby.

And we did.

After a cheap, fast breakfast at an insanely early hour the next morning, unbathed and groggy, we made our way, finally, to the Alamo. I vividly remember fighting back tears of disappointment and making sure my dad couldn't see how let down I was by the place itself. The small building of yellow stone was nothing like the vast, noble structure of my imagination. The inside was full of dusty mannequins and displays and gift shop gewgaws. How had the heroes of the Alamo had room to reload their long rifles? Where were the tall walls that Mexican soldiers had had to use ladders to scale? It was all wrong.

I dutifully trotted around and through the building for about thirty minutes, and then Dad herded us back to the car for the drive home. Our trip had taken less than twenty-four hours.

So what was it about this particular place that lit such a fire under my father to behave in a way so utterly out of character? Obviously, it was intensely important to him. Yet none of us ever mentioned the trip to each other again. In fact, it's only in relatively recent years that it occurred to me how truly bizarre this story is, and it's only very recently that I began to try to make meaning of and take meaning from the experience. I offer this bit of Dunbar family drama to interrogate the power of place and the hold place can have over memory and experience as well as how we make meaning of and describe memory and experience.

Human beings feel connections to the places where we live, work, and play, and no place will elicit identical responses from any two people. A place becomes invested with a kind of power, and when enough people invest themselves in a place, it becomes much more than the stone and mortar and landscaping. As Tim Cresswell writes, "Place, then, needs to be understood as an embodied relationship with the world. Places are constructed by people doing things, and in this sense are never 'finished' but are constantly being performed" (37). The Alamo and its mythology are an ongoing performance, and it is the myth that drew my family to San Antonio so many years ago.

Texans tend to feel a connection to and ownership of the Alamo—at least, I think this is true of my generation. From the John Wayne movie version of the battle to public school history classes to street names in almost every Texas town, we are immersed in Alamo lore and participate in the mythologizing process, even when the actual place, complete with gift shop and well-watered landscaping in densely built-up downtown San Antonio, clashes mightily with that mythology. In a very real sense, we have "learned" the Alamo.

Rhetoricizing an Icon

So what can it mean to "remember the Alamo"? Certainly every Texas "remembers" the Alamo, but few Texans remember—or even know—the specifics of the siege and its aftermath, much less the political factors contributing to and leading up to the battle. Our remembrances have been overpowered by popular culture and overweening pride peculiar to Texas and Texans. As Kendall R. Phillips writes in the introduction to *Framing Public Memory*:

> The study of memory is largely one of the rhetoric of memories. The ways memories attain meaning, compel others to accept them, and are themselves contested, subverted, and supplanted by other memories are essentially rhetorical. As an art interested in the ways symbols are employed

to induce cooperation, achieve understanding, contest understanding, and offer dissent, rhetoric is deeply steeped in a concern for public memories. These memories that both constitute our sense of collectivity and are constituted by our togetherness are thus deeply implicated in our persuasive activities and in the underlying assumptions and experiences upon which we build meanings and reasons. (2–3)

Like any good symbol, the Alamo is a potent yet flexible rhetorical tool to be used to serve a variety of purposes as needed. Our sense of what it means to "remember the Alamo" emerges from the collectivity of memories and the resulting collectively built meanings and reasons.

Nostalgia and romance are a powerful rhetorical couple, and it can be difficult to resist the pleasure of rhapsodizing about a place that triggers emotional responses. In *Unreliable Truth*, Maureen Murdock writes, "Memory is rarely whole or factually correct. If the image of the event we have participated in does not match the image of the self we have carefully constructed, then we rarely remember the facts of the event at all. What we remember is a reconstruction of image and feeling that suits our needs and purposes" (5). The men who died in the Battle of the Alamo are martyred heroes, whether or not that is factually correct (and it isn't, for the most part), because collectively we have reconstructed "image and feeling that suit our needs and purposes" without being conscious of that reconstruction. Although every publicly schooled Texan takes a full year of Texas history in seventh grade, unpopular interpretations are glossed over by the teacher, the textbooks, the students, or all. I even took an extra semester of Texas history during my senior year and can recall no lesson refuting the example of Lieutenant Colonel William B. Travis, commander of the Alamo, drawing a line in the sand to decide who would stay and fight to certain death and who would leave. It's a dramatic moment that likely never happened, but it's a moment so ingrained in every Texan's sense of Alamo history that it will not be dislodged.

In 1836, the year of the battle we all allegedly remember, the Alamo was one part of a large mission complex of buildings. In fact, the size of the complex was one reason the defenders (possibly as many as 250) were defeated: the compound was too big and too spread out. And the building so lovingly restored had little connection to the battle. In *The Alamo: A Cultural History*, Frank Thompson remarks, "The Alamo as it now stands is, in a very real sense, no longer *itself*, but a *monument* to itself" (12). That is, the mission building restored today is more like a plaque to the battle than the site of the battle; what we're remembering when we remember the Alamo is technically not that building. Just as the Alamo has influenced what it means to identify a place as helping shape our identities as Texans and Americans, we have in turn shaped and created the Alamo.

Of course, the actual battle and circumstances before and after were complicated; the defenders included not only Davy Crockett and Jim Bowie but also a ragtag group of individuals from the United States and Mexico who had numerous reasons of their own for wanting to resist Santa Anna and Mexican rule. The line in the sand, the number of defenders, who left, who stayed, why they left, why they stayed, how people died—all have been described and defined and redescribed and redefined according to our needs and political consciousnesses. "The myth of the Alamo is in an almost constant state of revision," writes Thompson (17).

In my own case, despite my awareness of the ways I don't *really* know or remember the Alamo, I nevertheless feel an intense affection for the shrine, both the actual place and the place that exists in my own imagination. Cultural geographer Yi-Fu Tuan writes in *Topophilia*, "Awareness of the past is an important element in the love of place" (99). I would argue that this is true even when one's awareness of the past is awash in myth. I love the mythology of the Alamo, I love my father's surprising and heartfelt affection for the Alamo, I love the gaudy spectacle of the present-day Alamo.

I can only speculate about my father's attachment. He was a George Wallace Democrat who hated anyone named Roosevelt and loved Audie Murphy (born and raised on a farm in the same Texas county as my father). My dad felt a testy, complicated allegiance to the United States. His experiences in the Philippines in World War II were horrific, and he suffered lifelong damage from severe physical wounds as well as what we now understand to be post-traumatic stress disorder. He once told me that if I were a boy, he would have driven me to Canada to keep me out of Vietnam and away from the experience of war. But he felt no conflict about identifying as a Texan with a connection to a rich, feisty, in-your-face history with clear-cut heroes, men who drew lines in sand and made a choice to cross that line.

My father dropped out of high school because he hated it. He hated farm labor and had no desire to continue farming as he had been raised to. He hated his time in the military and kept in contact with no one he had served with. He only occasionally found pleasure in his jobs with Borden's milk company—generally with some of his coworkers, none of whom he socialized with. Yet in his way, he loved Texas. He left the state rarely and reluctantly and always made it clear that it was the best place in the world.

Placing Ourselves

So how do we analyze our relationships to place? In what ways are we aware of the places we love, and in what ways do these places become like water to fish? Tuan has named the affection for and sense of connection to place "to-pophilia," which he defines as "the affective bond between people and place 203 or setting" (4). He explains, "Environment. . . is not just a resource base to be used or natural forces to adapt to, but also sources of assurance and pleasure, objects of profound attachment and love" (xii).

In another form of attachment and pleasure, psychogeographers—such as Guy Debord, Iain Sinclair, Will Self, and others—work to aestheticize place by consciously defamiliarizing themselves from their immediate environment. The focus on the materiality of place is a major tenet of psychogeography, which requires that the individual attend closely to the physical space around her or him, noticing what generally goes unnoticed, such as the sidewalk, the detritus of urban life (psychogeography is largely an urban phenomenon), the sounds. Merlin Coverly begins his small book *Psychogeography* by pointing to the ambiguity of the term's definition: "no one seems quite able to pin down exactly what it means or where it comes from" (9). Historically most connected with Paris and London, and with roots in surrealism and Dada, psychogeography can be traced to Paris of the 1950s and situationist Guy Debord, who defined it as "the study of the precise laws and specific effects of the geographical environment, consciously organized or not, on the emotions and behavior of individuals" (8).

Debord's definition stresses the importance of the specific ways our experience of place affects us emotionally and behaviorally—whether or not we are conscious of these effects. Clearly he argues that these effects are worthy of study; however, the ways that *study* has been defined and interpreted have taken a variety of forms. For Debord, psychogeography is an urban endeavor, and the psychogeographer becomes "one who explores and reports on psychogeographical phenomena" (51). The term *dérive* defines, to a certain extent, the psychogeographer's means of exploration: "a technique of transient passage through varied ambiences" (51). In other words, observant strolling. Broadly speaking, the psychogeographer walks the streets scrutinizing everything around him. He works to see—really see—his environment rather than merely passing through it.

Will Self, for example, gave himself the project of walking from London to New York City—that is, he would walk from his home in London to Heathrow, then from JFK Airport to his hotel in Manhattan. His purpose was (at least) twofold. One purpose was to experience the part of any trip that most of us experience as "empty" time driving or being driven through locations actively hostile to pedestrians, driving or being driven through *no*where to get to the place that will take us *some*where. Another purpose was to realize a personal connection to the two locations, examining his American mother's relocation from New York to London. In a certain sense, his walk served as a kind of biography. The connection was surprising and unexpected in part because he was walking defamiliarized ground. The relationship between the individual and the geographic environment is deeply personal and multifaceted, as his long "walk" demonstrates.

Making a personal connection to a monument everyone shares and for which many people feel a sense of ownership, however, complicates the psychogeographer's process. Consider the fact that until recently, the person owning the largest collection of Alamo memorabilia was British pop musician Phil Collins. His decision to give the collection to the Alamo for future display was announced late in 2014. There's a certain irony that until the return and display in a new visitors' center, "Davy Crockett's bullet pouch, Jim Bowie's sword, Sam Houston's snuff box, and more than two hundred other artifacts" resided in Collins's home in Switzerland. The power and romance of the Alamo story are at the heart of the collection and the transaction, as Collins claims that he "still gets goose bumps when he thinks about holding the same documents and weapons held by soldiers at the battle." The former Texas land commissioner who negotiated the return of the artifacts adds, "'We want to make sure that people know this battle, and that people know this battle, and that war, was between tyranny and liberty, not between Mexicans and Texicans'" (Hamilton). The artifacts help reify the myth rather than grapple with the complexity.

In *Framing Public Memory*, Phillips writes:

> As one examines the mutability of repeated memories one must also be mindful of the underlying struggles by various groups to maintain or resist memories. As we speak of cultural responsibility and/or absolution we should also be mindful of the hegemonic tendencies that want to inscribe memories—of triumphs or tragedies—in stone and fix them in seeming immutability. (10)

The former Texas land commissioner wants to make sure we "inscribe" our memory of the Alamo in terms of liberty versus tyranny, erasing the complicated and complicating factors of race, politics, and power that served to fuel much of the process of Texas's settlement, independence, and statehood. If we focus on liberty versus tyranny, we don't have to address topics like slavery and colonization.

Personal Arguments

As Texas demographics and landscapes change with alarming speed, we can see the appeal of a stable icon of nobility and sacrifice. Individual memories shift and prove slippery; cultural memory offers an illusion of possibility for shared experience and understanding. The Alamo gets a big buildup for every Texan. Hence we are told to "remember" it. To see the Alamo is to see, as Walker Percy terms it, the "symbolic complex" of what we're supposed to remember—not the little yellow stone building in and of itself. In "The Loss of the Creature," Percy points to our desire to see—*really see*—the Grand Canyon, but what we see is always mediated and distorted by what we expect to see because of the postcard images that color our expectations. Percy writes that the "term of the sightseer's satisfaction, is not the sovereign discovery of the thing before him; it is rather the measuring up of the thing to the criterion of the preformed symbolic complex" (47). I recall my sense of disappointment when I first saw the Alamo and could not believe that was all there was to it. The "preformed symbolic complex" promised drama and sacrifice and romance, but the building itself largely offered only postcards.

Of course, pleasure is produced by that symbolic complex, and that pleasure should not be easily dismissed or disdained. When my little family took our twenty-hour vacation to the Alamo, I have no doubt that my father wanted me to see firsthand an icon representing a clear line drawn in the sand, of a war with heroes and motives that made sense to everyone fighting, of a war very different from the one he had survived in the Pacific. Certainly, World War II has its own mythology and icons and inscribed triumphs, but my dad had lived through too much ugliness and too many examples of collateral damage (including his own serious injuries) and officer incompetence to buy into many of those myths. A third-generation Texan, my father was emotionally and touchingly invested in this Texas shrine and its myth. The Alamo, in a real sense, belonged to him. As Maureen Murdock notes, "Myth owes its longevity to its power to express typical human emotions that have been experienced throughout successive generations" (24), perhaps especially when individuals themselves cannot express them. Myth also provides a sense of stability in a world where stability is a rare commodity.

Geographically, intellectually, professionally, we tend to perceive our lives materially in terms of place. We are all embodied as we look at where and how we place ourselves, as well as where and how we are placed. The places that figure in our imagination and sense of ourselves many times offer complicated combinations of myths and realities, the romantic and the mundane. In a very real sense, Texans perform as well as remember the Alamo. And just in case we might forget, we have internet access to a twenty-four-hour webcam.

In this essay, I have attempted to unpack something of my complicated relationship with the place I live and the father who raised me in this place, as well as to make a bigger argument about the importance of not just foregrounding and including personal, material experiences and memories in the research we do but also blending and using both to complicate and enrich each other. I contend that such an interweaving, to use Rose's term once more, reveals and deepens the relationships that exist between scholarship and the experience of the body, memory, and place.

Works Cited

Coverly, Merlin. *Psychogeography*. Oldcastle Books, 2006.

Cresswell, Tim. *Place: A Short Introduction*. Wiley-Blackwell, 2004.

Debord, Guy. "Definitions." Knabb, pp. 51–52.

———. "Introduction to a Critique of Urban Geography." Knabb, pp. 8–12.

Hamilton, Reeve. "Phil Collins Collection Arriving at the Alamo." *The Texas Tribune*, 26 Oct. 2014, texastribune.org/2014/10/26/phil-collins-collection -arriving-alamo-week/. Accessed 26 Oct. 2014.

Knabb, Ken, editor and translator. *Situationist International Anthology*. Bureau of Public Secrets, 2006.

Murdock, Maureen. *Unreliable Truth*. Seal P, 2003.

Percy, Walker. "The Loss of the Creature." *The Message in the Bottle: How Queer Man Is, How Queer Language Is, and What One Has to Do with the Other*, edited by Percy, Farrar, Straus and Giroux, 1954, pp. 46–63.

Phillips, Kendall R. *Framing Public Memory*. U of Alabama P, 2004.

Rose, Mike. *Lives on the Boundary*. Penguin, 1989.

Thompson, Frank. *The Alamo: A Cultural History*. Taylor Trade, 2001.

Tuan, Yi-Fu. *Topophilia: A Study of Environmental Perception, Attitudes, and Values*. Columbia UP, 1974.

WEST TEXAS

Barry Brummett,
University of Texas–Austin

17. NOTES FROM A TEXAS GUN SHOW

*G*ravel, concrete, and discouraged patches of grass turning to mud . . . an armada of pickup trucks and SUVs . . . men in denim and camo jackets—this is what you see as you drive up to Texas gun shows. You may find such shows offered every other month or so in cities and burgs all over the republic. From Odessa to Houston, no matter the size and wealth of the city, the gun shows are remarkably the same. They are held in old, converted warehouses, failed Kmarts, third-tier local arenas. Faded paint announcing businesses of yesterday is covered over by big temporary banners declaring, "Gun Show today!" The look and feel of a Texas gun show reflect a consistency of the culture that supports them. What is that culture?

That culture, which just for convenience we might call gun culture, is as strong in Texas as anywhere else in America, maybe stronger. Gun culture nationally, in an important sense, *is* Texan. The popular images of the pickup truck with the shotgun rack over the rear window, of the shirt bulging with the concealed weapon underneath, of rifles standing inside closets and revolvers lying on nightstands may be more widely true in the Lone Star State than in any other. When a cowboy rides into the sunset on his horse, six-gun securely holstered on a hip and a lever-action Winchester housed in the saddle scabbard, when the wind whistles down the sendero and coyotes howl, when this vision plays out in movies, television, country western songs, or daydreams, the location is Texas, regardless of what the official plot says. Never mind that cowboys also roamed the Badlands of the Dakotas and the prairies of Kansas, and the OK Corral was in Arizona; get on a horse with a gun, you are in Texas. The armed cowboy, the tall, lean sheriff, the desperado, the small rancher defending his land (it's always a "he"), these images all merge into Texas identities. This is the state where country singer Billy Joe Shaver could shoot a man in the face in a bar and get acquitted on what is popularly known as the "some ol' boys need shootin'" defense. How guns work in American culture may be well and fairly assessed by coming to ground zero of firearms and their culture: Texas.

There are very few real cowpokes still around, and some of those may be found in Texas, but they are as rare as a live armadillo by a highway. Most people don't run into them much, anyway. Oh, you can see the guy in the Levi's and western-style shirt with the big belt buckle and the cowboy hat in stores and such, especially in the South and Southwest, but real cowboys doing cowpokish things, not so much. You can see movies—mainly old movies—of the cowboy life, and country western songs still echo with the scream of the wild cougar, but to really be immersed in the fantasy that is the armed cowboy, one has few places to go. But you can go to the gun show to get as close as makes no never mind.

Clearly, the gun is key to the cowboy image. The gun may morph into the black rifle of today's military conflicts, the snub-nosed revolver of film noir, or the various weapons of first-person shooter video games, but their common ancestor is the cowboy gun, whether six-shooter pistol, double-barrel coach shotgun, or lever-action rifle. Every gangster film like *Scarface* is the shootout at the OK Corral in drag. Some people who collect (or accumulate) guns specialize in one genre or another, but I think most gun enthusiasts have a variety of types. As dogs are all basically wolf, from shih tzu to Great Dane, so all guns are essentially where they began in modern form, and that is, especially in America, with the post–Civil War cowboy and buffalo hunter guns. That means that guns have a unity of feeling and affect, and resonance with one is at some level resonance with them all, of all eras and circumstances.

Probably the central gun culture consistency I want to stress is that the cowboy myth and its variations are all working class. Likewise, guns in the American imagination—and I think likely in fact—are connected to the working class. Certainly people of means have firearms, but the popular imagination puts them in the hands of poor and middle-class working people. This is consistent right across the range of gun-representing popular culture. The cowboy in reality and on-screen is not wealthy and in fact is little more than an itinerant seasonal worker. The marshal or sheriff is not wealthy and is likely to sleep in the back room of the jail. Occasionally one will see a person from a wealthy or privileged background (for example, in the film *The Ghost and the Darkness*) connected to guns, but it is usually in a context of work and poverty (such as building a railroad in Africa). The title character in *Scarface* lives by the gun and become wealthy, but he began life in poverty, and his riches buy him only wretchedness.

There are two paradoxes in gun culture today that I want to mention. The gun is deadly for real and in earnest: these things are meant to kill something, and they do. Hunting, yes, often. But people, bad guys, them varmints, not so much. When it comes to the killing associated with the cowboy (or gangster) myth, the gun is a contradictory bundle of restrained potential. It fairly hums with the power for dealing death and the realization that you'd better not do that. For all the violence in the media, and in particular for people linked to the gun culture at gun shows, these instruments of death that are found everywhere hardly ever deal death, although that's their main purpose.

A second, related paradox is that gun culture, in particular as found at gun shows, is both performative and simulational. By performative, I mean people are projecting an image. It may be a true image, but it's a carefully crafted image, just as the manager of an office may perform a managerial role. If you get up and put on certain kinds of clothing to project an image, if you walk and talk in a certain way, if you groom yourself in predictable ways, then you are performing an identity, even if that identity really is "you." And by simulational, I mean that much of the performance of gun culture is sort of like a video game in that it isn't "real." It's a simulation. You may be performing a cowboy, but odds are that you are not really a cowboy. This loops back to the idea that guns are deadly serious instruments of death but hardly ever used for that purpose on other people. The gun enthusiast who collects six-shooters and cowboy coach shotguns will never face down Wild Bill in the street, but be assured that a fantasy of doing so plays through that person's head regularly. The doomsday prepper who arms for the zombie apocalypse will likely never experience that catastrophe but nevertheless invests a lot of thought and emotion in planning and mentally rehearsing for it. These fantasies make gun ownership highly simulational.

Put these observations together with my claim that gun culture is working class, and we see strong parallels between that class position and gun culture. Working-class people are likely to experience life in terms of frustrated potential, the first gun paradox I discussed above. Many of the working class think with good reason that they coulda been contenders, but circumstance and class restrictions prevented them. And when these working-class people go to gun shows, where they may display their tail feathers for their kind to see, it is the working class that they perform. This is true no matter how much they may have in the bank, and so often the performance of the working-class status is simulational. To participate in American gun culture, you need to be willing to project some kind of working-class image and perhaps even identity.

Everybody has opportunities to perform the dimensions of their identities that are most important to them, that seem central to who they are or want to be. Think of the gun show, in Texas or elsewhere, as a miniconvention for performance and simulation of the cowboy, working-class identity. The old boys who go there perform their knowledge of guns. If they are veterans, they wear insignia to let you know that. Jeans, cowboy hats, gimme caps, belts with big buckles, western shirts, the whole nine yards, you find it here. It takes special circumstances and a hard skin to show up at a gun show in a suit and tie; probably nobody will say anything to you, but you would know you are performing the wrong identity for this occasion. As people perform these cowboy identities, they do so in a simulated environment that is sealed off from the twenty-first-century outside. Nowhere else will you find such a profusion of guns, knives, holsters, scabbards, camouflage gear and clothing, military surplus, tooled leather, and the like. To enter the gun show is to enter into a simulation that, while you are there, is encompassing. By way of illustration, let me just walk you through what you might experience at the gun show in Texas.

But first, who am I to be walking you through a gun show? I don't have the knowledge or discipline to say that I collect guns, but I accumulate them. I have more of them than I have years. I hunt. I was a Life Member of the NRA until I resigned over a political disagreement. I have a concealed carry permit in the state of Texas, and I carry whenever and wherever I legally can. As a youngster, I dreamed of being a cowboy, a fantasy fueled by my father's origins in the panhandle, and was never without a cap pistol. I am a gun nut. You are in good hands.

I have never been to a gun show in a new, tidy, well-kept-up facility. Without fail, they are in minor, failing local arenas or in defunct big-box stores and warehouses opened just for the event. Parking lots are fields of broken concrete. In a real sense, this is the lone prairie transferred to the context of cities and middle-size towns (it seems not to be worth the while of gun show operators to hold events in small rural areas, despite the rural resonances of the cowboy image). It is a low-overhead environment entirely in keeping with a working-class sensibility.

You park your car and walk through rows of pickup trucks and utility vehicles. If gun show patrons own sports cars or hybrids, they don't drive them to the shows. Many of these trucks sport stickers and decals expressing memberships in sports or firearms clubs, conservative political opinions, or military experience. You will find a few men—and it's almost entirely men who come to the shows—in the parking lot walking to and from the venue, sometimes with sons in tow. Some of them carry guns they want to sell into the building, some are coming out with the day's haul.

People at the gun shows dress in working men's garb: denim, overalls, cowboy hats or gimme caps advertising agricultural or firearms products, belts with enormous detachable buckles, and so forth. On the way in, a few take some last pulls from their cigarettes and leave them in the sand buckets by the entrance. Signs generally forbid even legal concealed carry, likely for insurance reasons, since the clientele is surely offended by such notices. If an election is pending, you will see some campaign signs here and there as you enter.

You walk in and pay your fee, usually around five dollars or a little higher, and get your hand stamped as proof that you have paid, so you can get back in if you leave the building temporarily. A table nearby is manned by police officers who are inspecting guns that people bring in, usually for sale or trade, to make sure they are not loaded. Here and there, other police officers stand by, friendly and watchful—they seem not to be expecting any trouble.

And so you are in, and the world of the gun show lies before you like the pleasant Land of Counterpane. Tables displaying goods for sale are laid out in long blocks stretching nearly the length of the hall. To work a gun show systematically, you start on one side and walk up and down between the blocks. Vendors sit in folding chairs within these blocks. They are there for the long haul and have brought coolers, boxes, and cases for selling their wares. Many have dogs. These vendors form a community within the community of the gun show. Most are friendly with one another; most will watch another's table if someone needs to go to the bathroom. They have paid a modest fee for the right to rent tables, usually for two days. Many of these men have wives or daughters with them, but it is predominantly a male group of vendors. If you ask a question of a woman, she may often call to the man in charge. She is there mainly to take money and make sure nothing gets stolen.

Many of these vendors are federally licensed dealers. Some are ordinary citizens who may sell their guns legally so long as they are not making a living at it. So you will find the fellow who is retiring, downsizing a collection, or moving house and wants to shed some guns, knives, gun leather, oddly assorted ammunition, knives, and such. The licensed dealers must follow all the rules any other dealer does, including requiring firearms buyers to fill out federal forms and wait while the information is phoned in to Washington. A private individual is not bound by these rules and may sell to anyone he thinks could otherwise legally buy a gun—but this assumption is never really checked on. This is the so-called gun show loophole, which is a misnomer. You may go next door in most states and buy a gun from your neighbor without having to pass a background check, so long as your neighbor is not a licensed dealer. All a gun show does is to bring together such private individuals for greater convenience of sale. It is in this regard a market but not a black market. The gun show is thus a mishmash of authority and legal constraint and individual citizen action on the edge of the law. In that sense, it somewhat resembles the Wild West.

Most of the tables at a gun show display, who knew, guns. But many of them display knives, some mixed in with guns. Some larger knife dealers will have extensive displays of only knives, machetes, and so on. There will be several tables displaying military surplus clothing and equipment: boots, jackets, vests. Some tables will have trays of surgical equipment, no doubt for sale to doomsday preppers equipping themselves for amateur bullet extractions. Some tables will sell holsters of leather or synthetic fabric, for pistols or long guns. Some of these sell bandoliers for carrying lots of readily available ammunition across the chest or in belts. A few vendors will sell books of militaria, cowboy history, gun lore, and other related subjects. Perhaps the most marginal of the vendors still linked to gun culture are those who sell bumper stickers and posters, all of a conservative bent, castigating former president Obama, declaring an intention to shoot trespassers, and so forth.

A feature of every gun show I've ever seen, which I can't claim to comprehend fully, is the presence of distinctly nongun vendors. Someone is usually selling roasted nuts or candy, jams, meat jerky, homemade honey, and such. Reliably, you can find at least one vendor offering porcelain figures or women's jewelry, and a more out-of-place kind of commodity for a gun show can scarcely be imagined. Are these gifts to take home to placate a spouse for yet another gun purchase? Are they an echo of the civilizing touch that the schoolmarm brought to the frontier town? Your guess is as good as mine, but the consistency with which you find these unicorn vendors is remarkable.

The aisles between the blocks of tables are packed tight with gun enthusiasts threading their way slowly past the displays. This is no stroll through luxurious surroundings; it is more like the crowded saloons of the Westerns to which the dusty cowboys go after a season in the wide open spaces. Gun people are fond of repeating the old chestnut that an armed society is a polite society. We hope it is true, at any rate, but some attention to manners is required as one winds through these tight spaces. Every now and then, passage must be created for a man in a wheelchair, maybe a veteran facing long recovery from wounds. One constantly begs pardon for the inevitable jostling needed to progress through the crowd. This physical proximity to others reinforces a sense that there is nothing fancy about those in attendance. You will never smell cologne. You will from time to time get a whiff of body odor or clothing that has been worn to work in. You will physically encounter people up close and personally.

If manners are expected to be performed while squeezing through the aisles, a more rigid code of conduct is in force for interaction with the vendors selling merchandise, specifically those selling guns. Sometimes these rules are expressed in signs that are posted, but more often they are just commonly understood. Chief among them is that one should ask permission of the vendor to pick up a gun on display. Vendors selling guns, especially the licensed dealers, will have scores of pistols, rifles, and shotguns on display, sitting in boxes if new, sitting out on the table if used. It is considered bad form simply to pick up a gun and examine it. Sometimes it's not physically possible to do so because a security cable is running through many of the guns and must be disconnected before an examination is even possible. You may be reprimanded if you forget to follow this rule.

If the dominant performance of gun culture is working class, then it is white working class. That is by far the overwhelming demographic of the shows. Occasionally one will see an African American or Asian. In Texas, one will see Latinos not infrequently, but still not in proportion to their share of the state's population. This demographic fact is consistent with the cowboy myth if not the cowboy reality. In fact, many historical cowboys were African American or of Mexican heritage, but try to find those groups represented in classic Western movies. It's all white cowboys and their deadly enemies, the Indians, with the occasional tragic half-breed to spice up the plot line. I have never seen outright racism or microaggressions at a gun show, but the performative message is strong that this is a white-dominated culture.

The buzz of conversation at the shows is in earnest. Accents are southern or southwestern in Texas. Even in the North, accents will never be perceived to be upper class. Vocabulary choice also is working class, simple and straight-forward. I don't at all mean to imply that people at the shows are unlearned; I am friends with a Mensa member and organization officer who frequents the shows and points out to me vendors from that group. It's that people express themselves plainly and simply. You will hear snippets of hunting stories as you walk along. Some buyers or vendors may be discussing hunting dogs they are training, selling, or buying. A few are growling out conservative political views, which is consistent with the bumper stickers and posters available at some tables, which dish up a fair bit of vitriol toward Obama, the United Nations, Michael Bloomberg, and the like. These are good ol' boys, and they talk like that.

When you do hear specialized talk with technical vocabulary, it will be in discussions of the guns. Most of the men here, whether show patrons or vendors, have some kind of specialized knowledge of history, firearms, or ammunition. It is genuine knowledge, carefully assembled over a lifetime of experience and learning about the subject. You will hear historical stories of particular guns, of notable feats of marksmanship, of the use of certain guns in war or law enforcement or on the frontier, and so forth. You will hear the technical merits of different guns and cartridges discussed in exquisite detail. Some of this talk is the performance of expertise and knowledge, a display of mastery within a very specific field of knowledge. Here, the old and middle-aged are generally in their glory, drawing on lifetimes of experience and learning to create performances of expertise.

The gun show is an escape from restrictions and conformities of big business, in many ways. If you go to a brick-and-mortar store for firearms, the selection is inherently limited. Most such stores will be stocking dealers for the big names in firearms manufacturing: Ruger, Browning, Glock, and the like. Many varieties of guns may be offered, but they will all be what is current and newly available on the market. Gun shows, on the other hand, draw private individuals who have combed through their closets to find old, strange, discontinued guns and obsolete cartridges. The "kitchen table" licensed dealers who show up are always doing business on a much smaller scale than are their brethren in the big-box stores, so they must supplement their stock with a wide range of used guns taken in trade or purchased used from customers. In fact, you can always find customers walking the floor who are selling their own guns, and they wear signs advertising the fact.

What all this means is that the odd, strange, wonderful, and even legendary in guns, cartridges, and gear may be found at a gun show much more commonly than at a regular store. You will simply not predictably find an old Colt Peacemaker revolver in a regular store, but you can at a gun show. You will find obscure guns brought back from the European or Pacific theater of World War II, or the Korean or Vietnamese War, and you will be able to talk to the veteran who brought them back—but you can't do that at a regular store. The gun show is therefore a site of the unique, the individual, the storied. To reference a distinction made by Walter Benjamin, you will find guns that began as mechanical reproductions but have through age and history and association become nearly unique works of art (Benjamin). The gun show is a kind of museum, an archive, of individuality and uniqueness that I think can speak strongly to the working-class individual who dreams of riding free through the western wilds. It is a kind of escape from the regulation and repetitive drudgery of most workplaces today.

If I attend a gun show with someone I know personally from other contexts, I am always impressed with how that person and I manage to conform ourselves so as to belong to the crowd. Whether one is "fronting," though, I claim that the gun show is perhaps the most simulational and performative focused site in the country. A parallel example might be the annual motorcycle rally in Sturgis, South Dakota, in which all manner of upper-middle-class professionals perform outlaw motorcycleness alone with the "real" outlaw motorcycles. That is performative and simulational. But for the most part, the gun culture crowd is always performative and simulational because those firearms are so rarely pulled out and used.

We may then think of the gun show as a great site of yearning: yearning to be a cowboy, a Texan, a rude mechanical, working-class person. People yearn to master the power and violence of the gun. They yearn to fling defiance in the face of authority. Yet none of this really happens at the gun show. It is highly performative and bound within the parameters of a simulation, much like Helmglot's apocryphal porpoise (Brummett et al.). It is a place where grownups can go to exercise their imaginations, but imaginations only.

Perhaps in some way this truth informs us of other dimensions of Texan culture. Much of what we do when we barbecue, ride pickups, wear cowboy gear, pile our hair up like beehives is a yearning for an identity that is hard if not impossible to actually achieve. The fatuous threats and hints that Texas may secede and become its own republic again are understood even in Texas to be so much hot air. This is Texas: we have our dreams, and they are strong ones, but the dreams do not always survive the morning light.

Works Cited

Benjamin, Walter. *Illuminations.* Translated by Harry Zohn and edited by Hannah Arendt. Schocken Books, 1968.
Brummett, Barry, et al. "NSFW: Experiencing Immanentism or Transcendence upon Hearing Gilbert Gottfried's Rendition of Fifty Shades of Grey in the Postmodern Workplace, or Liberatory Criminology," *Science Journal of Sociology and Anthropology*, Dec. 2014, vol. 2014, doi:10.7237/sjsa/235.

Brian McNely,
University of Kentucky

18. EL PASO, PLASTIC BAGS, AESTHETICS

*I*n an iconic scene from the 1999 film *American Beauty*, two characters sit side by side in a darkened room, gazing at a television, mesmerized by the lilting, delicate movements of a white plastic bag dancing among fall leaves against a red brick background. "Do you want to see the most beautiful thing I've ever filmed?" one character asks the other, who sits silently, watching, slightly (we may infer) in awe—of the animate plastic bag, of the young man next to her, of the odd, quotidian sublimity of the situation. This is a moment in which ordinarily invisible and tacit phenomena are made visible and explicit: the electricity that presages a snowstorm, the capricious breezes that cause the bag to float and shift, the understated aesthetics of everyday life and affect and care.

"That's the day I realized that there was this entire life behind things," the videographer says. And that's likely the day he realized, too, that places are made, in part, among the lives of *things*. That red brick wall, in that particu-
220   lar spot, will resonate differently. The place is changed, made, *invented* by its

association with vital matter, with beauty, with epiphany. As Heidegger has argued, we rarely notice what surrounds us, what participates in our understandings of places, what envelops us. We willingly evade things, in fact. But Shaviro, channeling Heidegger, notes that matter often erupts into our consciousness: a white plastic bag, dancing in the breeze, no longer ignored, seen for what it is, for where it goes, for what it does. A white plastic bag may reach out to us, from across distances both physical and metaphysical, and our perceptions may both respond to and be affected by its disclosures (Shaviro 117).

"When objects encounter one another," Shaviro argues, "the basic mode of their relation is neither theoretical nor practical and neither epistemological nor ethical" (52). Instead, "every relation among objects is an *aesthetic* one" (53). In approaching things aesthetically (as they approach each other), humans may feel objects for their own sake (53); we grasp and marvel and contort at momentary eruptions of *worldishness* (Heidegger's notion of world-*making*). In Shaviro's terms, the animate white plastic bag propositions us, lures us into new possible relations with things, places, and times (54–55). When we respond to such propositions, we encounter new possibilities, we *feel* something we would not have otherwise felt (55).

My eight years in El Paso, Texas, are punctuated by visions and sounds of plastic bags. Steel blue Walmart bags caught in thorny blooming yuccas or razor wire. White convenience store sacks borne on the formidable West Texas wind, circling like buzzards above the desert. THANK YOU THANK YOU THANK YOU bags shredded yet still legible in a clutch of prickly pear. Plastic bags are inescapably yoked to my understanding of El Paso, of my time there, of their relation to other things beautiful and tawdry, sublime and lurid, visible and

invisible. I watched plastic bags swoop up and over El Paso's ubiquitous rock and mortar walls. I watched them race up the steep slopes of the Franklin Mountains in summer windstorms, bright white spots violently visible through the dust, sand, and dirt of my neighborhood. I saw in them the scale of consumption in my city and region. I watched them defile the border. I watched them bloom, like desert poppies, among hearty ocotillos.

This chapter considers how place is invented in part through aesthetic encounters with things—humble, utilitarian, ubiquitous plastic bags. During my time in El Paso, they often erupted into my consciousness, pixelating the desert and urban landscape, forming aesthetic, inventional relations with *my* El Paso. In my El Paso, matter is vibrant (Bennett); plastic bags, mundane and ordinary, are not passive "but immanently active, productive, and formative" (Shaviro 99). Autoethnographic vignettes and fieldwork photographs accompany—and extend—reflections on both theory and method in the remainder of this chapter.

Commute

From 2001 until 2009, I drove at least twenty to thirty minutes each day— each way, morning and evening—from my home in northeast El Paso, in the foothills of the Franklin Mountains, to downtown. Heading south in the morning on Patriot Freeway, I saw the Chihuahuan Desert yawning in the distance to my left, the rocky, sparse Franklin Mountains, with elevations of seven thousand feet, bathed by early light, to my right. Mornings were often still, quiet, and cool. To preserve both gas and freon, I'd drive with the rear windows of my car rolled down, the smell of dust, diesel, and creosote in the

air. When I eventually merged onto Interstate 10 westbound, the morning commute was more like being *on* the world than being *in* the world (Ingold). Ciudad Juárez, sprawling south across the desert, to my left, the point of the Franklin Mountains and the heart of El Paso to my right, downtown straight ahead, the city at sixty-five mph big, impersonal, distanced.

The drive home was more intimate. Near Fort Bliss, heading north, I would leave Patriot Freeway for Railroad Drive, a nearly derelict stretch of asphalt through parts of town intentionally unseen by most El Pasoans. At fifty-five mph, with far less traffic than the freeway, Railroad was a respite from commuting anxieties. On my right, train tracks and endless desert scrub, on my left, a military golf course giving way to warehouses, an occasional squat saloon, manufacturing facilities, and miles of gunmetal chain-link fence, often topped by razor wire, glinting in the evening sun as it dropped mercifully behind the mountains. Along this backroad, plastic bags found purchase. They fluttered in the evening winds, were buffeted by passing trucks. Not beautiful, not ugly. Bright emblems, instead—points of contrast against the relentless dusty, brown cityscape. Hanging on to the last bits of human development at the edge of the desert, yearning toward passersby, waving, waving.

Aesthetic Intensities

In arguing for speculative philosophy's aesthetic dimension, Shaviro notes that "nothing is hidden; there are no more concealed depths. The universe of things is not just available to us but increasingly unavoidable" (43). Plastic bags do not necessarily carry meaning, they just are: inescapable, mobile, vital facets of a place and a time and a way of being in the world. "Things are active and interactive far beyond any measure of their presence to us," Shaviro suggests. So a thing "is always more than its qualities; it always exists and acts independently of, and in excess of, the particular ways that we grasp and comprehend it" (49). Our encounters with such things may surface as momentary intensities—"regularly, intermittently, urgently, or as a slight shudder" (Stewart, *Ordinary Affects* 10).

In his efforts to bring together the work of Alfred North Whitehead with the speculative realism of scholars such as Graham Harman and Levi Bryant, Shaviro turns to aesthetic engagements as a way of understanding such human-nonhuman (and nonhuman-nonhuman) intensities. Aesthetics, Shaviro argues, "has to do with things insofar as they cannot be cognized or subordinated to concepts and also insofar as they cannot be utilized, or normatively regulated, or defined according to rules" (53). Indeed, an aesthetic interaction is potentially noncorrelational, the obverse of phenomenological apprehension and response. Aesthetic experience, Shaviro adds, "is always asymmetrical: it needs to be posed in terms of a subject, as well as an object. A world of objects is really a world of experiencings" (63). In other words, an immanent subjectivity is at play among both humans and nonhumans, writ large (64).

This understanding of human-nonhuman relations is radically different from the "default metaphysics" of Western culture (Harman 25), which contends "that the world is necessarily beholden to our ways of shaping and processing it" (Shaviro 66). But the world and its things "cannot in any way be contained or constrained by the question of our *access* to" them (66). Things exist without correlation or reconciliation to our thoughts about them. Indeed, one could reverse this metaphysics: we exist as we are because of our relation and response to things that exist as they are. We are inescapably situated by such interactions (see McNely). As Shaviro suggests, "We are alluding to objects—and objects to one another—almost all the time" (70). And in these allusions and relations, "we can be aesthetically *moved* by objects or causally *affected* by them even when we do not (and cannot) actually know or cognize them" (70).

In troubling Harman's take on speculative realism, therefore, Shaviro argues that "knowledge is just one particular sort of relation—and not even an especially important one at that" (105). We need not obsess about *knowing* a place; I need not *know* why plastic bags circulate, seemingly unchecked, to experience that they do. I need not *know* about the climate patterns that drive El Paso's infamous afternoon winds, but that the two things encountering one another—winds and plastic bags—create something that affects me and my experience of being in place. Rhetorical invention, it follows, need not equate (or even aspire) to knowledge claims.

Our perceptions, therefore, need not be only or always filtered through epistemic correlations. Rather than developing knowledge of a thing, we might instead posit that "no amount of information can ever *exhaust* the thing" (117). We cannot know, and do not *need* to know, to credibly invent and engage. Perception, in an aesthetic key, would be better conceived "as a nonrepresentational process of continual feedback, response, and adjustment" (118). One object's contact with another may be noncognitive yet palpably suasive. "A thing may affect me," Shaviro argues, "without my having access to the 'inner life' of the thing, or it to mine" (144). He adds, "I am always being affected and altered by things that call to me, or brush up against me, or delight or repulse me, or otherwise superficially encounter me" (144). Things produce "contact at a distance," a kind of affect, often aesthetic, that is formative and inventive "without knowledge and without phenomenological intentionality" (147). Aesthetics, he concludes, "is the realm of immanent, noncognitive contact" (148). "Through aesthetics," then, "we can act in the world and relate to other things in the world without reducing it and them to mere correlates of our own thought" (156).

"The question of composing worlds," Kathleen Stewart argues in a manner congruent with Shaviro, is a question of "how forces of all kinds take form and how forms take on a charge and enter circuits of reaction" ("Autoethnography" 660). Another way of stating this, following Latour, is that our inventional practices around place are interagentive rhetorical efforts both thrown together and deliberative. Attunements to rhetorical ambience (Rickert), to our relations with things, can pull inventional practices "into alignment with phenomena" (Stewart 661), a form of research and writing that performs important kinds of work, that accounts for circulations, reactions, thrownness (McNely). Descriptive detours, both visual and discursive, through and around aesthetic relations might "note the incommensurateness of the elements [of experience] throwing themselves together" (Stewart 661). Stewart suggests, beautifully, that such work "might become a hinge onto the commonplace labors of becoming sentient to whatever is happening" (661).

In the Interstices

I have long admired desire paths—those well-trod throughways from one place to another, sanctioned not by urban planners and municipalities, but by the wisdom and pragmatism of everyday life. Alleys, too, comfort me—not-quite-official spaces, the backs of places, interstices. To travel these routes is to feel the city differently, to hear and smell it differently, to see it differently. The gravity of interstices is disproportionate to their size; they inordinately pull things such as plastic bags into their orbit. The bags live, for a time, in such places, perhaps for the same reasons that I am drawn there, perhaps for reasons alien to me.

In the interstices, you can sidestep the world's relentless bother for a moment. Things get quiet, and you find shelter from the winds. You find shade. The pungent smell of urine is a deterrent for many, but not for you. You deal with it—fuck, you *embrace* it—because it means fewer people, more time and space to think and be. This isn't where you'll stay forever. It was never meant to be that kind of space. It is instead a waypoint, a stopover, a shortcut to someplace else, a respite until the time comes to move on to an avenue or boulevard.

In an alley, or along a shrouded, dusty trail that few will travel, you hear the plastic bags among displaced breezes. Embracing razor wire or enveloped by thorned weeds, they rustle and wheeze. The clarity of their sound—the sometimes gentle, sometimes angry twisting of plastic bags—means the white noise of the city is elsewhere, the belching engines and cell phone conversations and horns and walk signs distanced. These bags dissemble by day, seemingly content; they move when you're not looking. They do not offer themselves to you, necessarily, but they make no attempt to hide their availability, for now. Those embracing razor wire will eventually disassemble, their parts moving on to new encounters elsewhere in the city, perhaps eventually beyond it.

[Visual] Autoethnography

Autoethnography, according to Denzin, explores the particularity of lives lived and grounded in specific historical moments (x). Interpretation, from a researcher's perspective, "works forward to the conclusion of a set of acts taken up by the subject while working back in time, interrogating the historical, cultural, and biographical conditions that moved the person to experience the events being studied" (x). A foundational question for autoethnographic work, then, is this: "How do [people] give meaning to their lives and perform these meanings in their daily lives?" (x). As a methodology, autoethnography is unique in its affordances for exploring the specificity of experience. Autoethnography, then, is especially suited to explorations of specific objects (plastic bags) in a specific place (El Paso, Texas) during a specific time (the first decade of the twenty-first century).

An overarching metaphor in Denzin's theory of autoethnography is *pentimento*: "something painted out of a picture which later becomes visible again" (1). A trace, a something made tangible. In autoethnographic inquiry, there is no single truth, "only multiple images and traces of what has been, what could have been, and what now is" (1). For these reasons, and several others, autoethnography is a methodology that many researchers actively resist. Stewart notes that autoethnography is "unsettling for some, [but] a relief for others" (659). What is unsettling? The usual methodological peccadilloes—no recourse to an easy grasp on reliability, validity, and the dream of objectivity. But also unsettling is the power of writing, as a mode of invention and a way of bringing forth worlds. There are those who might be offended by a "world presented starkly as a composition of elements thrown together into something with texture, density, and force" through writing. And this methodology presents other discomfiting textures for some, presentations of "how things are the way they are without laying out just what this might mean (what it might do) in the scheme of how we think and feel about things" (659).

This kind of noncognitive, noncorrelational inquiry should feel familiar by now.

I'm happy in these tensions. Contemporary autoethnography, in my home discipline of rhetoric, is a scholarly interstice. It is a mode, Stewart contends, of processual reaction—"you write from a place in which the world is reacting to something: it's animated, incited, thrown together into something" (660). Autoethnography is a methodology for reimagining subject-object relations and circulations. "The objects of autoethnography" Stewart adds, "are tellingly diffuse yet precise." Autoethnographic inquiry "is one route into a broader-ranging, more supple exploration of what happens to people, how force hits bodies, how sensibilities circulate and become, perhaps delicately or ephemerally, collective." For rhetoricians, autoethnography "composes a world perturbed by the singularities of events in ways that can be generative" (661).

Whether it is primarily evocative or analytic (Anderson), autoethnography is "a way of calling up the textures and densities of worlds of all kinds formed out of this and that—identities, situations, scenes, sensory conditions, bodies, meanings, weights, rhythms, absence" (Stewart 667). As a methodology, it is "a hinge onto a moment of some world's legibility." Autoethnography, then, "can be a way to forge a linkage between self and world, the abstract and concrete, the massive and minute, the fuzzy or smudged yet precise. It is a composing that attunes to forces coming into form" (667). It is an approach to engaging ambience and worldishness.

Visual autoethnography enlarges the scope and scale of a world's legibility. Drawing on Laruelle, Shaviro argues that photography "'*lets things be*' without standing in for them or representing them." Photography "exemplifies a mode of thought that *presents* things without being *about* them—that is, without representing them or *intending* them as objects" (130). All too often, the scholarly use of visuals in my field is tautological: images merely illustrate discursive arguments. Videographic data, when collected at all, is criminally reduced, turned into verbal transcripts and treated like texts. But visualizing field sites, participants, sensory engagements, and circulatory intensities offers "active engagement with the material of the world" in mutually generative processes (Liggett 103). Visual methods, in other words, may promote "sites of participatory reading" and understanding (Liggett 118)—between researchers and research sites, between researchers and audiences, and between research sites and audiences.

Here I share with you in writing the El Paso I knew. In fieldwork photographs, composed several years after leaving, I share with you an El Paso both as I see it and as it persists. Visual fieldwork, therefore, is not a view of a hidden El Paso, but an El Paso stuffed to bursting with vivid and vibrant things, scenes, and spaces that we typically unsee. These visual arguments sometimes overlap with the written, but they always make arguments of their own too.

They afford aesthetic engagements. They both provoke and let things be.

Anthropomorphisms

Where does a plastic bag want to be? Does it want to stay with others, its full length and width luridly and persistently pressed up against seemingly identical companions in the unused stack at the end of a Walmart checkout counter? Does it want to fly like a buzzard above the desert, held aloft on unseen thermals, sage and rocks and dying postthunderstorm rivulets its fleeting domain? Does it want to disassemble and foster flight elsewhere, its contiguousness shredded and parceled out as material in so many bird nests? Does it want to see the city from the rear window of a hatchback, loosely holding juice boxes and bags of potato chips? Does it want to line a litter box? Does it yearn for the thorny embrace of prickly pear?

When you are a plastic bag, you are born to encounter others, to hold and care and move others. You can stretch and contract, accommodate and recede. Fingers and hands and beaks and claws move inside you, yank you up, pull you back, crush you and tear you and throw you. Your plans are rarely their plans. You will outlive all these others. You will eventually approach and engage others like you—razor wire, chain-link fences, steady, salty ocotillos. You move, move, move, your timescale unfolding across decades rather than days. You might take ten years to traverse Segundo Barrio. You might spend four years tucked inside an unseen fold of plaster and brick, an embracer

embraced and sheltered and unbothered. You might spend three years hold-ing a stack of newspapers in the corner of a garage. You might spend a year hanging from a rusty nail in dim light, holding sandpaper, wood filler, and a plastic putty knife. Eventually, you'll move.

Shaviro explores Levi Bryant's notion of a "democracy of objects" from the perspective of both Whitehead and object-oriented ontology. He notes that both approaches recognize that "perception, feeling, and aesthetics are universal structures, not specifically human ones." All entities, therefore, feel other entities. And anthropomorphizing what nonhumans feel and perceive might actually work against anthropocentrism (61). Moreover, "if all entities have feelings and exert agency, this means that they are all . . . vital, active, and creative" (62). Vitality may be "unevenly distributed, but it is at work everywhere" (63).

Inverting Heroic Copulations

In *On Photography*, Susan Sontag claims that early photographs were to be "idealized images" in the tradition of painting. But photography, to her dis-may, eventually revised "definitions of what is beautiful and ugly," relishing in particular the mundane and everyday. Sontag argues that "to photograph is to confer importance," since in some way all photographs "accord value to their subjects" (28). This led, she argues, to the "polemical pursuit of the trivial and vulgar" by American photographers of note (29). In one of her most arresting criticisms, Sontag argues that "photography is a kind of over-statement, a heroic copulation with the material world" (30).

Yet in autoethnographic inquiry, Stewart claims, "it may sometimes be possible for a detail to remain a detail." Such details need not "become the symbol of a meaning"; instead, autoethnographic work, particularly visual autoethnography, pivots on "the tactile compositions of the living out of things." This is the labor of theory, Stewart adds, the "pulling into proximity to the ordinary work of becoming sentient to a world's bodies, rhythms, ways of being in noise and light and space" (668).

In other words, we may invert Sontag's claims through these approaches. It is Sontag who overstates and overreaches, ascribing meaning to photo-graphic practice and ascribing intentionality to photographers. Sometimes a detail remains a detail, a moment simply a moment, an understanding of place composed of such details and moments. Noncognitive, noncorrelational aesthetic calls and responses. Because, as Shaviro notes, it may be impossible to exhaust the characteristics and aesthetic potentials of a thing (117), visual and discursive reflection may well be understatement.

In this way, theory can be slow and small, its epistemological reach un-certain and unsettled.

Works Cited

American Beauty. Directed by Sam Mendes. DreamWorks Pictures, 1999.

Anderson, Leon. "Analytic Autoethnography." *Journal of Contemporary Ethnography*, vol. 35, 2006, pp. 373–95.

Bennett, Jane. *Vibrant Matter: A Political Ecology of Things.* Duke UP, 2010.

Bryant, Levi. *The Democracy of Objects.* Open Humanities Press, 2011.

Denzin, Norman. *Interpretive Autoethnography.* 2nd ed., Sage, 2013.

Harman, Graham. *Prince of Networks: Bruno Latour and Metaphysics.* re.press, 2009.

Heidegger, Martin. *Being and Time.* Translated by Joan Stambaugh. SUNY P, 2010.

Ingold, Timothy. "Bindings against Boundaries: Entanglements of Life in an Open World." *Environment and Planning A*, vol. 40, 2008, pp. 1796–1810.

Laruelle, François. *The Concept of Non-Photography.* Sequence/Urbanomic, 2011.

Latour, Bruno. "Another Way to Compose the Common World." The Executive Session of the Annual Meeting of the American Anthropological Association, 2013, Chicago. Keynote Address.

Liggett, Helen. *Urban Encounters.* U of Minnesota P, 2003.

McNely, Brian J. "Circulatory Intensities: Take a Book, Return a Book." *Rhetoric, through Everyday Things*, edited by Scot Barnet and Casey Boyle, U of Alabama P, 2016, pp. 139–54.

Rickert, Thomas. *Ambient Rhetoric: The Attunements of Rhetorical Being.* Pittsburgh: U of Pittsburgh P, 2013.

Shaviro, Steven. *The Universe of Things.* U of Minnesota P, 2014.

Sontag, Susan. *On Photography.* Picador, 1977.

Stewart, Kathleen. "An Autoethnography of What Happens." *Handbook of Autoethnography*, edited by Stacy Holman Jones et al., Left Coast Press, 2013, pp. 659–68.

———. *Ordinary Affects.* Duke UP, 2007.

Jillian Sayre,
Rutgers University–Camden

19. WEARY LAND: THE SPACE AND PLACE OF WEST TEXAS

> From early morning to late in the evening to have nothing before
> you but the self-same hills, the self-same interminable plains, the
> self-same kind of dry soil, to meet hardly any one, and to see only a
> few small villages in the distance, —how can such a journey be called
> anything but wearisome?
> —Carel Willem Meredith van de Velde, *Narrative of a Journey*
> *through Syria and Palestine in 1851 and 1852*

"Every Story Is a Travel Story—a Spatial Practice"

When the frontier romance reached the Great Plains that separated the Near
West—the first West—from what would become the Far West, the rocky,
arid land where "West" would become formalized as a genre (the Western),
it wrote the landscape as a vast inland sea. Between the shores of *near* and *far*
intervened an expansive self-same universe of waving grasses and unbroken,
forever-extended horizons. James Fenimore Cooper, whose Leatherstocking
had thrived in the wooded, game-rich world of New York and Ohio, offers his
frontiersman the mercy of death as he tires and weakens in this opening up
of the landscape. At the close of *The Prairie*, Leatherstocking's monument,
the lingering sign of his passing, comes to serve as a waypoint for those who
manage to cross over this uncanny ocean and reach that alien land (forev-
er-far) beyond. Beyond the sea, beyond the tiresome prairie, beyond death,
that *farther* West is conceived in advance as an exhausted, weary space.

I am from the part of the West where the earth long ago shattered that
unending flatness, rose up against it in ranges that now stretch the length of
the continent. If the Central Lowlands and Great Plains can be characterized
by a quiet, enervating force, then the mountains are loud in their disruption,
reinvigorating. The mountains are a spectacle of distinction, and nestled in
the front range of the Rockies, I grew accustomed to the way this land calls
attention to itself, shaping my locative capacities, the intertwined narrative
of space, place, and direction. Am I headed north or south? Look up. Which
side are the mountains on? Soon I didn't have to look up anymore. I felt them.

232

I carried them with me, an internal compass. These grand referential monuments are, relative to myself, eternal, and their size and antiquity attached a sense of security to my understanding of where I am and where I am headed. And movement itself is important for this spatializing; it functions, as Michel de Certeau notes, as a "practice" of space in which reside intricacies of lived space that exceed representations of them. In thus dividing practice from representation, Certeau includes narrative in the former category: "Every story," he writes, "is a travel story—a spatial practice." These stories we tell, in and about the places that surround us, "simultaneously producing geographies of actions and drifting into the commonplaces of an order, do not merely constitute a 'supplement' to pedestrian enunciations and rhetorics. . . . They make the journey, before or during the time the feet perform it" (115–16). The space I have constructed as home is not simply produced by an anthropocentric and theoretical idea of geography, of man's construction of space through the generalized experience of a situated interaction with it, but also shaped in important ways by affective inscriptive powers of the land on the individual who encounters it. With the important attention paid to the social production of space (Lefebvre; Certeau; Massey), it is important to remember that this sociality includes geological and other nonanthropological interlocutors. If, at home, my movement feels certain, assured, this has much to do with the spectacular, interruptive, and relatively fixed mountains themselves.

When I moved to Texas, I had to travel west to go home. I traced and retraced my way across central and northwestern Texas, hypnotized by the flat, hard, unchanging landscape that moved past at the same pace, no matter what speed I was driving. Whereas the mountains back home were grand, towering above the plains and marking off a bounded space, here the land is vast, opening up too much, pushing past the horizon. On these trips, I spent hours moving through the Llano Estacado, the mesa that makes up most of northwestern Texas, staring into its smooth—tiresome—expanse. When Francisco Coronado arrived here in 1541, he described it as "tan sin seña como si estuviéramos engolfado en la mar," so desolate, without landmark, that he and his men felt as though they had been swallowed up by the sea. There, he says, they wandered, uncertain of their location, "porque en todos [los llanos] no hay una piedra, ni cuesta, ni árbol, ni mata, ni cosa que lo parezca" (263). Almost half a millennium later, the road keeps me from wandering, from getting lost, but I am still drawn to Coronado's apophasis[1]; I am similarly dislocated by the lack that surrounds me, the overwhelming feeling of a place that is here and a space that is *not here*: no rocks, Coronado wrote, nor hill, nor tree, nor shrubs, nor anything that looks like it. On one trip through the llano, my truck, surprised by snow, catches the slush mounded up between tire tracks on the highway. It spins twice and goes off the road, where I find myself dazed, unsure whether I am pointed in the right direction, uncertain which way to go when I pull out of the grass. The fresh blanket of white in front of and behind me aggravates the sense of expansive sameness underneath. To that exhausting repertoire, I added journeys directly west, to that space between the straight and curved lines of national and state borders, imaginary (even when "natural") lines that travel hundreds of miles before collapsing into each other: the Trans-Pecos; the Far West of West Texas. These lands, this West and farther West of Texas, seem so full of nothing, brimming over with it, and in laboring to move through it, I become overwhelmed, even misled by its expanse. When objects appear on the horizon, they do not move for hours, despite my dogged pursuit of them at seventy-five miles per hour. I begin to wonder if the testimony of my movement in the beige flashes outside my car window is illusory; the roadside moves along, but everything else seems to be standing still. When I stop, when I stand still in the landscape, I do not find it any easier to grasp. Walking on the train tracks outside Valentine, Texas, I feel the open and undifferentiated landscape as an endless reflection of itself, a suspension of space. As if someone held up a mirror to the world. I feel worn down by its apparent vacancy. I feel weary of its repetition.

To experience and announce one's weariness may seem like a strange position from which to engage with place, a concept laden with a priori assumptions about space, time, and the perceiving subject, but the production of weariness in the encounter with this landscape might help us better understand the ways in which the vast and self-same environment of West Texas resists, overwrites, and overwhelms our productions of space. Michel de Certeau argues that "space occurs as the effect produced by the operations that orient it, situate it, temporalize it." "Space," he writes, "is like the word when it is spoken, that is, when it is . . . situated as the act of a present (or of a time), and modified by the transformations caused by successive contexts" (117). Space, then, is produced out of an encounter with place by the locative—and thus narrative—capacities of the perceiving subject, a "spatial practice" that organizes the relation between physical components of the place *and* the temporal quality of those components. Certeau asserts this spatial practice as the other of the distant voyeur, whose totalizing view produces representations of space; the voyeur reads space, while the practitioner writes it (92–93). But unlike the urban environments on which he predicates this division (the voyeur is lifted above New York City to see the "whole," while the "walker" makes use of spaces both visible and invisible to the voyeur while at the same time is able to see only a small portion of the whole), the vast open space of West Texas places me in two positions at once; I am both distant witness and intimate practitioner. Nothing hides from my view save that portion beyond the horizon, yet it resists the sense of closure attached to panoptic or cartographic representation (Massey 109).

Moving through this space, then, I am forced to grapple simultaneously with the small portion of my immediate experience and the enormous excess that surrounds it and yet doesn't cohere into an accessible representation. Nothing hides from my view, but nothing seems to coalesce either. Instead, like Coronado, I experience the presence of the land as a neither . . . nor, a structure that Maurice Blanchot would describe as the Neutral, an idea he attaches to the experience of weariness, a position that "does not seek to hold two substantive features, two positivities, together in the mind at once, but rather attempts to retain two negatives or privative ones, along with their mutual negation of each other" (Jameson 180). This is the weariness that begins Blanchot's *Infinite Conversation*, an affect both produced by and requiring a representational suspension, making possible the work of "putting [the world] at a distance from itself in order to give voice to the otherwise of writing that precedes and exceeds the founding of any world" (Hill 288). Weariness is both a symptom of the limits of language (having exhausted its possibilities, one is exhausted at its im-possibilities) and a generative opening onto a nonnarrative counterstructural *place*, one that unworks the practices of space that render it legible.

If weariness can be understood as both a recognition of limits and an erosion of distinctions by which we order space, language, and the speaking subject, then it is important to remember that weariness and exhaustion are temporal concepts; they draw attention to experience in and through time. If the vast expanse of West Texas is produced as weariness upon the subject, it is because the exhausting openness of the landscape affects the time of the spatializing practice of movement; it is made vacant by the vastness. "Weariness is repetition," Blanchot writes, "a wearing away of every beginning" (xx). In the expansive sameness of the West Texas landscape, weariness is produced upon the body by its experience of excess *not its own*, the excessive unlocatable land itself.

"You Were Tired by Something, but Exhausted by Nothing"

While traveling through West Texas, I read to pass the time. And because I am laboring to pass the time in this space, I read Cormac McCarthy's *No Country for Old Men*, the 2005 novel that details the attempt to trace/track a "psychopathic killer" through this same landscape. The novel's minimalist style matches the landscape perfectly. Containing spare, terse dialogue, without elaborate descriptions, even without standard punctuation, the novel seems marked, as does the land, with the presence of *lack*. So full of nothing. Hundreds of miles separate sparsely populated towns, land that is crossed in cars, in buses, on foot, and on horseback, with the sheriff always arriving too late. Instead, he collects what remains, the dead men in the canyon and burning cars on the roadside that all mark the aftermath of events he no longer believes he can prevent. The central trope of pursuit forces the lawman of "a county the size of Delaware" to acknowledge as untenable his ability to regulate the expansive space of "outland country" (45, 25). Instead, Bell retreats from this fruitless pursuit to lament a futurity from which he seems both excluded and dragged into unwillingly.

If I have made the landscape of the novel appear as a large concern of its story, then my motivation for this essay has encouraged me to mislead you. While the vast, hard, and ungovernable country reflects—perfectly and endlessly—the protagonist's crisis of faith, there is a notable failure of spatializing effects in the text; the land is withheld, passing by in silence. In pursuit of the killer Chigurh, who is in turn pursuing the citizen Llewelyn Moss, Sheriff Ed Tom Bell crosses more than 1,500 miles of West Texas, but that movement passes by unmarked. Reading the text while traveling through the same landscape, I pull out an atlas to calculate Bell's mileage. Sanderson to Huntsville, three times in the first paragraph. We haven't even gotten to the story yet and Bell remarks that he made this trip "two or three times. Three times" (3). That's about 1,500 miles. Bell could have traveled all the way to the Atlantic Ocean in less time. No, I correct myself. That doesn't get him back home on those three trips. It's actually 2,940 miles, 200 miles more than driving from New York City to Los Angeles. The total is startling in its excess. I start to pay more attention to the outline of the pursuit in which towns are mentioned but travel itself is never narrated. Invoked and concluded, but otherwise passed over in silence; the economic prose does not make room for it. Bell goes from Sanderson to Sonora and back: 300 miles; Eagle Pass and back: 350 miles; a trip to Odessa puts 300 miles on the car; 400 more to get up to Van Horn and back. Tired of moving back and forth from atlas to book, I stopped mapping out the smaller trips. I finish the book long before we get home, and having nothing else to do, I fall asleep. "You were tired by something," Deleuze writes, "but exhausted by nothing" (4).

Bell is, of course, not the only traveler in this story. In the desert where the reader first meets Llewelyn Moss, we see the veteran sharpshooter scanning the West Texas landscape, locating the antelope he is hunting "a little under a mile away" on the edge of the "baked terracotta terrain of the running borderlands" (8). He selects a spot about half a mile away from which to shoot, noting with disappointment that it would "take the better part of an hour to get there." The distances are all marked as approximate; the journey across it is asserted. Then he is there. The spatializing practice of movement is narratively undermined by the silence in which it takes place. We don't know it. We can't know it. And when Moss reaches his perch, he understands that he can't know it either. "He knew the exact drop of the bullet in hundred yard increments," our laconic narrator notes. "It was the distance that was uncertain" (9). He shoots. And in the inverse of the missing hour-long journey to this moment, the time of the text expands as the bullet crosses the "uncertain" distance between man and animal:

> Even with the heavy barrel and the muzzlebrake the rifle bucked up off the rest. When he pulled the animals back into the scope he could see them all standing as before. It took the 150 grain bullet the better part of a second to get there but it took the sound twice that. They were standing looking at the plume of dust where the bullet had hit. Then they bolted. Running almost immediately at top speed out upon the barrial with the long whaang of the rifleshot rolling after them and caroming off the rocks and yawing back across the open country in the early morning solitude. (10)

Moss watches as the sound of the rifle chases the antelope and fills the floodplain, but only after the failure of his bullet and his own recovery from the concussion of the fired gun. The belated sound draws the reader's attention not only to the speed of the shot but also to the space in which it occurs, the medium for an encounter with an open and lonely country. But the sound fades, the antelope move out of sight, and the story pivots to other pursuits.

On his way to discovering the failed drug deal that attaches him to Bell's story, Moss passes a ridge "etched with pictographs perhaps a thousand years old. The men who drew them hunters like himself. Of them there was no other trace" (11). The marks are an echo that has lost its origin, untethered from the community upon which their legibility relies, and in their absence, we have a sense of the incommensurability of geological and anthropological time, the man that passes and the rocks that remain. Blanchot writes that indifference is the truth of weariness. Perhaps my weariness, then, is a trace of what cannot be moved. If the land resists me, exhausts me, perhaps it is because it just doesn't care.

"Something to Uncommunicate"

In a rare descriptive moment, Sheriff Bell takes note of the silence that surrounds him while staring out over his desert county. "So quiet," he thinks to himself. "Low hum of wind in the wires. High bloodweeds along the road. Wiregrass and sacahuista. Beyond in the stone arroyos the tracks of dragons. . . . That god lives in silence who has scoured the following land with salt and ash" (45). In contrast to the laconic anti-ambient text that surrounds it, the brief passage seems florid, baroque. The land, which has been rendered largely invisible by the elliptic movement of the characters and the focus on action, comes back into focus for a moment. The passage is quiet in subject and in structure, listing without comment the contents of the vista. But even in its subdued description, the irony of the passage, which requires a greater presence for Bell's voice in the service of naming both the quiet of the land and the silence of an absent creator, continues to re-mark a gap that such positive listing might seem to fill. And in god's silence, Coronado's apophasis becomes Bell's apophatic theology; to encounter "the following land" is to acknowledge the limits of our mortal knowledge. God, like the land, is without voice. Its knowledge withdrawn, the world held in abeyance just outside our reach. Bell gets back in his car and drives away.

As endless as the experience of West Texas may seem, as empty as the landscape appears, as weary as its effect on us may be, eventually we all get back in our cars and drive away. The journey ends, and on the other side, I can recognize a boundary to that space that makes it easier to understand. I start to feel restored when I see the Capulin Volcano in New Mexico. The Clayton-Raton volcanic field punctures the flat landscape, and I know that the mountains aren't far off. But before moving out of that space, staying instead at this experience of limit contained within the limitless landscape, I want to return to weariness not merely as disorientation or capitulation but rather as a wearing away—of expectations, of hierarchies, of knowledge—as an opening onto an unworking of spatial practices that allows us to experience the *placeness* of place and importantly the specific placeness of *this place*. Tim Morton writes that "whether we think of nature as an environment, or as other beings (animals, plants, and so on), it keeps collapsing either into subjectivity or into objectivity. It is very hard, perhaps impossible, to keep nature just where it appears—somewhere in between" (41). I do not offer the experience of weariness here as a correction to this collapse, as a resolution or synthesis of that division, but the "generative movement" of weariness can offer us an experience of limits and the breaking down of limits that might function as a yet-to-arrive revelatory affect (Muckelbauer and Donovan 857), even as it perhaps undermines representation and narrative. Blanchot writes:

> Let us admit that weariness makes speech less exact, thought less telling, communication more difficult; does not the inexactitude proper to this state reach through all these signs a kind of precision that would also finally serve exact speech by offering something to uncommunicate? But immediately this use of weariness again seems to contradict it, to render it more than false, suspect, which is in the way of its truth all the same. (xx)

Note

1. In *Ecology without Nature,* Timothy Morton aligns *apophasis* to a broader understanding of negative imagery rather than its limited definition as a rhetorical device of invoking an idea by denial of it. In this way, Morton links *apophasis* to *apophatic theology,* which defines the qualities of God in the negative rather than the positive: "As with rhythm, there is such a thing as negative imagery, or *apophasis*—saying something in the negative" (45). For more on this connection, see the third section of this essay.

Works Cited

Blanchot, Maurice. *The Infinite Conversation.* Translated by Steven Rendall. U of Minnesota P, 1993.

Certeau, Michel de. *The Practice of Everyday Life.* Translated by Steven Rendall. U of California P, 1984.

Cooper, James Fenimore. *The Prairie.* 1827. Penguin, 1987.

Coronado, Francisco Vazquez. "Carta a su Magestad, de Francisco Vazquez Coronado (20 de Octubre de 1541)." *Colección de documentos inéditos: relativos al descubrimiento, conquista y organización de las antiguas posesiones españolas de América y Oceanía, sacados de los archivos del reino, y muy especialmente del de Indias,* vol. 13, edited by Joaquín Francisco Pacheco et al. Imprenta de José María Perez, 1870, pp. 261–68.

Deleuze, Gilles. "The Exhausted," translated by Anthony Uhlmann. *SubStance,* vol. 24, no. 3, 1995, pp. 3–28.

Hill, Leslie. "Weary Words: L'Entretien Infini." *Clandestine Encounters: Philosophy in the Narratives of Maurice Blanchot,* edited by Kevin Hart, U of Notre Dame P, 2010, pp. 282–303.

Jameson, Fredric. *Archaeologies of the Future: The Desire Called Utopia and Other Science Fictions.* Verso, 2005.

Lefebvre, Henri. *The Production of Space.* Trans. Donald Nicholson-Smith. Blackwell, 1992.

Massey, Doreen B. *For Space.* SAGE, 2005.

McCarthy, Cormac. *No Country for Old Men.* Vintage, 2005.

Morton, Timothy. *Ecology without Nature: Rethinking Environmental Aesthetics.* Harvard UP, 2007.

Muckelbauer, John, and Tim Donovan. "To Do Justice to This Moment: Between Exhaustion and Totality." *JAC,* vol. 24, no. 4, 2004, pp. 851–70.

Contributors

Index

CONTRIBUTORS

Editors

Casey Boyle is an assistant professor in the Department of Rhetoric and Writing at the University of Texas–Austin, where he researches and teaches digital rhetoric and media theory.

Jenny Rice is an associate professor at the University of Kentucky and the author of *Distant Publics: Development Rhetoric and the Subject of Crisis.*

Contributors

James J. Brown Jr. is an associate professor of English and the director of the Digital Studies Center at Rutgers University–Camden. His book *Ethical Programs: Hospitality and the Rhetorics of Software* addresses the ethical and rhetorical dimensions of software.

Barry Brummett worked at Purdue University and the University of Wisconsin–Milwaukee before moving to the University of Texas–Austin, where he is the Communication Studies Department chair and the Charles Sapp Centennial Professor in Communication Studies. His research interests are in the rhetoric of popular culture and literary theorist and critic Kenneth Burke.

William T. Burdette is the program coordinator of the Digital Writing and Research Lab at the University of Texas–Austin. His research looks at the ways food and communication travel together through networked ecologies.

Jennifer D. Carlson is a cultural anthropologist. Her research on energy transitions engages ordinary senses of plentitude, uncertainty, and struggle as a resource for environmental action. She is a visiting research fellow at Rice University's Center for Energy and Environmental Research in the Human Sciences and was a 2017 Carson Fellow at the Rachel Carson Center for Environment and Society in Munich.

Donna Dunbar-Odom is the head of the Department of Liberal Studies and a professor of English at Texas A&M University–Commerce.

Doug Eskew is an associate professor of English and the director of writing at Colorado State University–Pueblo, where he has been a faculty member since 2008. His work has appeared in *Early Modern Literary Studies, Cahiers Élisabéthains*, and *Exemplaria*.

Jordan Frith is an associate professor at the University of North Texas. He is a coauthor of the book *Mobile Interfaces in Public Spaces*, and his latest book is *Smartphones as Locative Media*. His research is interdisciplinary, melding human geography, rhetoric, and media studies.

Megan Gianfagna happily spent her graduate school years in Austin, the city at the center of her research on rhetorics and ethics of placemaking. Now a Cincinnati resident, she continues to pursue her interest in place-based narratives through work as a communications strategist for a global NGO.

Cynthia Haynes is a professor of English at Clemson University whose research interests are rhetoric, composition, critical theory, games studies, and the rhetorics of war and terrorism. Her publications include *The Homesick Phone Book: Addressing Rhetorics in the Age of Perpetual Criticism* and numerous journal articles and book chapters.

Nate Kreuter lived in Texas while attending the University of Texas–Austin. He is now an associate professor of rhetoric at Western Carolina University, where he misses Lone Star Beer, seventy-five-mile-per-hour speed limits, and hunting feral hogs. He has been described by friends, colleagues, and enemies alike as "experienced at poking snakes."

Brian McNely works in the Department of Writing, Rhetoric, and Digital Studies at the University of Kentucky. His research and teaching explore professional and technical communication, rhetorical theory, and research methodologies and methods.

Michael Odom teaches painting at Texas A&M University–Commerce. His essays and reviews have appeared in *Artforum, Art Papers, Glasstire*, and numerous exhibition catalogues in the United States and Canada. His psychogeographic videos have been shown in several venues in Texas and the Midwest.

James Chase Sanchez is an assistant professor of writing at Middlebury College, where he studies cultural rhetorics, protest, and writing assessment. His work has appeared or is forthcoming in *CCC, Present Tense*, and *WPA*. Sanchez is a 2015 winner of the CCCC Scholars for the Dream Travel Award.

Jillian Sayre is an assistant professor of English at Rutgers University–Camden, where she teaches American literature and literary theory. She has current and forthcoming work in *Papers of the James Fenimore Cooper Society, Networked Humanities*, and *Americanist Approaches to* The Book of Mormon.

Ryan Skinnell is an assistant professor of rhetoric and composition at San José State University, where he teaches rhetoric and writing classes. He is the author of *Conceding Composition: A Crooked History of Composition's Institutional Fortunes* and a coeditor of *What We Wish We'd Known: Negotiating Graduate School.*

Victor J. Vitanza is a professor of English and the founding director of the PhD program in rhetorics, communication, and information design at Clemson University. He is the Jean-François Lyotard Professor at the European Graduate School, Saas-Fee, Switzerland, in philosophy, art, and critical thought. And he is the publisher and editor of the journal *PRE/TEXT.*

Anna M. "Amy" Young is an associate professor of communication and the chair of the Communication and Theatre Department at Pacific Lutheran University in Tacoma, Washington. Her work appears in venues such as *Quarterly Journal of Speech* and *Communication and Critical/Cultural Studies.* Her most recent book is *Prophets, Gurus, and Pundits: Rhetorical Styles and Public Engagement.*

INDEX